"In his *The Case for Biblical Archaeology: Uncovering God's Old Testament People*, John D. Currid provides a introduction to the discipline of archaeology and its the Old Testament.

"The work is divided into three parts. The first part comprises chapters that cover a general introduction to the geography and topography of the land of the Bible, a general introduction to the history of the field of archaeology as it relates to the ancient Near East, the nature of biblical tells and their excavation, and a brief survey of the history of the lands of the Bible from the earliest times about which archaeology can provide information to the beginning of the Babylonian exile.

"The second part explores the land of biblical Israel in more detail, with separate chapters on each of the main geographical regions of Palestine that treat their most important archaeological sites. The third major part of the book provides the reader with an overview of the results of archaeology as they relate to some key features of the culture of Israel in the Old Testament period. These chapters are particularly valuable because they provide concise but readable overviews of a number of topics, such as agriculture and burial practices, about which good introductory treatments are hard to come by.

"Several features of the book make it especially well suited for use as a textbook for an introductory course on biblical archaeology or a seminary-level general introductory course to the Old Testament. The main text is supplemented by several appendices that provide historical and chronological information and a glossary of terms used in archaeological literature. Among the appendices is a summary of extrabiblical references to the kings of Israel and Judah that both students and teachers of the Bible will find helpful in setting the biblical accounts in their proper historical context. In addition, most sections conclude with a list of key terms, a number of discussion questions, and suggestions for further reading that will enable students to pursue more in-depth study of topics of interest, and that teachers can use as the basis of additional assignments as needed.

"In its breadth, its readability, and its organization, *The Case for Biblical Archaeology* provides a valuable resource to pastors, teachers, and students who would like to learn about the real world of biblical archaeology and the myriad ways that it has cast light on our understanding of the world of the Bible in the Old Testament period."

—**David L. Adams**, Associate Professor of Exegetical Theology (Old Testament), Concordia Seminary, St. Louis

"In some respects, this book is a needed update to Dr. Currid's *Doing Archaeology in the Land of the Bible*, which is now twenty years old. Yet it's much more than an update. Currid not only discusses the 'nuts and bolts' of the work of archaeology in Bible lands, but describes in detail the geographic attributes of each region and provides appendices that include timelines, king lists, and extrabiblical references to biblical personages, as well as crucial discussions on aspects of society (agriculture, burial practices, and water management).

"This book is a must for all serious Bible students, whether they plan to excavate in Israel or to work from their 'armchairs.' Dr. Currid is to be applauded for creating such a manual. It is hard to imagine anyone with more experience and knowledge of biblical archaeology. Thus, the book is not only helpful to the beginning student, but also highly authoritative, written by someone who has 'dirtied his boots' in the field. I cannot imagine teaching a course on ancient Israel without referring to this resource often. Furthermore, I cannot imagine a beginning excavator who did not have this book in his or her backpack while in the field. In fact, in my upcoming Study Abroad experience in Israel and Jordan, I plan to have this book in hand!"

—**Mark W. Chavalas**, Professor of History, University of Wisconsin–
La Crosse

"While many such introductory studies use either an archaeological or a biblical approach, Currid's geographical approach is fresh and helpful as an introduction to the subject for a beginning student, layperson, or traveler to the Holy Land. His view of the role of archaeology in the study of the Bible is exactly right. His key terms, discussion questions, and suggestions for further reading at the conclusion of chapters extend the volume's usefulness. Part 2 could even be used as a travel guide for a first-time visitor. The only thing missing is a chapter on Transjordan. The appendices, too, add value. Altogether, this volume stands out from the competition."

—**Lawrence T. Geraty**, President Emeritus, La Sierra University;
former president, American Schools of Oriental Research (ASOR);
longtime director, Madaba Plains Project (Jordan)

"In this book John Currid provides the reader with a wonderful introduction to important geographical, historical, and cultural aspects of the Bible. Readers will benefit from the archaeological and textual knowledge found here."

—**Richard S. Hess**, Distinguished Professor of Old Testament and
Editor, *Denver Journal*, Denver Theological Seminary

"Over the years, I have asked my students to use John Currid's easy-to-read book *Doing Archaeology in the Land of the Bible*, and also encouraged tour members to purchase his book in preparation for the Israel tours I have led. I was delighted to see Currid's new manuscript, *The Case for Biblical*

Archaeology: Uncovering the Historical Record of God's Old Testament People, a book well suited to the classroom and a guide to the layperson interested in archaeology. His inclusion of discussion questions and specific reading suggestions for the various chapters will be helpful for further study. Currid's new work is well organized and leads the reader from the broader areas of the history and work of archaeology in the Holy Land, to specific consideration of archaeological work in the various regions of the land, and finally to important factors relating to life in ancient Israel. Currid's new work will be welcomed among those of us who desire a clear presentation of the geography, archaeology, and everyday life in the land of the Bible. I strongly recommend his new book."

> —**H. Wayne House**, Distinguished Research Professor of Biblical and Theological Studies, Faith International University and Faith Seminary

"*The Case for Biblical Archaeology* provides an excellent entry point into the archaeology of Israel and the ancient Near East. Unlike other books of this type, its organization by topic, rather than by archaeological era, makes it especially useful. Currid's masterful summaries of burial practices, ceramics, architecture, etc. from the Neolithic through the Iron Ages open 'the fifth gospel' to his readers and will leave them longing to traverse these lands for themselves."

> —**Catherine McDowell**, Associate Professor of Old Testament, Gordon-Conwell Theological Seminary

"Currid provides an accessible handbook for an excavation volunteer or a traveler to Israel. This book provides an introduction to archaeology in the Holy Land, as well as a robust guide to the tourist or pilgrim who wants an understanding of the role that archaeology plays in revealing the history of the region. This handbook explains how the archaeological enterprise has transformed our understanding of the land of Israel. It is a valuable reference for archaeology students going on their first dig, tourists on a pilgrimage tour, pastors, or tour leaders."

> —**Steven M. Ortiz**, Professor of Archaeology and Biblical Backgrounds, School of Theology, and Director, Charles D. Tandy Institute of Archaeology, Southwestern Baptist Theological Seminary

"In this excellent work, John Currid starts by giving readers what the title promises—an explanation of how to practice archaeology in the land of the Bible. He also then takes readers on a tour of that land and explains numerous important facets of the biblical culture. Currid's work obviously flows from the mind and heart of a person who well understands the discipline of archaeology and related fields, drawing from decades of excavation and study and ministry."

—**Boyd Seevers**, Professor of Old Testament Studies, University of Northwestern–St. Paul, Minnesota

THE CASE FOR

Biblical Archaeology

THE CASE FOR

Biblical Archaeology

Uncovering the Historical Record of God's Old Testament People

JOHN D. CURRID

PUBLISHING

P.O. BOX 817 • PHILLIPSBURG • NEW JERSEY 08865-0817

Library of Congress Cataloging-in-Publication Data

Names: Currid, John D., 1951- author.
Title: The case for archaeology : uncovering the historical record of God's
    Old Testament people / John D. Currid.
Description: Phillipsburg, New Jersey : P&R Publishing, 2020. | Includes
    bibliographical references and index. | Summary: "We gain encouragement
    and helpful background to Scripture in studying the land of the Bible
    (the "fifth gospel"). Archaeologist and biblical scholar John Currid
    overviews areas of inquiry and discovery"-- Provided by publisher.
Identifiers: LCCN 2019054129 | ISBN 9781629953601 (paperback) | ISBN
    9781629953618 (epub) | ISBN 9781629953625 (mobi)
Subjects: LCSH: Bible--Antiquities. | Bible--Geography. |
    Palestine--Antiquities. | Middle East--Antiquities. | Bible.
    O.T.--Criticism, interpretation, etc. | Excavations
    (Archaeology)--Palestine. | Excavations (Archaeology)--Middle East. |
    Bible--History of Biblical events.
Classification: LCC BS621 .C86 2020 | DDC 221.9/3--dc23
LC record available at https://lccn.loc.gov/2019054129

To my students (1980–2020)

Contents

Illustrations

Foreword

THERE ARE COUNTLESS reasons to delve into archaeology. Many people love studying archaeology for its own sake. The thrill of discovery and the immense quantities of new historical data are enough to keep us hooked. Perhaps we were lured in years ago by visiting museum exhibitions of exquisite golden artifacts from Mesopotamian Ur or from the tombs of Egyptian pharaohs such as King Tut. Others of us grew up digging in our backyards, with childhood dreams of unearthing a relic from years past, thrilling to the discovery of an old soda bottle or a bovine shoulder bone. Some of us remember watching Indiana Jones movies, only later to learn that only rarely does the modern archaeologist need to fend off Nazis, murderous religious sects, and space aliens with a whip and brash resolve. No, excavation is a much slower and more mundane process that involves methodically taking 4-meter squares of soil down centimeter by centimeter with a brush and a hand trowel. Whatever has led us to love archaeology, a book about excavating in biblical lands is right up our alley.

Others come to archaeology hoping to substantiate treasured historical documents, perhaps seeking evidence to corroborate biblical history. This has long motivated people to dig in sites such as Troy (to validate Homer), to pursue evidence for the route of Alexander the Great through the Near East, and to study Egyptian hieroglyphs on tomb walls in hopes of discovering a lost pharaoh. Bible students are by no means alone in such interests, even if we may have extra motivation to assert the historical validity of our holy text. But we may acknowledge a cautionary tale in Heinrich Schliemann's nineteenth-century race to uncover Homer's Troy at Hissarlik in Turkey. Schliemann plowed through layers of archaeological material, taking relatively few notes and destroying millennia of evidence. He then overhyped his findings and ultimately misidentified the correct historical strata for the Homeric city. In the quest to validate written sources, it is certainly possible to be too hasty in making identifications and to be unprofessional in archaeological procedure. Similarly, biblical archaeology has made mistakes in the past, even amid a vast quantity of careful research and many truly important discoveries. What is needed is a trustworthy guide to help us weigh the evidence cautiously and confidently. In John Currid's book, you possess just such a reliable volume.

Finally, still others realize that perhaps the greatest value from archaeology for biblical studies stems from how excavations illuminate ancient culture, facilitating better interpretations of the biblical text. While relatively few artifacts exposed in a dig speak directly to the historicity of the Bible, every archaeological discovery informs us a little bit more about ancient culture and about life in Bible times. This is important because it relates to how we humans converse with one another. We are constantly relying on our shared experiences of culture to fill in the gaps in our speech. Communication is as much about what we do *not* say as about what we say. As we recount events from our lives, there are many things that we do not have to verbalize because they are implicitly known to everyone in our society, and so we omit such matters from our speech and writing.

For example, I can declare: "Last night my wife and I hired a babysitter, and we went to a movie." Presumably that makes good sense to you. Now imagine an audience of people who have not yet fallen under the sway of Western pop-culture hegemony—perhaps they live deep in a beautiful rainforest or high up in a remote mountain village; these folks might have never seen a movie theater and may well have different customs surrounding child-rearing. Would my sentence make sense to them? They would undoubtedly have many questions, such as: "What is a babysitter? How do you hire babysitters, and what do you use to pay them? What is a movie? Why did you have to hire a babysitter in order to go to the movie? Where did you see this movie? How did you get there? Why did you do this at night? Was this for fun or for work?" In short, why is it that some may have difficulty understanding my sentence, while the rest of us comprehend it immediately? Those who grasp the meaning also typically share the same culture. In my sentence, I had intentionally omitted details that I assumed my reader would know based on shared culture, but in the process my sentence might well confuse someone who has not experienced life in twenty-first-century America.

Consequently, when we read the Old Testament, which is culturally removed from us by more than twenty-five hundred years, there could be entire portions that mystify us or that we misinterpret simply because we do not comprehend the societal assumptions that the original authors shared with the people of their day. Thus, any student of the Bible (or of any other ancient book, for that matter) can hone his or her ability to interpret the text by getting to know the cultures of antiquity. This immediately propels us into the arms of archaeologists, for the main data that we have about those ancient Old Testament societies must come to us from digging in the dirt.

John Currid helpfully observes throughout this fine volume that we discover firsthand evidence in archaeology of everything from ancient burial practices to the daily stuff of life. We encounter inscriptions, ostraca, and papyri that have provided the vast bulk of our knowledge of ancient literature. We observe the layout of Bronze and Iron Age buildings—from houses to storerooms, water tunnels to city gates, temples to palaces. We also get marvelous glimpses into what such structures contained. We witness the very idols and shrines of the surrounding ancient Near Eastern nations, which served as such a great temptation to the Israelites. And we learn about patterns of everyday life in food, agriculture, family life, construction, ceramics, jewelry, transport, warfare, scribal practices, and so on.

Whatever motivates your interest in archaeology and in the Bible, this book serves as a masterly introduction to the field. Currid draws on decades of experience as a field archaeologist, and his excellent training is evident on every page. You will quickly recognize that John is summarizing meticulous research from his previous books on biblical geography, Egyptology, and the study of the ancient Near East. Moreover, his extensive experience in writing accessible academic commentaries on (by current count) at least nine Old Testament books means that Professor Currid is eminently suited to make good and proper connections between the biblical text and archaeological discovery. John's years of seminary teaching and pastoral ministry have also equipped him to communicate even the most technical matters in ways that all of us can understand and enjoy. As John leads you through the many Old Testament locales and as he takes you, discovery by discovery, through ancient buildings and artifacts, you can read with the confidence that you are learning from a pro.

David W. Chapman
Professor of New Testament and Archaeology
Covenant Theological Seminary

Preface

AS THE SUBTITLE of this book indicates, it is an introduction, meant to be a mere door into the field of archaeology during the Old Testament period. By nature, it is selective and not exhaustive. Although it is introductory, I have included much bibliography throughout, so that the student who desires more in-depth study may easily pursue it. In a nutshell, my goal is to provide an initial overview of the main areas of inquiry, discovery, and study of archaeology as it relates to the Hebrew Bible.

Many introductions to the archaeology of Old Testament times survey the material remains according to the sequence of archaeological periods. So one chapter covers the remains of the Early Bronze Age, and then the next chapter gives an overview of the Middle Bronze Age, and so forth in chronological fashion. This is a good and valuable approach to the topic. I have taken a somewhat different tack by providing an overview of the material topically and chronologically. For example, I survey the burial practices in Canaan from the Neolithic period to the end of the Iron II period. This approach to the archaeological finds in the Old Testament time period will perhaps be helpful.

It is hard to believe that I have been working in the field of archaeology and in the "field" of excavation for almost fifty years. I began my study as an undergraduate student when I attended the field school of Tell Qasile, under the direction of Ami Mazar, in 1972. That spurred a lifelong interest in archaeology and how it illumines our understanding of the Old Testament. More in-depth training came when I served as a field supervisor at the excavation of Carthage in Tunisia under the oversight of Larry Stager. At that time, Professor Stager was teaching at the University of Chicago, and he served as my PhD dissertation supervisor. Later staff positions at Tell el-Hesi, Bethsaida, and Lahav added to the training. I am deeply indebted to all those who trained me in excavation methodology over the years.

I have written this introduction with my students in mind, both past and present. Over my many years of teaching archaeology to both undergraduate and graduate students in Israel and in the US, I have learned as much from them as they have learned from me. Therefore, this book is dedicated to them.

Abbreviations

AASOR	*Annual of the American Schools of Oriental Research*
ABD	*Anchor Bible Dictionary*, ed. David Noel Freedman (Yale: Yale University Press, 1992)
ABR	Associates for Biblical Research
AJA	*American Journal of Archaeology*
ANET	*Ancient Near Eastern Texts Relating to the Old Testament*, ed. James B. Pritchard, 3rd ed. (Princeton: Princeton University Press, 1969)
APEF	*Annual of the Palestine Exploration Fund*
ASOR	American School of Oriental Research
AUSS	*Andrews University Seminary Studies*
BA	*Biblical Archaeologist*
BAR	*Biblical Archaeology Review*
BASOR	*Bulletin of the American Schools of Oriental Research*
BDB	Brown, Francis, S. R. Driver, and Charles A. Briggs, *A Hebrew and English Lexicon of the Old Testament* (Oxford: Clarendon Press, 1975)
EAEHL	*Encyclopedia of Archaeological Excavations in the Holy Land*, ed. Michael Avi-Yonah, 4 vols. (Jerusalem: Israel Exploration Society and Masada Press, 1975–78)
EB	Early Bronze (Age)
EI	*Eretz Israel*
ESV	English Standard Version
HALOT	*The Hebrew and Aramaic Lexicon of the Old Testament: Study Edition*, ed. Ludwig Koehler, Walter Baumgartner,

	and Johann Jakob Stamm, trans. M. E. J. Richardson, 2 vols. (Leiden: Brill, 2001)
IEJ	*Israel Exploration Journal*
JBL	*Journal of Biblical Literature*
JNES	*Journal of Near Eastern Studies*
JPOS	*Journal of the Palestine Oriental Society*
JSOT	*Journal for the Study of the Old Testament*
LB	Late Bronze (Age)
MB	Middle Bronze (Age)
NEA	*Near Eastern Archaeology* (formerly *Biblical Archaeologist*)
NEAEHL	*The New Encyclopedia of Archaeological Excavations in the Holy Land*, ed. Ephraim Stern, 5 vols. (Jerusalem: Israel Exploration Society & Carta; New York: Simon & Schuster, 1993–2008)
PEF	Palestine Exploration Fund
PEQ	*Palestine Exploration Quarterly*
PN	Pottery Neolithic (period)
PPN	Pre-Pottery Neolithic (period)
PPNA	Pre-Pottery Neolithic A (period)
PPNB	Pre-Pottery Neolithic B (period)
PPNC	Pre-Pottery Neolithic C (period)
TA	*Tel Aviv*
VT	*Vetus Testamentum*
VTS	*Vetus Testamentum, Supplements*
WTJ	*Westminster Theological Journal*
ZDPV	*Zeitschrift des deutschen Palästina-Vereins*

CHAPTER 1

Introduction

"O God, we have heard with our ears, our fathers have told us, what deeds you performed in their days, in the days of old." (Psalm 44:1)

BARGIL PIXNER MADE the following statement regarding the land of the Bible: "Five gospels record the life of Jesus. Four you will find in books and the one you will find in the land they call holy. Read the fifth gospel and the world of the four will open to you."[1] Pixner was probably quoting Jerome, who, in the fourth century A.D., was the first commentator to call the land of the Bible "the fifth gospel." He believed that the geography, topography, and site remains add a new dimension to one's understanding of the Bible. In the preface to his work on Chronicles, Jerome states, "Just as Greek history becomes more intelligible to those who have seen Athens . . . man will get a clearer grasp of Holy Scripture who has gazed at Judaea with his own eyes and has got to know the memorials of its cities and the names . . . of the various localities."[2] Jerome is absolutely correct. The Old Testament scholar George Adam Smith (1856–1942), who served as the principal at the University of Aberdeen, agreed with Jerome when he poignantly said at the end of the nineteenth century that the land is "a museum full of living as well as ancient specimens of its subjects."[3]

But, specifically, in what ways does a study of the land of the Bible give us greater understanding of the Bible itself? A primary purpose of archaeology and its related disciplines is to shed light on the historical and material contexts in which the events narrated in the Bible occurred. Archaeology helps to provide a life setting for biblical texts, that is, a *Sitz im Leben*. In that respect, archaeology can be a confirmatory tool, especially when the textual and archaeological evidence converge. A good example of how archaeology illumines the Bible is the conquest of Judah by Nebuchadnezzar, king of

---

1. Bargil Pixner, *With Jesus through Galilee according to the Fifth Gospel* (Collegeville, MN: Liturgical Press, 1996), back cover.
2. J. N. D. Kelly, *Jerome: His Life, Writings, and Controversies* (London: Duckworth, 1975), 120.
3. George Adam Smith, *The Historical Geography of the Holy Land*, 16th ed. (London: Hodder and Stoughton, 1910), 40.

Babylon, during the decade of the 580s B.C. During the early years of the sixth century B.C., Judah came under the control of the Babylonians and, in fact, the Babylonians set up the Judean Zedekiah as a puppet king over Judah and Jerusalem (597–586 B.C.). Toward the end of Zedekiah's reign, the Egyptians began to flex their muscles in Syro-Palestine. Zedekiah, believing the Egyptians would come to his aid, revolted against the Babylonians. Nebuchadnezzar responded quickly. He captured the outlying fortresses of Judah and then conquered Jerusalem after a siege that lasted a little more than a year. The conquest of Judah and Jerusalem is described in detail in 2 Kings 25 and 2 Chronicles 36.

Most of the cities of Judah from this period that have been excavated contain destruction layers from the Babylonian invasion. Major sites, such as Beth Shemesh, Gezer, and Lachish have huge burn layers that reflect the devastation. Excavations at Lachish in the 1930s under the supervision of J. L. Starkey uncovered eighteen ostraca in the burnt debris of a guardroom between the inner and outer gates of the city.[4] The date of the ostraca, based upon stratigraphical analysis, is commonly understood to be just prior to the destruction of Lachish at the hands of the Babylonians. A military leader named Hoshaiah wrote some of the letters to another commander named Yaosh. A common scholarly reading of the texts understands Yaosh to be the commander of Lachish, and Hoshaiah, in charge of a fortress outside of Lachish, to be writing to him. Others, such as the Israeli archaeologist Yigael Yadin, in an alternate reading, believe Hoshaiah to be the commander of Lachish, writing to Yaosh, who was a high official in Jerusalem.

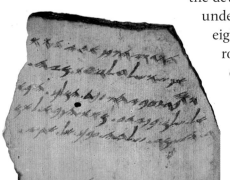

Fig. 1.1. Lachish Ostracon

One of the letters closes with Hoshaiah commenting, "And let (my lord) know that we are watching for the signals of Lachish, according to all the indications which my lord hath given, for we cannot see Azekah." Hoshaiah was speaking about fire signals that would have been transmitted from one city of Judah to another, and the particular setting of this letter appears to be the advance of the Babylonian army through the Lachish region. Azekah, located about 12 miles north-northeast of Lachish, was apparently not sending signal fires and, therefore, was perhaps under siege or had been destroyed by the Babylonians.

The destruction layer at Lachish from the Babylonian attack has been exposed through archaeological investigation. Many scholars agree that the

4. Ostraca (*sing.* ostracon) are pottery sherds containing inscriptions written in ink.

ash layer of Level II at the site reflects the attack of Nebuchadnezzar. The city gate was destroyed at this time, and its ash layer seals the occupation layer beneath it; that occupation layer contains the Lachish ostraca and Late Judean pottery. One of the letters embedded in the destruction debris opens with a date, "In the ninth [year] . . ." This date should bring to mind 2 Kings 25:1, which says, "And in the ninth year of his reign [i.e., Zedekiah], in the tenth month, on the tenth day of the month, Nebuchadnezzar king of Babylon came with all his army against Jerusalem and laid siege to it."

All the data—biblical, archaeological, and linguistic—come together to provide an accurate and helpful picture of what happened at Lachish during the destruction of Judah by the Babylonians. Archaeological investigation provides background material and some substance to the events described by the prophet Jeremiah: "Then Jeremiah the prophet spoke all these words to Zedekiah king of Judah, in Jerusalem, when the army of the king of Babylon was fighting against Jerusalem and against all the cities of Judah that were left, Lachish and Azekah, for those were the only fortified cities of Judah that remained" (34:6–7). This convergence of the biblical text and archaeology is not unique. The biblical authors set events like the invasions of Pharaoh Shishak (1 Kings 14:24–26) and Sennacherib (2 Kings 18:13; 19:16; 2 Chron. 32:1–22) and the revolt of Mesha, king of Moab, against Israel in their proper chronological framework and setting.[5] These events are confirmed and filled out by contemporary ancient Near Eastern texts, specifically the Bubastite Portal at the Temple of Amun at Karnak, the Prism of Sennacherib, and the Moabite Stone. Excavation work has also brought to light numerous destruction layers in Israel that reflect these campaigns.

It is our contention that the purpose of archaeology (and related fields) is not to prove the Bible. The Bible doesn't need to be proved. It stands well enough on its own. As Charles Spurgeon once remarked, "Scripture is like a lion. Who ever heard of defending a lion? Just turn it loose; it will defend itself." As George Ernest Wright once commented, "Our ultimate aim must not be 'proof,' but truth."[6] Biblical archaeology serves to confirm, illuminate, and give "earthiness" to the Scriptures. It helps to demonstrate that the events related in the biblical accounts actually took place in history. This is especially important in our day and age for two primary reasons. First, the common thinking of our generation is *ahistorical*. That is, for many people, history is irrelevant, is meaningless, and has little application to modern existence. These days, people are obsessed with technological innovation and cultural

---

5. Source-critical scholars have a difficult time explaining such convergences. It has been reported that at a national meeting of biblical scholars, J. Maxwell Miller asked John Van Seters, who holds to a postexilic date for the writing of Kings, how the author of Kings put Shishak "in the right pew." Reportedly, Van Seters responded, "I wish I knew."

6. George E. Wright, *Biblical Archaeology* (Philadelphia: Westminster Press, 1962), 27.

change that arrives with lightning speed. There is little interest in history, which is seen as boring and the domain of dusty scholars who are lost in the maze of the past. One cultural critic agonized over this state of affairs by concluding that the Westerner's view and scope of history does not precede breakfast! In reality, the ahistorical worldview is one consequence of postmodernism, post-Christian thinking, and deconstructionism. The dismissal of history is a core part of deconstructionism, in which the modern reader is encouraged to read and interpret the Bible in any way he or she sees fit. The lens of interpretation thus becomes one's own self and experiences. A major argument of deconstructionism is that the reader cannot get at true history because all historical writing is propagandistic and reflects the bias of the historian. Therefore, the question has become, Is there really such a thing as history? Because of the very physical nature of archaeology, its study helps to ground us in the realia (i.e., the "real things") of what has happened in the past.

Second, the common thinking of our generation is biblically and historically *uninformed*. A recent Barna survey revealed that at least 12 percent of adults believe that Joan of Arc was Noah's wife, and another survey indicated that 50 percent of graduating high school seniors thought that Sodom and Gomorrah were husband and wife! A recent study by Kelton Research concluded that Americans are more familiar with the ingredients of a Big Mac than they are with the Ten Commandments. The uninformed are easy prey to movements such as "pop" archaeology, in which staggering discoveries are announced—the ark of the covenant (with blood still on it!) or Egyptian chariot wheels in the Red Sea—and then the discoverers make careers out of speaking on these so-called finds that have never been produced. Tried and true archaeological research and study fortifies one to resist such bogus claims.

WHAT IS ARCHAEOLOGY?

Archaeology may be defined as *the systematic study of the material remains of human behavior in the past*. It is concerned with the realia, that is, the physical, material remains of antiquity. Roland de Vaux describes it this way: "Archaeology, therefore, is limited to the *realia*, but it studies all the *realia*, from the greatest classical monuments to the locations of prehistoric fireplaces, from art works to small everyday utensils . . . in short, everything which exhibits a trace of the presence or activity of man. Archaeology seeks, describes, and classifies these materials."[7]

The objects of archaeological discovery are in various stages of preservation. Most of the artifacts found are preserved in a ruined or fragile

---

7. Roland de Vaux, "On Right and Wrong Uses of Archaeology," in *Near Eastern Archaeology in the Twentieth Century*, ed. James A. Sanders (Garden City, NY: Doubleday, 1970), 65.

condition. That reality highlights Stuart Piggot's famous dictum that archaeology is the "science of rubbish." In contrast to Hollywood's depiction of archaeologists making "the great find" (e.g., the ark of the covenant), the reality is much less exotic. Archaeologists spend their time and efforts in long-forgotten heaps of ancient refuse: shattered pottery, broken small finds, destroyed buildings, and few, if any, crumbling documents. So, for example, archaeologists are excited when they uncover a *midden deposit*, which is an archaeological term for a garbage or trash heap. Middens resulted from deliberate human discarding of trash—food remains, broken pottery, and other domestic materials—into a pile. They contain all kinds of remains that reflect numerous cultural behaviors. These garbage dumps can provide insights into human diet, wealth, status, subsistence patterns, trade, and so forth. Such debris sometimes contains *coprolites*, which are fossilized feces. Examination of coprolites can provide the researcher with the diet of the human and perhaps shed light on prevalent diseases and on what animals might have been domesticated. When all is said and done, Patty Jo Watson hits the nail on the head when she says about archaeologists, "We are all, by definition, middenophiles."[8]

Another example of such remains is the discovery of a *favissa*. This is a pit that has been dug near or in a temple and contains sacred objects no longer in use. For instance, the Fosse Temple at Lachish was destroyed by a violent attack in the thirteenth century B.C. A number of favissae were discovered just outside this temple complex, and they contained an abundance of small finds. Amihai Mazar reports, "Among these finds were ivory fragments of a statue, including a palm of a hand and an eye. Presumably, these fragments belonged to a composite statue of a deity made of ivory, wood, and cloth."[9] These discoveries may not be glamorous, but they highlight the reality of archaeological research as "trashology," or "garbology," which deals with what has been thrown away.

THE AIM OF ARCHAEOLOGY

The primary goal of archaeology is *to discover, observe, preserve, and record the buried remains of antiquity and to use them to help reconstruct ancient life*. It needs to be noted up front, however, that archaeology is by no means exhaustive in what it provides; it is a limited tool. No excavation can paint

---

8. Patty Jo Watson, "The Idea of Ethnoarchaeology: Notes and Comments," in *Ethnoarchaeology: Implications of Ethnography for Archaeology*, ed. Carol Kramer (New York: Columbia University Press, 1979), 282.

9. Amihai Mazar, *Archaeology of the Land of the Bible, 10,000–586 B.C.E.* (New York: Doubleday, 1990), 254–55.

a complete picture of a site; it gives only a slice of the material remains that exist there. For instance, excavations have taken place at the site of Tell Ras Shamra almost every year since the initial excavation under the direction of Claude Schaeffer in 1929.[10] Great finds have been made there, such as the Ugaritic texts (which are the main source for the Canaanite language). Yet much of the site is unexcavated. That is true of every major site. Megiddo, in northern Israel, has been the subject of the most extensive excavations in the land, beginning in 1903 and continuing almost unabated ever since, yet only part of the mound has been excavated. What archaeology provides for the reconstruction of culture is by nature fragmentary, piecemeal, and incomplete.

Fig. 1.2. Megiddo Excavations

The limitations of archaeology should not be surprising. In Israel, for example, more than 6,000 ancient sites have been surveyed, yet less than 500 have been excavated. Of those, less than 50 have been exposed to major excavation work. These statistics underscore the reality that in the process of reconstructing ancient cultures, archaeology is only part of the equation. It cannot stand on its own. Other disciplines are also valuable and must be brought to bear on this endeavor; fields of study such as anthropology,

---

10. The only hiatus was during the years surrounding World War II (1939–48). See William M. Schniedewind and Joel H. Hunt, *A Primer on Ugaritic: Language, Culture, and Literature* (Cambridge: Cambridge University Press, 2007), 5–30.

geography, geology, history, and linguistics provide critical keys to unlocking the past. Even with its limitations, however, archaeology is an important
investigative tool in the attempt to recover and reconstruct ancient life.

Another example will help to demonstrate the part that archaeology
can play in restoring our understanding of ancient life and events, and how
it works with other disciplines to achieve that understanding. We read in
2 Chronicles 32 about an Assyrian threat to Jerusalem during the reign of
Hezekiah, king of Judah, near the end of the eighth century B.C. In response
to the peril, Hezekiah "closed the upper outlet of the waters of Gihon and
directed them down to the west side of the city of David" (v. 30). The Gihon
Spring was the main and most dependable water source for the city of Jerusalem. It was located, however, outside the city walls near the base of the
Ophel (hill). The problem for Jerusalem was that the inhabitants would be
cut off from this water source during times of siege or attack. A nineteenth-
century explorer named Charles Warren discovered a vertical shaft that was
cut through bedrock, allowing the people of Jerusalem to have access to the
spring from behind the walls of the city. The Jebusites probably dug it during
the Late Bronze Age, and it may have been the shaft that David's soldiers
used to penetrate the city and capture it from the Canaanite inhabitants
(2 Sam. 5:6–8). During the time of Hezekiah, the king used part of that old
system and then excavated a new tunnel that sloped gently away from the
Gihon Spring to allow water to flow into the city of Jerusalem at the Pool of
Siloam (2 Chron. 32).

Hezekiah's tunnel has been found, and we basically know how the tunnel was originally dug because a Hebrew inscription was discovered in the
tunnel approximately 20 feet from the entrance to the Siloam Pool. It reads:

> [. . . when] (the tunnel) was driven through. And this was the way in which
> it was cut through: While [. . .] (were) still [. . .] axe(s), each man toward
> his fellow, and while there were still three cubits to be cut through, [there
> was heard] the voice of a man calling to his fellow, for there was *an overlap*
> in the rock on the right [and on the left]. And when the tunnel was driven
> through, the quarrymen hewed (the rock), each man toward his fellow, axe
> against axe; and the water flowed from the spring toward the reservoir for
> 1,200 cubits, and the height of the rock above the head(s) of the quarrymen
> was 100 cubits.[11]

Two teams moving toward one another, one beginning at the Gihon Spring
and the other from the Siloam Pool, cut the tunnel. The tunnel was serpentine because of the change in terrain. The two teams adjusted their paths
as they drew near to one another, perhaps being directed by engineers from

---

11. William F. Albright, "The Siloam Inscription," in *ANET*, 321.

above. The inscription describes the last moments prior to the meeting of the two teams of cutters.

Information gleaned from various disciplines—archaeology, biblical studies, geography, linguistics, and topography—comes together in order to provide a full picture of the episode of Hezekiah's construction of a water tunnel at the close of the eighth century B.C. Each discipline provides relevant material for the reconstruction that the other disciplines do not provide. Archaeology is only one of the disciplines that contribute to this multidisciplinary approach to reconstructing ancient life and culture.

KEY TERMS

archaeology

coprolite

favissa

midden deposit

ostracon (*pl.* ostraca)

realia

Sitz im Leben

DISCUSSION QUESTIONS

1. How would you argue against the modern Western thought that debunks the significance of history? What role does archaeology play in your argument?
2. Why is it important to see and understand that God revealed the Bible in the contexts of particular historical periods, places, and settings?
3. "Pop archaeology" is a common phenomenon today, in which claims of spectacular finds are used to prove the Bible. How are Christians to respond to such claims?

FOR FURTHER READING

Currid, John D. "What Is Archaeology?" in *ESV Archaeology Study Bible*, ed. John D. Currid and David W. Chapman, xix–xx. Wheaton, IL: Crossway, 2017.

Glueck, Nelson. *The Other Side of the Jordan*. Cambridge, MA: ASOR, 1970. For a fascinating discussion of the definition of archaeology and its purposes, see pp. 5–39, "What Is Biblical Archaeology?"

Wright, George E. *Biblical Archaeology*. Philadelphia: Westminster Press, 1962. See, especially, pp. 17–28 on the purposes of archaeology.

PART 1

SETTING

CHAPTER 2

Geography of the Land of the Bible

"God created war so that Americans would learn geography."—Mark Twain

THE LAND OF Promise, the land where the Israelites settled after their escape from Egypt, sits at a critical geographical juncture in the ancient Near East. It serves as a land bridge between three continental landmasses: Asia, Africa, and Europe. In antiquity, Palestine[1] was located between three great civilizations of the ancient Near East: Egypt, Mesopotamia, and the land of the Hittites (Hatti in modern-day Asia Minor). Human settlements first appeared in these three regions, and the shift from food-gathering economies to agricultural economies can be seen in them during the Neolithic period. Inevitably, over time, trade contacts were established between these major regions, and prominent international highways developed and connected the three areas. Many of the routes went directly through Palestine and Transjordan. It was only natural that the international thoroughfares would traverse the region, since it was bordered on the west by the Mediterranean Sea and on the east by the Arabian Desert.

Egypt was perhaps the most advanced civilization in the ancient Near East. In many areas of human culture, the ancient Egyptians surpassed other nations of the time, such as in architecture, literature, and other arts. In medicine, for instance, modern physicians would find much to emulate. As David Mininberg comments, "Many of the practices followed by today's physicians are legacies of the skills and knowledge gained by ancient Egyptian physicians."[2] The Old Testament signifies that there was much contact

1. Throughout this book, I use the name Palestine merely as a geographic designator for the Land of Promise. This usage is along the lines of William F. Albright's groundbreaking work *The Archaeology of Palestine: A Survey of the Ancient Peoples and Cultures of the Holy Land* (Harmondsworth, UK: Penguin Books, 1949). There is no intention of making a political statement with the use of that designation.

2. David T. Mininberg, "The Legacy of Ancient Egyptian Medicine," in *The Art of Medicine in Ancient Egypt*, by James P. Allen and David T. Mininberg (New York: Metropolitan Museum of Art; New Haven: Yale University Press, 2005), 13.

between the Hebrews and the land of Egypt. Abraham spent time in Egypt (Gen. 12:10–20), and Joseph was imprisoned in Egypt, where he eventually rose to prominence (Gen. 37–50). The Hebrews were enslaved in Egypt for more than four centuries, but were redeemed from there through divine intervention.

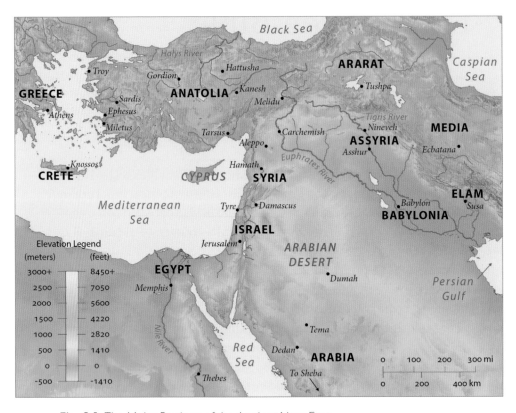

Fig. 2.1. The Major Regions of the Ancient Near East

The history of the Hittites encompassed much of the second millennium B.C. They were particularly strong and influential during the New Empire period (1400–1200 B.C.). During that time, they controlled much of Syria, just to the north of the land of Canaan. There was much contact between the Hittites and the Egyptians during the Late Bronze Age, and it took the form of treaties, trade, and sometimes war. In 1296 B.C., for example, the military forces of both nations met in the famous battle of Kadesh, next to the Orontes River in Syria. Although Pharaoh Ramses II claimed victory, the evidence appears "to favor the conclusion that the battle was indecisive."[3] Excavations in both lands have revealed treaty documents between the two powers.[4]

3. Siegfried J. Schwantes, *A Short History of the Ancient Near East* (Grand Rapids: Baker, 1965), 47.
4. *ANET*, 199–203.

Mesopotamia was home to some of the earliest human remains, which were found in the Zagros Mountains. It was a land situated between the Tigris and Euphrates Rivers, and the great nations of Assyria and Babylonia were founded there. The patriarch Abraham and his family were natives of that land (Gen. 11:31), and only later in life did he immigrate to Canaan. Assyria, under the rule of Sargon II (722–705 B.C.), conquered the northern kingdom of Israel in 721 B.C. and deported its upper classes. Nebuchadnezzar, a powerful Babylonian monarch, destroyed Judah and Jerusalem in 586 B.C. (2 Kings 25).

Much of the contact between these major ancient Near Eastern powers, whether trade or war or diplomacy, took place in or went through the land of Palestine. "The key to power in the ancient Near East was to control Palestine, and particularly the road system that traversed it."[5] George Adam Smith, in his classic work on the geography of the Holy Land, sums it up perfectly when he says that it was "the passage for the earliest intercourse and exchanges of civilization."[6]

THE GEOGRAPHIC AND TOPOGRAPHIC REGIONS OF PALESTINE

Although the land of Palestine is small, roughly the size of the state of Vermont, it displays a wide range of different physical features. Palestine is a land of contrasts in geography, topography, climate, and vegetation. George Adam Smith recognized this reality long ago, when he said,

> We are able to appreciate in some degree the immense differences both of temperature and fertility, which are due, *first*, to the unusual range of level—from 1300 feet below the sea with a tropical atmosphere to 9000 feet above it with an Alpine, and, *second*, to the double exposure of the land—seawards, so that the bulk of it is subject to the ordinary influences of the Mediterranean basin, and desert-wards, so that part of it exhibits most of the characteristics of desert life.[7]

A good example of these variations is the differences in climate, topography, and vegetation between Jerusalem and Jericho. The two sites are a mere 14 miles apart. Jerusalem lies in the central hill country about 2,400 feet above sea level, whereas Jericho is located near the Dead Sea at about 1,300 feet below sea level. Jerusalem receives an average of 21 inches of rain

---

5. John D. Currid and David P. Barrett, *Crossway ESV Bible Atlas* (Wheaton, IL: Crossway, 2010), 18.

6. George Adam Smith, *The Historical Geography of the Holy Land*, 16th ed. (London: Hodder and Stoughton, 1910), 12.

7. Smith, *Historical Geography of the Holy Land*, 63.

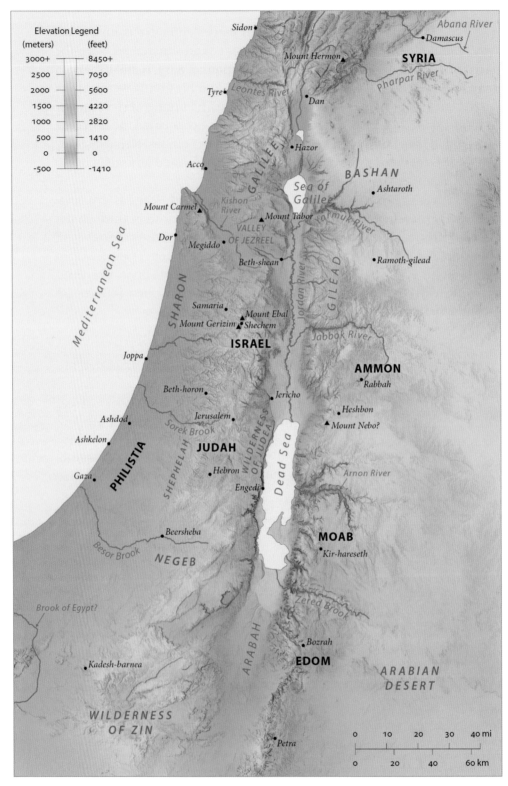

Fig. 2.2. The Natural Geographic Regions of Palestine

per year and has an average temperature of 64°F, while Jericho gets a scant 6 inches of precipitation per year and has an average temperature of 77°F. Jerusalem was in a highly forested area in antiquity, but Jericho was and is an oasis region.

We will now explore the various geographic regions of the Land of Promise, beginning from a north to south direction, and then we will proceed from west to east. The discussion and description of these regions will be foundational for a later, major part of this book, when we will analyze individual excavation sites according to their regional settings.

GALILEE

Galilee was the northernmost region occupied by ancient Israel. It consists of alternating valleys and ridges running east to west, and "it measured no more than approximately 50 miles north-south and 25 miles east-west."[8] Galilee is part of the Mediterranean wet zone, which is characterized by a relatively high average annual precipitation (about 14 inches per year). Because of its rainfall patterns, the area contains many forests, and its main trees are evergreen, oak, and terebinth.

Galilee is divided into two districts called Upper and Lower Galilee. They are divided by the Beth Kerem Valley, which runs from Acco on the Mediterranean coast to the area of Safed, north of the Sea of Galilee. A rugged, mountainous terrain characterizes Upper Galilee, with some mountains reaching a height of 4,000 feet. This region was captured by the Israelites during Joshua's northern campaign (Josh. 11:6–15). It was allotted for settlement to the tribes of Naphtali, Dan, and Asher. In antiquity, Upper Galilee was a frontier region that contained a small population, and few significant cities were found there besides Dan and Hazor.

Lower Galilee is less rugged, with hills reaching only to about 2,000 feet. The district contains numerous valleys that run through it laterally, and some of these are particularly lush and fertile; perhaps the most prominent is the fruitful Jezreel Valley. These many valleys allow for easy travel and commerce in the region. After the Israelite invasion, the land of Lower Galilee was inherited for settlement by the tribes of Issachar, Zebulon, and Naphtali. It proved to be, however, a region of much conflict between the Israelites and the Canaanites (e.g., Judg. 5:1–31). Lower Galilee was central to the Galilean ministry of Jesus (e.g., John 2:1–11; Luke 7:11–17). It also became the center of Talmudic studies after the destruction of Jerusalem in A.D. 70.

8. Barry J. Beitzel, *The Moody Atlas of Bible Lands* (Chicago: Moody Press, 1985), 18.

THE JUDEAN WILDERNESS

A few miles southeast of the city of Jerusalem, the wilderness of Judea begins. It has a desert climate with sparse fauna, flora, and rainfall. Any water in the region comes from numerous wadis that cut through the landscape. These are seasonal streambeds that bring water from the central highlands during the winter. A noteworthy example is the Wadi Qelt, which flows from Jerusalem to Jericho, and it parallels the main ancient roadway between the two cities (see Luke 10:29–37).

Fig. 2.3. A Wadi in the Negev

The primary reason for the lack of rainfall in the area is the location of the central highlands immediately to the west. Winter winds bring rain from the Mediterranean Sea into Palestine, but the central mountain range blocks the rain from continuing eastward. There is, therefore, a precipitous drop in rainfall on the eastern slopes of the Judean Mountains. Also, the top geological layer of the eastern slopes is Senonian limestone, which is not permeable. Therefore, the landscape of the area is characterized by barren hills. The prophet Ezekiel predicted, however, that one glorious day a great river would flow through this wilderness (Ezek. 37:7–8), and the prophet Isaiah proclaimed that a time would come when the rocky hills of the Judean desert would be made flat and straight (Isa. 40:3–4).

THE NEGEV

The Negev was the southernmost region occupied by ancient Israel. In Old Testament times, the Negev denoted the barren wilderness south of the Judean highlands that encompassed the land down to the oasis of Kadesh-Barnea. It included the area east and west of Beersheba. The Negev is an area hostile to human settlement. Although there are some wells in the vicinity of Beersheba, the water supply is mostly dependent on rainfall. Its precipitation, however, is minimal (ca. 8 inches of annual rainfall), and it occurs mainly in the winter. Vegetation is sparse and is normally found near wadi beds. Acacia trees are plentiful in the landscape of the northern Negev.

Although the environment of the area is forbidding, many Old Testament events took place there. The patriarchs, for instance, lived much of their lives in the Negev, and the site of Beersheba played an important role in their stories (e.g., Gen. 21:32). The wandering Israelites settled for a time at Kadesh-Barnea, and from there Moses sent spies to reconnoiter the land of Canaan (Num. 12:16–13:3). When fleeing from Saul, David spent much time in the Negev, and even lived at the site of Ziklag, from where he campaigned against desert tribes from the southern Negev (1 Sam. 27:1–8).

We will now turn to consider the various natural regions of Palestine moving from west to east. This brief analysis is based on the appearance of five parallel longitudinal regions: the coastal plain, the Shephelah (foothills), the central highlands, the Jordan Valley, and the Transjordanian Plateau. Although parallel with one another, each region displays unique terrain, climate, and geography.

THE MEDITERRANEAN COASTAL PLAIN

In general, the coastline of Palestine may be divided into four regions, and we will consider them in order from north to south. The first region, including the plains of Asher and Acco, extends from Rosh Hanikra in the north to Mount Carmel in the south. The Plain of Asher is one of good agricultural productivity because it contains a deep layer of topsoil, due to erosion from the mountains of Upper Galilee, and has sufficient drainage. South of it is the Plain of Acco, which, in contrast, contains much swampland. It has an overabundance of water because of two rivers traversing the region (Kishon and Na'aman) and insufficient drainage. Sisera's army, as described in Judges 4–5, found out how dangerous this swampland could be! The area had few important sites in antiquity, except ones directly on the coast, like Dor and Acco.

The next section to the south is the Sharon Plain, which extends from the Mount Carmel region, near modern-day Haifa, to the city of Tel Aviv /

Jaffa on the Jarkon River in the south. Its landscape is defined, first of all, by three sandstone ridges, called kurkar ridges, that run north-south through the area. Numerous small rivers traverse the region and help to make it swampy. Agricultural efforts were doomed in antiquity and, therefore, the Sharon Plain was not densely populated. It also lacks natural harbors for the construction of deepwater ports. During the Roman period, Herod the Great built an artificial harbor at the site of Caesarea along the Sharon Plain.

The third coastal region is Philistia, which stretches from the Jarkon River at Tel Aviv / Jaffa to the Besor Brook just south of the site of Gaza. It is primarily grassland with no forests. The soil is mainly alluvium, which makes the land agriculturally rich and productive. This was the settlement area of the Philistines, one of the groups of Sea Peoples that came from the northern Mediterranean and settled there about 1200 B.C. The Philistine Pentapolis (five capital cities) of Ashdod, Ashkelon, Ekron, Gath, and Gaza were established as major cities in the region. The Philistines were mortal enemies of the Israelites, and, thus, many Old Testament events took place in Philistia.

The final geographic region is the coastland of Sinai. It is a semiarid climate zone with sandy dunes and little precipitation. Meager human settlement took place here in ancient times. It is most important as a thoroughfare leading up from Egypt. Known as the Great Trunk Road, it was a primary route for commerce and military incursions. The Old Testament refers to the highway as the "way of the land of the Philistines" (Ex. 13:17), and the Egyptians called it the "way of Horus."

THE SHEPHELAH

The term *shephelah* derives from a Hebrew verb meaning "to be or become low," and it is a technical term in the Old Testament for a strip of "lowlands" lying between the coastal plain and the Judean highlands (e.g., Josh. 9:1; 10:40; 12:8). It is an area of low, rolling hills through which some broad valleys cross from east to west. These valleys served as areas of transit between the coast and the highlands, and they were areas of military conflict between the two. In these valleys, the Philistines and the Israelites met in battle, such as in the Valley of Elah (1 Sam. 17:1–2). Some major cities, like Gezer and Lachish, were established in this region.

THE CENTRAL HIGHLANDS

The next longitudinal zone to the east is the central hill country. This mountainous spine runs from north to south for about 90 miles. It is divided into two parts: the Samarian highlands in the north and the Judean hills in the south. The Samarian range begins at the southern tip of the Jezreel Valley near Mount Gilboa and then continues southward to the site of Shechem, which is bookended by the mountains of Ebal and Gerizim. From there the spine moves into the Judean hills to the city of Hebron, and it ends in the south with the appearance of the Negev.

Fig. 2.4. The Central Hill Country

The differences in terrain between the coastal plain and central highlands are striking. For example, the coastline at the Mediterranean is sea level, and the land rises up to Jerusalem, which is 2,400 feet above sea level, in a mere 35 miles. At its highest point, the coastal plain ascends to about 650 feet, whereas the highlands contain peaks that rise over 3,500 feet. The hill country is composed mainly of hard limestone, and along with its rugged, hilly terrain, the region is agriculturally unproductive in comparison to the coastal plain. In addition, the highlands in antiquity were forested, including trees such as evergreen oak, terebinth, and Jerusalem pine. Due to deforestation, many of these forests have disappeared, although some remnants can still be seen.

The central hill country played a major role in biblical history. It was the primary settlement area of the Israelites, and the two capital cities, Samaria (north) and Jerusalem (south), were both located in it.

THE JORDAN VALLEY

The fourth zone from west to east is the Jordan River Valley, which descends from Mount Hermon in the north to the Dead Sea in the south. It is part of the major fault that runs from modern-day Turkey down into Africa, which is called the Rift Valley. It is a precipitous drop from the central highlands to the Jordan Valley, which is below sea level. It may be divided into four geographical districts that descend from north to south.

The Upper Jordan

At the northernmost point of the Jordan Valley sits Mount Hermon, and its peak is 9,200 feet above sea level. Melting snow from the top of Mount Hermon, along with fresh water springs at its base, serve as feeders for the headwaters of the Upper Jordan River. That river flows from the area of Banias / Caesarea Philippi for about 25 miles south, until it empties into the Sea of Galilee near the New Testament city of Bethsaida.

In some biblical texts, Mount Hermon is designated as the most northern point of the Promised Land (Josh. 12:1). Other passages defined Israel's inheritance as extending "from Dan to Beersheba" (e.g., 1 Sam. 3:20; 2 Sam. 3:10). Dan lies near the foot of Mount Hermon, a few miles west of Banias / Caesarea Philippi. The upper Jordan Valley was a frontier zone in Old Testament times, and only two major sites existed there: Dan and Hazor. Both sites, however, were of critical importance in biblical times (e.g., Josh. 11:10–11; 1 Kings 9:15; 12:28–30). They have both been extensively excavated.

The Sea of Galilee

The Sea of Galilee is a fresh-water lake, 13 miles long and 8 miles wide. Its surface is 680 feet below sea level, and its depth reaches to 145 feet at its deepest part. In Old Testament times, the sea was called Kinneret, and it did not play a significant role in biblical narratives. It was primarily a geographical marker in border descriptions (Deut. 3:17; Josh. 12:3; 13:27; 19:35). During the New Testament period, on the other hand, the sea had a prominent position, especially as a principal setting for the Galilean ministry of Jesus. Much of his early ministry occurred at sites on the northern and western shores of the sea, such as at Capernaum, Bethsaida, and Chorazin.

The Lower Jordan

The Jordan River exits the Sea of Galilee in the south, and from there it descends approximately 65 miles, where it empties into the Dead Sea. The river, however, does not follow a straight line; rather, it meanders for more than 200 miles between the two large bodies of water. In its twisting course, the Jordan drops about 600 feet, and its descent becomes more precipitous as it nears the Dead Sea. The name of the river perhaps reflects this downhill current; in Hebrew, the name "Jordan" means "descending/downward."

Human settlements first appeared in Palestine in the immediate vicinity of the Jordan River. A continual water source was necessary for survival. During the historical periods, however, no large cities were built on the banks of the river. This may be due to the fact that the river is not navigable, and the people of the time were able to control their water supply better than the early settlers. Even so, many important biblical events took place in the Lower Jordan River basin. The Israelites, for example, miraculously crossed the river to enter the Land of Promise (Josh. 3:14–17). Elijah divided the river, crossed over on dry ground, and then was taken to heaven in a whirlwind; Elisha returned from that episode by dividing the waters himself (2 Kings 2:6–14). The Syrian commander Naaman was cured of leprosy in the river (2 Kings 5:13–14). In New Testament times, it was here that Jesus was baptized by John the Baptist (Mark 1:4–11).

The Dead Sea

The biblical "Salt Sea" (Gen. 14:3; Num. 34:3, 12; etc.) measures 49 miles long and 8 miles wide. The surface of the sea lies at the lowest place on earth, at 1,300 feet below sea level. At its deepest, the Dead Sea bottoms out at another 1,300 feet below sea level. There is, thus, no outlet for the water except evaporation; because the region is so hot and arid, the rate of evaporation is high. In the heat of summer, the water level can decrease by as much as an inch per day. The streams that feed the sea are saline, and when evaporation occurs, it leaves salt and other deposits. The salt concentration is eight times as dense as seawater. Because of the salinity, plant and marine life do not exist in the sea.

Due to the environment, few ancient settlements were built on the shores of the Dead Sea, and few biblical events took place there. The cities of Sodom and Gomorrah were located in the area (Gen. 19:23–26), and there Lot's wife turned into a pillar of salt: she was saline, just like the region around her. David hid out in the canyons on the western side of the sea. The most famous is Ein Gedi (En-gedi), where David spared Saul's life (1 Sam. 24:1–7). It was along the western shore that the Dead Sea Scrolls were produced and later discovered. A separatist sect that labored at the site of Qumran from the second century B.C. to the first century A.D. probably wrote them. The site of Masada, not far from Qumran, was important during the Jewish War (A.D. 66–73), in which Jewish zealots held out for seven years against the Roman Tenth Legion.

TRANSJORDAN

The final region for our consideration is what the Bible calls the land "beyond the Jordan eastward" (Josh. 13:8; 18:7). The modern name for the area is Transjordan, that is, "across the Jordan" from the perspective of one standing in Palestine. The region is a plateau that extends from Mount Hermon in the north to the Red Sea in the south, a distance of about 250 miles. Its width varies, but it averages about 50 miles from east to west. The plateau can be imposing because the peaks of the mountains can reach to heights over 5,000 feet above sea level. It can be divided into five geopolitical regions, and we will consider them from north to south.

Bashan

The land of Bashan is located to the east of the Upper Jordan River, and it extends about 35 miles from Mount Hermon in the north to the Yarmuk River in the south. The name Bashan means "smooth or fertile," and it was famous in biblical times for its lush grazing lands (Ezek. 39:18). The prophet Amos complained, for example, about the women of Samaria being greedy and gluttonous like the "cows of Bashan" (Amos 4:1). Prior to the conquest, the region belonged to Og, king of Bashan, but Israel wrested it away from him (Num. 21:31–35). It was then allotted to the half-tribe of Manasseh, which settled it heavily until the time of the destruction of the northern kingdom in 722 B.C. During the time of Solomon, one section of Bashan called Argob contained "sixty great cities with walls and bronze bars" (1 Kings 4:13).

Gilead

The land of Gilead lies between the Yarmuk River in the north and the Jabbok River in the south. In contrast to Bashan, Gilead is hill country (e.g., Gen. 31:21). In ancient times, the region was famous for its production of spices and medicines (Gen. 37:25; Jer. 46:11). This reputation gave birth to the incredulous question, "Is there no balm in Gilead? Is there no physician there?" (Jer. 8:22). After the conquest, the half-tribe of Manasseh settled the area. A few important biblical events took place in Gilead, many of them involving acts of loyalty by the men of Jabesh-gilead (1 Sam. 11 and 31; 2 Sam. 21).

Ammon

The land of Ammon is located roughly between the Jabbok River in the north and the Arnon River in the south. The exact boundaries are difficult to define because the geopolitical territory of the Ammonites increased or decreased, depending on the military might of the Ammonites at any particular time. The capital city of the Ammonites was Rabba, which sits on the banks of the southern tip of the Jabbok River. Important excavations have taken place in the region, such as the major digs at the site of Heshbon. The Ammonites were often in conflict with Israel. They opposed Israel's march through their land during the wilderness wanderings, and thus Israel conquered this region that was under the rule of Sihon (Num. 21:21–30). In the land allotments, the tribe of Gad received the northern part of Ammon, and the tribe of Reuben the southern part. Discord between Ammonites and Israelites, however, continued throughout the settlement and early monarchic periods of Israel's history (Judg. 11; 1 Sam. 11; 2 Sam. 10:1–5).

Moab

The heartland of ancient Moab was between the Arnon River in the north and the Zered Brook in the south. Again, the northern border must be understood as fluid; at times, the Moabites controlled areas north of the Arnon, and some major cities belonging to them were located there, such as Dibon and Aroer. The region between the Arnon and the Zered is a high plateau that receives minimal precipitation. In antiquity, its economy was principally herding. Moab played a central role in the narratives of Israel passing through Transjordan prior to the conquest of Canaan. The Moabites offered little resistance to Israel, because they were militarily weak and under the subjugation of Sihon (Num. 21:26). Their king Balak, however, did hire the seer Balaam to put a curse on Israel (Num. 22–24). The divination had no effect. Israel fell into idolatrous sin with the Moabites by worshiping their god Baal Peor (Num. 25:1–9). During the monarchic period, Mesha, king of Moab, sent huge tribute to King Ahab of Israel. But after Ahab's death, he revolted (2 Kings 3:4–5). This episode was confirmed by the Moabites themselves on the so-called Moabite Stone / Mesha Stele.

Fig. 2.5. Moabite Stone (Mesha Stele)

Edom

The final geopolitical zone of Transjordan is the southernmost, and it is the land settled by the Edomites. It extends from the Zered Brook to the Gulf of Aqaba. Its main topographic feature is a high, narrow ridge that runs north to south for about 75 miles, but is only a few miles wide. To the west is the Arabah, an arid and rugged desert region south of the Dead Sea. To the east lies the Arabian Desert. The Edomites were primarily a seminomadic people who relied on a vast trade network for their subsistence. They were hostile to the Israelites throughout biblical history; they refused to give Israel free passage through their land during the wilderness wanderings (Num. 20:14–21). Saul fought against Edom (1 Sam. 14:47), as did David (1 Kings 11:15–16). The Edomites also played a part in the destruction of Jerusalem at the hands of the Babylonians in 586 B.C. The prophet Obadiah prophesied that Edom would get repaid for their role in Judah's destruction.

This chapter provides only a general overview of the geography of the regions in and immediately surrounding the Land of Promise. If you desire a more in-depth look at the land, consider some of the more recent literature.[9] In part 2 of this book, we will consider the major sites that have been excavated in each geographical region that we have just discussed. This is called regional archaeology, which is defined as the study of the material remains of a geographical area that covers numerous sites.[10]

KEY TERMS

Kurkar Ridge
Pentapolis
Shephelah

DISCUSSION QUESTIONS

1. Why is it so significant that the Land of Promise was located between the two great ancient Near Eastern civilizations of Egypt and Mesopotamia? How did this geographical setting affect the lives of the Hebrews?
2. Why is it important for readers of the Bible to recognize and understand the topographical variability of the Land of Promise in interpreting the Bible? Can you provide a specific example from the Old Testament?

9. See, e.g., Yohanan Aharoni et al., *The Carta Bible Atlas*, 4th ed. (Jerusalem: Carta, 2002); Zev Kallai, *Historical Geography of the Bible: The Tribal Territories of Israel* (Jerusalem: Magnes, 1986); Efraim Orni and Elisha Efrat, *Geography of Israel*, 4th ed. (Jerusalem: Israel University Press, 1980); Carl Rasmussen, *NIV Atlas of the Bible* (Grand Rapids: Zondervan, 1989).

10. John D. Currid, *Doing Archaeology in the Land of the Bible* (Grand Rapids: Baker, 1999), 33.

3. How does the fact that Israel was primarily a hill-country people affect the way that they lived? For instance, one result of Israel's central settlement being in the inner highlands of Canaan was that they were not a sea-faring people. Can you think of another consequence of the location of their habitation?

FOR FURTHER READING

Baines, John, and Jaromir Malek. *Atlas of Ancient Egypt.* New York: Facts on File, 1980.

Beitzel, Barry J. *The Moody Atlas of Bible Lands.* Chicago: Moody Press, 1985.

Currid, John D., and David P. Barrett. *ESV Bible Atlas.* Wheaton, IL: Crossway, 2010.

Orni, Efraim, and Elisha Efrat. *Geography of Israel.* Jerusalem: Israel Universities Press, 1980.

Rasmussen, Carl G. *Zondervan Atlas of the Bible.* Grand Rapids: Zondervan, 2010.

CHAPTER 3

The Archaeological Study of the Land of the Bible

"I need to go to a freakin' archaeologist. What are those people called?
The ones who crack your back?"—Paris Hilton

THE DISCIPLINE OF archaeology, in a modern sense, began with the excavations at the site of Herculaneum, located along the Bay of Naples on the Tyrrhenian Sea.[1] When Mount Vesuvius erupted in A.D. 79, the area of Herculaneum and Pompeii were engulfed by volcanic material. Herculaneum itself was submerged under pyroclastic surges and flows that solidified to a depth of at least 15 meters (ca. 50 feet). The site was not "re-discovered" until 1709, when a local farmer attempted to dig a well through the volcanic material and in the process discovered some ancient marbles from the city. In 1738, excavations began under the auspices of King Charles of Bourbon, and they continued until 1765. The excavators dug vertical shafts and tunnels through the volcanic debris, and they recovered magnificent statuary that can be seen today in the Naples Museum. Karl Weber drew accurate architectural plans of the site, including a general, overall mapping of the town. Excavations were eventually shut down because of the extreme labor intensity needed to chop through so many meters of volcanic material that covered the site in order to get to the ancient remains.

Excavations soon followed at Pompeii in the year 1748. The first area excavated was called La Civita, and it was not difficult digging because the volcanic debris in the area was light and not heavily compacted. The first buildings investigated included "the smaller theatre (or Odeon, 1764), the Temple of Isis (1764), the so-called Gladiator's barracks (1767), and the Villa

---

1. William Foxwell Albright, *From the Stone Age to Christianity*, 2nd ed. (Garden City, NY: Doubleday, 1957), 26.

of Diomedes outside the Herculaneum Gate (1771)."[2] Karl Weber, again, was a primary participant in the Pompeii excavations, and his work sought to provide evidence of the ancient culture at the site with plans, drawings, and commentary. His goal contrasted with that of many of his contemporaries, who were little more than treasure hunters looking for valuable objects.[3]

Systematic archaeological work also began in North America during the eighteenth century. It appears that Thomas Jefferson was the first person to excavate a site using stratigraphic analysis, that is, according to basic modern methods of excavation.[4] Jefferson excavated an Indian barrow that was located in his home state of Virginia, and concluded that the remains were deposited in various strata and that the topmost stratum was the latest in date. Jefferson's insights were prescient, as William Peden points out: "An amateur archaeologist, among the very earliest on the North American continent, Jefferson anticipated by a century the aims and methods of modern archaeological science."[5]

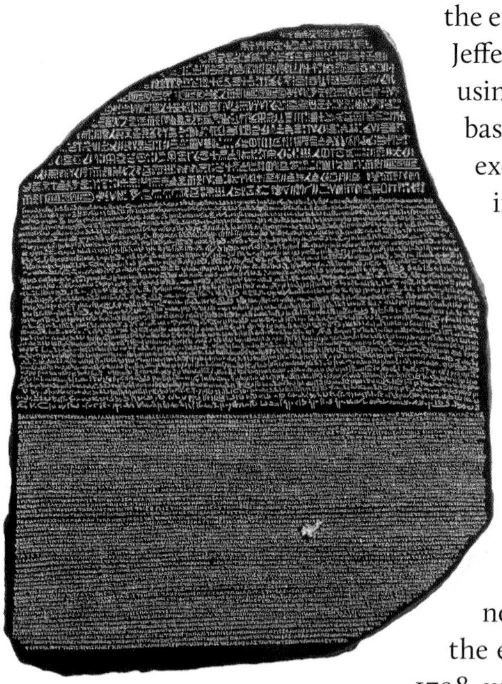

Fig. 3.1. Rosetta Stone

Systematic archaeological work did not begin in the Near East until the close of the eighteenth century. It started in the year 1798, when Napoleon invaded Egypt. As part of his force, Napoleon included architects, draftsmen, and scholars whose duty was to survey the ancient monuments of Egypt.[6] The French leader was well aware of the importance of history; as he gathered his troops at the foot of the pyramids for battle against the Mameluke army (July 21, 1798), Napoleon declared to his troops, "Soldiers! From atop these pyramids, fifty centuries look down upon you!"

Perhaps the greatest archaeological find ever was made by this expedition at the site of Rosetta in the Nile Delta next to the Mediterranean Sea. There they found what came to be known as the Rosetta Stone:

---

2. Egon Gersbach, "Herculaneum and Pompeii," in *The Oxford Companion to Archaeology*, ed. Brian Fagan (New York: Oxford University Press, 1996), 275.

3. See Christopher Parslow, *Rediscovering Antiquity: Karl Weber and the Excavation of Herculaneum, Pompeii and Stabiae* (Cambridge: Cambridge University Press, 1998).

4. William Stiebing, "Who First Excavated Stratigraphically?," *BAR* 7 (1981): 52–53.

5. Thomas Jefferson, *Notes on the State of Virginia*, ed. William Peden (Chapel Hill, NC: University of North Carolina Press, 2011), cited in Stiebing, "Who First Excavated," 53.

6. To view the engravings produced by this expedition, see Gilles Néret, *Description de l'Egypte* (Berlin: Taschen, 2007).

It proved to be invaluable because it was the key to unlocking ancient Egyptian hieroglyphics, a picture script unutilized for over fourteen hundred years. Dating to the time of King Ptolemy V (204–180 B.C.), the Rosetta Stone is inscribed in three scripts: demotic, Greek, and hieroglyphs. The Greek proved to be a translation of the ancient Egyptian language on the stone.[7]

The decipherment of hieroglyphics was the key to unlock the world of ancient Egypt. As Carol Andrews concluded, it "marked the beginning of the scientific reading of hieroglyphs and the first step toward formulation of a system of ancient Egyptian grammar, the basis of modern Egyptology."[8]

The French expedition also did some work in the important Valley of the Kings, where Egyptian pharaohs of the New Kingdom (1550–1070 B.C.) built royal tombs for themselves on the west bank of the Nile River across from ancient Thebes. The first to identify the site was the Jesuit priest Claude Sicard (1677–1726), but he did no archaeological work at the site. The valley contains over sixty tomb complexes, although not all of them belong to royalty. Major excavation work has taken place in the valley since the middle of the nineteenth century. The most well-known discovery was the tomb of Pharaoh Tutankhamen (1333–1323 B.C.), found by Howard Carter in 1922. No royal tomb has been found in the area since then, although in 2005 Otto Schaden uncovered a mummification storage area (he named it Tomb KV 63) that perhaps belongs to a larger tomb complex yet undiscovered.

The discovery of hieroglyphics not only unlocked the ancient culture of Egypt, but also had an almost immediate impact on the study of the Hebrew Old Testament. Translation soon took place of a monumental triumphal relief on the Bubastite Portal of the main temple of Amon at Karnak.[9] The relief provides confirmation and verification of the biblical account of Shoshenq I's invasion of Israel in the tenth century B.C. (see 1 Kings 14:25–26; 2 Chron. 12:2–4).

Archaeological investigation also began in Mesopotamia in the first half of the nineteenth century. George Roux explains:

> But in 1843 Paul Emile Botta, Italian-born French consul in Mosul, started at Khorsabad the first archaeological excavations in Iraq, discovered the Assyrians and opened a new era. Almost at once (1845) an Englishman, Sir Henry Layard, followed his example at Nimrud and Nineveh, and soon a number of tells were excavated.[10]

7. John D. Currid, *Doing Archaeology in the Land of the Bible* (Grand Rapids: Baker, 1999), 18–19.
8. Carol A. R. Andrews, "Rosetta Stone," in *Oxford Companion to Archaeology*, 620.
9. See, in particular, Kenneth A. Kitchen, *The Third Intermediate Period in Egypt (1100–650 B.C.)* (Warminster: Aris and Phillips, 1973).
10. Georges Roux, *Ancient Iraq* (repr., Baltimore: Penguin, 1976), 43.

Great strides in the decipherment of the Akkadian language were also taking place in the mid-nineteenth century. The key to unlocking cuneiform, and ultimately the Akkadian language, was the discovery and translation of the Behistun Inscription, which is a rock relief found on a cliff at Mount Behistun in western Iran. Much like the Rosetta Stone, this relief contained an inscription written in three different languages: Old Persian, Babylonian (a dialect of Akkadian), and Elamite. The Assyriologist Henry Rawlinson played a major role in the decipherment process; he, with the help of others, deciphered and translated the Old Persian text of the inscription.[11] This led to the decipherment of Akkadian, which by the late 1950s was considered a *fait accompli*.

Excavation work and translation work in Mesopotamia yielded much more material relevant to the study of the Old Testament than did Egypt. For example, the annals of Sargon II (722–705 B.C.) were discovered at Khorsabad, and the Assyrian king claimed in them, "I conquered and sacked the towns of Shinuhtu (and) Samaria, and all Israel." And again he boasts, "I besieged and conquered Samaria, led away as booty 27,290 inhabitants of it."[12] Sargon II made Israel a tributary province, and replaced much of its population with foreign peoples. The northern kingdom of Israel thus ceased to exist (2 Kings 17:24). The annals of Sargon II provide important details and confirmation of Israel's demise in the last quarter of the eighth century B.C.

Since our primary focus in this book is the archaeology of the Land of Promise, we will spend more time discussing the history of the discovery of ancient Palestine. Investigation of the land of Palestine has evolved greatly over time. In the early centuries after the New Testament period, ancient biblical sites were identified, many of them based on tradition, primarily as places for pilgrimage. Today, the study of the land is a discipline ruled by modern technology, computer analysis, and the incorporation of the physical and social sciences into its investigations. It is our intention to survey the history of archaeological research in Palestine from its humble beginnings during the pilgrim period to the modern time of vast information gathering and scientific study. I have divided this history into seven phases.[13]

---

11. Henry Rawlinson, *The Persian Cuneiform Inscription at Behistun, Deciphered and Translated with a Memoir on Persian Cuneiform Inscriptions in General, and on That of Behistun in Particular* (London: John W. Parker, 1846).

12. *ANET*, 284–85.

13. In my book *Doing Archaeology in the Land of the Bible*, 23–34, I structured the history into six phases, beginning with the individual explorers of the nineteenth century. I have added to that material here, and have included another phase that is important for the development of the discipline of archaeology.

PHASE 1: PILGRIMS (PRE-1838)

In the early centuries of the church, Palestine became a destination for pilgrims from various parts of the world because of the events of the Bible that had taken place there. Many of the sites visited were traditional in nature, that is, sites that were identified through an oral history that may or may not have been true. Biblical site identification for pilgrimage was promoted by Emperor Constantine (A.D. 306–337), who in 325 began a program to make sacred sites into public shrines. Queen Helena, Constantine's mother, was perhaps the primary mover in this process; she became a special patron of the Christian community in Jerusalem and in Palestine, and she supervised a religious building program there. For example, Helena played a significant role in the building of the Church of the Nativity in Bethlehem. The early fourth-century writer Eusebius comments that this traditional site of Jesus's birth was "adorned by the pious Empress with wonderful monuments, as she adorned the holy grotto there in manifold fashion." The earliest remains of the church date to the first half of the fourth century, and the church is still a site of pilgrimage today.

Some of the pilgrim sites were accurately identified through oral history. For instance, some of the important New Testament sites mentioned in the Gospels were places of pilgrimage for the early church. Theodosius, in A.D. 530, commented: "From Seven Springs (Tabgha) it is 2 miles to Capernaum. From Capernaum it is 6 miles to Bethsaida, where the Apostles Peter, Andrew, Philip, and the sons of Zebedee were born. From Bethsaida it is 50 miles to Panias: that is the place where the Jordan rises from the two places Ior and Dan."[14] The pilgrim Willibald visited the same area in 725: "From there [Capernaum, Willibald and his companions] went to Bethsaida, the city of Peter and Andrew: there is now a church there in the place where originally their house stood."[15] The geography described by those early travelers is essentially correct, and the sites they visited were historically accurate.

Over time, the locations of some of the pilgrim sites were lost. For example, the precise location of Bethsaida became uncertain, and its location became a matter of dispute until the present day. The recent investigations at et-Tel on the northern shore of the Sea of Galilee have confirmed that it is, in fact, the site of Bethsaida.[16] Recent excavation work at el-Araj, including the purported find of the "Church of the Apostles," has led the excavators to

---

14. John Wilkinson, *Jerusalem Pilgrims before the Crusades* (Warminster: Aris and Phillips, 1977), 63.

15. Wilkinson, *Jerusalem Pilgrims before the Crusades*, 128. See also Bargil Pixner, "Searching for the New Testament Site of Bethsaida," *BA* 48 (1985): 207–16.

16. See Rami Arav and Richard Freund, eds., *Bethsaida: A City by the North Shore of the Sea of Galilee* (Kirksville, MO: Thomas Jefferson University Press, 1995).

believe that it is the site of Bethsaida. A full assessment of that identification cannot be done until further excavation reports are published.

The location of many biblical sites during this period was a matter of speculation based on oral tradition, and some misidentified sites became places of pilgrimage. For instance, one of the most visited sites in Galilee throughout church history has been the traditional site of the Mount of Beatitudes. The New Testament gives no indication of the specific location of Jesus's Sermon on the Mount (Matthew 5–7). However, the Byzantines built a church in the fourth century A.D. at the foot of Mount Eremos that lies between Capernaum and Tabgha. This hill has been commemorated for over 1,600 years as the site of Jesus's greatest sermon, although its location is merely a matter of conjecture.

PHASE 2: PIONEERS (1838–65)

Amihai Mazar is correct when he says that "the research of the country started with systematic surface surveys and historical-geographic studies carried out by the American scholar E. Robinson."[17] Edward Robinson was professor of biblical literature, first at Andover Newton Theological Seminary (1830–33) and then at Union Theological Seminary in New York (1837–63). Prior to his academic appointments, Robinson studied in Germany for four years (1826–30), learning Hebrew under the great scholar Wilhelm Gesenius and studying "geography under the incomparable Ritter."[18] On his return to the United States, Robinson formulated a plan of study; he said, "I had long meditated the preparation of a work on biblical geography and wished to satisfy myself by personal observation as to points on which I could find no information in the books of travellers."[19] Robinson thus hoped to travel to Palestine and provide a systematic description of the topography and geography of the land.[20]

In 1838, Robinson, with his companion, Eli Smith, an American missionary in Beirut, traveled for four months throughout Egypt and Palestine. Their research was almost entirely topographical and geographical, but it was truly groundbreaking. They tried to map out as much of the land as possible, and they spent much time surveying areas that few researchers had ever studied. The sources of their labors consisted primarily of the Bible and site names and traditions from the local Arab population. Robinson and Smith did not

---

17. Amihai Mazar, *Archaeology of the Land of the Bible* (New York: Doubleday, 1990), 10.
18. William Foxwell Albright, *The Archaeology of Palestine* (Harmondsworth, UK: Penguin, 1949), 25.
19. Edward F. Robinson and Eli Smith, *Biblical Researches in Palestine, Mount Sinai and Arabia Petraea* (Boston: Crocker and Brewster, 1856), 1:36.
20. Albrecht Alt, "Edward Robinson and the Historical Geography of Palestine," *JBL* 58 (1939): 375.

employ traditions held by local monasteries or churches, because many of them were inaccurate. They described their route and discoveries in three volumes titled *Biblical Researches in Palestine and in the Adjacent Regions* (1856). Robinson made a second survey trip in 1852, and he published his findings in his book *Later Biblical Researches in Palestine and in the Adjacent Regions*.[21] Robinson and Smith's work, particularly their identifying of biblical sites, has proved to be essentially accurate. Albrecht Alt concludes that "in Robinson's footnotes are buried the errors of generations."[22]

Robinson's labors were a great leap forward in the historical study of the land of Palestine. Titus Tobler, who soon followed Robinson in doing survey work of Palestine, commented, "The works of Robinson and Smith alone surpass the total of all previous contributions to Palestinian geography from the time of Eusebius and Jerome to the early nineteenth century."[23] Equally important is the fact that Robinson and Smith's foundational survey work served as an immense stimulus to others to do further investigation of the land. As Neil Silberman points out, "Palestine witnessed an unprecedented flood of western travelers intent on following in the footsteps of the learned American professor and recovering the splendor of the biblical past."[24] For this reason, Robinson is often called "the founder of modern Palestinology" or "the Father of Biblical Geography."[25]

The most important succeeding investigations included an American expedition led by Lieutenant W. F. Lynch to map out the course of the Jordan River from the Sea of Galilee in the north to the Dead Sea in the south. Titus Tobler worked in Palestine for several seasons (1845–46, 1858, and 1865), and he produced a seven-volume publication of his finds. He was the first to provide a detailed examination of the Church of the Holy Sepulchre in Jerusalem. The surveying work of Victor Guerin soon followed, and it covered the areas of Galilee, Samaria, and Judah in vast detail (1852–75). A lot of Guerin's work was speculative in site identification, and, as Peter Moorey comments, "he made relatively few identifications which have survived subsequent scrutiny."[26] Albright's assessment of these post-Robinson surveys is correct when he says that "little of permanent value was accomplished," and that Robinson's work was so well done that "nothing was left for his successors but gleanings."[27]

---

21. Edward F. Robinson, *Later Biblical Researches in Palestine and in the Adjacent Regions* (Boston: Crocker and Brewster, 1856).

22. Alt, "Edward Robinson," 374.

23. Cited in Albright, *The Archaeology of Palestine*, 25.

24. Neil A. Silberman, *Digging for God and Country: Exploration, Archeology, and the Secret Struggle for the Holy Land* (New York: Knopf, 1982), 51.

25. James B. Pritchard, *Archaeology and the Old Testament* (Princeton, NJ: Princeton University Press, 1958), 57–58.

26. Peter R. S. Moorey, *A Century of Biblical Archaeology* (Louisville: Westminster / John Knox, 1991), 18.

27. Albright, *The Archaeology of Palestine*, 26.

This was a period of little excavation work, and what was done was primitive and bordered on treasure hunting. Frederic de Saulcy did some digging in Palestine, and he is most well known for having opened and cleared the so-called Tombs of the Kings in Jerusalem. Albright generously declared de Saulcy to be "the first modern excavator of a Palestinian site."[28] That is perhaps true, although artifacts had been dug up through excavation at earlier times; in fact, "the first archaeological artifact ever discovered by excavation in Palestine" was found by Lady Hester Lucy Stanhope in the early 1800s.[29] In reality, the study of Palestine between 1838 and 1865 was primarily geographical and topographical in nature. The "main achievement concerning the Old Testament period in this early phase of research was the identification of many biblical places with ruins and sites which in many cases preserved the ancient names."[30] Although the work was a mere baby step in the discipline of archaeology, it was an important one that laid the foundation upon which later archaeological work might be established.

PHASE 3: SOCIETIES (1865–90)

Much of the work done by the pioneers of phase 2 was individualistic. It consisted of one or two investigators, with compass and Bible in hand, who rode on horses throughout Palestine to identify and mark ancient biblical sites. This next stage was corporate, in that learned societies were established to promote archaeological inquiry in the Holy Land. The British created the first society dedicated to this purpose, and it was called the Palestine Exploration Fund; it was founded in 1865 and still exists today. In November of that year, the Fund sent its first expedition to Palestine under the oversight of Captain Charles Wilson. He was sent there to carry out a feasibility study and to "locate such spots as might merit the further investigation of the Fund."

Much of the work of this phase continued to be topographical, geographical, and survey investigation, but it was done in a more intense manner. For example, in 1871, the PEF sent two army lieutenants, Claude Conder and H. H. Kitchener, to Palestine to survey and map out the entire land west of the Jordan River.[31] They completed their work in 1877 and published four volumes

---

28. Albright, *The Archaeology of Palestine*, 26.
29. Silberman, *Digging for God and Country*, 26.
30. Mazar, *Archaeology of the Land of the Bible*, 10–11.
31. Kitchener was 24 years old when he joined the survey team. He later became famous as a British soldier who won the battle of Omdurman during the Second Boer War, became commander and chief of the army in India, and held the cabinet post of Secretary of State for War. Conder did not become as famous, although recently he has been accused of being the infamous Jack the Ripper!

in 1881 that gave the results of their survey that covered about 6,000 square miles.[32] Conder performed further survey work beginning in 1881, but this time he was exploring the area of Jordan (eastern Palestine). He completed some of the work before he was stopped by the Ottoman government, and then published his findings in 1889.[33] Kitchener also did further survey work by focusing on the region of the Dead Sea.

In 1870, the Society of Biblical Archaeology was founded in Great Britain. The purpose of this society was

> to collect from the fast perishing monuments of the Semitic and cognate races illustrations of their history and peculiarities; to investigate and systematize the Antiquities of the ancient and mighty empires and primeval peoples whose records are centered around the venerable pages of the Bible. In other words, an Association to bring into connexion the labours of individual scholars, and to utilize the results of private enterprize and national munificence—to accumulate data, and to preserve facts—to give a voice to the past, a new life to the future, and assistance, publicity, and permanence to the efforts of all students in Biblical Archaeology.[34]

Much of the labor of this society was publication and analysis of archaeological finds. Prominent figures in the archaeology of the ancient Near East during the nineteenth century were members of this society: Henry Rawlinson, F. de Saulcy, A. H. Sayce, Charles Wilson, and many others.

Although a lot of the work of this period continued to be survey, some important excavation work did take place. Perhaps the most important work at this time occurred under the supervision of Charles Warren, who was sent to Jerusalem by the PEF to excavate the Temple Mount (known to Muslims as Haram esh-Sharif). Although local authorities barred Warren from excavating the mount itself, the Englishman did dig thirty or so shafts in areas south and west of the mount. He discovered that the lower courses of the platform of the mount were in fact the very foundation upon which Herod's temple sat during the Roman period. According to Silberman, Warren also "succeeded in locating the southern and northern limits of the city, investigated an ancient subterranean aqueduct on the southern slope, and unearthed a number of pottery jar handles, stamped in ancient Hebrew with the words 'Belonging to the King,' which were the first genuine Biblical artifacts ever scientifically excavated in the Holy City."[35]

---

32. Claude Conder and Horatio H. Kitchener, *The Survey of Western Palestine (1871–1877)* (London: Palestine Exploration Fund, 1881).

33. Claude Conder, *The Survey of Eastern Palestine* (London: Palestine Exploration Fund, 1889).

34. These are introductory remarks given at the founding of this society; see *Transactions of the Society of Biblical Archaeology* 1 (1872): 1.

35. Silberman, *Digging for God and Country*, 94.

Archaeological work in Palestine was not the sole dominion of the British during this phase. Other countries established societies to explore, research, and publish findings from Palestine. In 1870, Americans founded the American Palestine Exploration Society, and they sent John Paine to Palestine to lead its first expedition.[36] It was not a particularly noteworthy endeavor; Paine's team made casts of some ancient inscriptions, put together a collection of foliage, and was able to identify the ancient site of Pisgah. The Germans entered the picture with the founding of the Deutscher Palästina-Verein in 1877, and much of their early work continued the survey of the land of Palestine. Gottlieb Schumacher, who would later excavate the site of Megiddo, surveyed the Golan region east of the Sea of Galilee in 1884. The French founded the École Biblique et Archéologique in 1890, although some Frenchmen, like Charles Clermont-Ganneau, had been working in the land prior to that time.

PHASE 4: TELL EXCAVATION (1890–1914)

One of the momentous and consequential events for the archaeology of Palestine was Heinrich Schliemann's excavation of ancient Troy, which began in 1871. Although his archaeological methodology was primitive by today's standards, Schliemann discovered that the site of ancient Troy was a mound consisting of a series of occupational layers, one lying on top of another. The mound was like a many-layered cake, in which one ruined city had been built on top of another, and the top layer was the latest in date. This discovery was the real beginnings of stratigraphy, which may be defined as the study of the deposition and relationships of the occupational layers of an archaeological site.

In 1890, an eccentric Englishman named William M. Flinders Petrie applied the important and groundbreaking work of Schliemann at Troy to the archaeology of Palestine. Petrie, an Egyptologist by profession, had been in the Middle East since 1880, when he came to Egypt to measure and study the great pyramids at Giza. Due to unstable political conditions in Egypt at the close of the decade, Petrie thought it prudent to leave the country. The British Palestine Exploration Fund immediately appointed him to direct the first systematic archaeological excavation in Palestine. Petrie chose to excavate Tell el-Hesi, a 34-acre mound located in the Shephelah (foothills) of Palestine. The archaeologist endured many trials and dangers at the site, but at the end of his time there he could remark, "I had six weeks work there, including the whole month of Ramadan, when work is very difficult for the

36. See Warren J. Moulton, "The American Palestine Exploration Society," *AASOR* 8 (1926–1927): 55–78.

fasting and thirsty Muslims. But in that time, and without disturbing the crops, I succeeded in unraveling the history of the place."

What Petrie did was to cut vertical sections in the slopes of the mound. By probing that way, he uncovered 60 feet of superimposed occupation, one living layer on top of another. He determined that there had been eleven cities in the history of Tell el-Hesi, covering a period of about 3,000 years. When one city was destroyed, another city was built on top of it. Petrie further observed that every city layer or period had broken pottery in it. He noted the style and type of pottery in every level, and he discovered that each period had its own typical pottery. He was then able to correlate the pottery of several layers at Hesi with pottery from Egypt, and thereby secure a relative chronology of the history of Hesi. These two features, what are now called stratigraphy and ceramic typology, are the backbone of modern archaeology. There is simply no dig in Palestine that does not base its research and findings on these methods employed by Petrie. Because of his labors at Hesi, Petrie has rightfully earned the nickname "the Father of Palestinian Archaeology."

Soon after Petrie's formative work, numerous excavations of significant mounds in Palestine began in earnest. F. J. Bliss continued Petrie's work at Tell el-Hesi, and there he built upon Petrie's method of stratigraphical analysis.[37] Then came major campaigns at Taanach, Jericho, Gezer, Beth-Shemesh, Megiddo, and Samaria. This was an important period for the development of archaeological methodology, as William Dever comments: "The foundations of the discipline were laid in the first appreciation of the true nature of the tell and how it was formed. Archaeologists began to learn how to disentangle the successive strata and to date each by its contents, particularly the pottery. . . . The result was that by 1914 a rough outline of the history and culture of ancient Palestine had been produced."[38]

Dever was correct in using the word "rough" in reference to these early excavations, because by today's standards their procedures were quite primitive and lacked consistency in excavation technique. For example, R. A. S. Macalister, digging at the site of Gezer (1902–9), was well aware of the importance of stratigraphy for excavation, but he abandoned it because "the complexity of the stratification of the mound itself made it difficult to carry through the work of description in the form proposed." Consequently, hardly a single object can be related to the stratigraphy of the site, and even the determination of the buildings in which items were found is speculative. Macalister justified himself by concluding, "The exact spot in the mound where any ordinary object chanced to lie is not generally of great

37. Frederick J. Bliss, *A Mound of Many Cities*, 2nd ed. (London: Palestine Exploration Fund , 1898).
38. William G. Dever, "Archaeological Method in Israel: A Continuing Revolution," *BA* 43 (1980): 42.

importance."[39] The use of ceramic for dating was also hit or miss. Gottlieb Schumacher's excavations at Megiddo (1903–5) are a case in point. His limited use of ceramic typology and basic disregard of stratigraphy make his findings virtually useless for reconstructing the history of the site.

Another important development at this time was the establishment of foreign archaeological institutions in Jerusalem: the École Biblique in 1890, the German Evangelical School in 1902 (under the direction of Albrecht Alt), and the British School of Archaeology in 1919. Typical of these institutions was the American School of Oriental Research, which was established in 1900. Its purpose was "to enable properly qualified persons to prosecute Biblical, linguistic, archaeological, historical, and other kindred studies and researches under more favorable conditions than can be secured at a distance from the Holy Land."[40] The first excavations of ASOR began in 1901 of tombs in Sidon, and this was followed by a major excavation at the site of Samaria in 1909 under the direction of G. A. Reisner.

PHASE 5: THE GOLDEN AGE (1918–40)

Between the two great world wars, archaeology made great strides in becoming an academic, scientific discipline, over against the image of mere treasure hunting. Archaeologists developed sound techniques for excavation and recording of materials that they found. Many of the excavators were associated with major educational institutions, and they displayed scholarly competence.[41] Along with advancing methodology of excavation, two further developments took place that were critical for the field. First, the chronology of the history of Palestine from the Neolithic period to the Roman period was settled in detail, and it remains the basic dating structure that is still used today. Although sometimes called into question, the chronology has stood the test of time. Second, scholars of this phase began to see how the history and archaeology of Palestine fit in with the study of the rest of the ancient Near East.

Two excavations during this period set archaeology as an academic discipline on solid footing. The first was undertaken at the site of Megiddo under the direction of C. S. Fisher, beginning in 1925. Fisher served as professor of archaeology at the American School in Jerusalem from 1925 until his death in 1941. He published his findings in 1929.[42] Fisher's most lasting

---

39. William G. Dever, "Gezer," in *EAEHL*, 2:434 (1976).

40. Philip J. King, *American Archaeology in the Mideast: A History of the American Schools of Oriental Research* (Philadelphia: ASOR, 1983), 27.

41. Dever, "Archaeological Method in Israel," 43.

42. Clarence S. Fisher, *The Excavation of Armageddon*, OIC 4 (Chicago: University of Chicago Press, 1929).

legacy was his systematic approach to excavation and a detailed recording system, so that what had been dug would not be lost. Fisher also excavated the major sites of Beth Shean and Beth-Shemesh.

The work at Megiddo was turned over to P. L. O. Guy in 1927. His supervision improved the excavation technique of Fisher, and he employed photography throughout (and even used aerial photography). Gordon Loud led the excavations from 1935 to 1939, and he published many of the findings of Megiddo. His report is still considered today to be a standard way to present archaeological remains from a site.[43]

The second excavation began in 1926 under the direction of William Foxwell Albright at Tell Beit Mirsim. The hallmarks of his work there were careful stratigraphic investigation and a clear ceramic typology. Albright's delineation of the Bronze and Iron Ages according to these procedures remains the standard for today's archaeological work. Philip King is right when he says that the excavations at Tell Beit Mirsim "marked such a significant step in the development of ceramic chronology that even today no student of Syro-Palestinian archaeology can afford to neglect the Tell Beit Mirsim publications."[44] Albright had great influence in the field, as he served as professor of Semitic languages at Johns Hopkins University from 1927 to 1958, and was the editor of *BASOR* from 1931 to 1968.[45] He trained many archaeologists, such as George Ernest Wright, who would play a significant role in the development of archaeology in Palestine. Although much of what Albright concluded is under great scrutiny by today's scholars, particularly his understanding of the relationship between the Bible and archaeology, what George Ernest Wright said about him still holds today: "It must be said that Albright created the discipline of Palestinian archaeology as we know it."[46]

Jewish archaeologists from Palestine became active during this period.[47] Among these scholars were Benjamin Mazar (Ramat Rahel in 1931 and Bet She'arin in 1936–40), E. L. Sukenik (Jerusalem in 1925–27 and Hammat Gader in 1932), and Michael Avi-Yonah (Hosifa in 1931 and Nahariya in 1941). These early Jewish excavators laid the foundation for the later Israeli school of archaeology that began in the 1940s.[48] Also, the influential Department

---

43. Gordon Loud, *Megiddo II*, OIP 62 (Chicago: University of Chicago Press, 1948).

44. Philip J. King, "The American Archaeological Heritage in the Near East," *BASOR* 217 (1975): 60.

45. For a study of Albright's influence, see P. D. Feinman, *William Foxwell Albright and the Origins of Biblical Archaeology* (Berrien Springs, MI: Andrews University Press, 2004).

46. George Ernest Wright, "The Phenomenon of American Archaeology," in *Near Eastern Archaeology in the Twentieth Century*, ed. James A. Sanders (Garden City, NY: Doubleday, 1970), 27.

47. For an overview, see William Foxwell Albright, "The Phenomenon of Israeli Archaeology," in *Near Eastern Archaeology in the Twentieth Century*, ed. James A. Sanders (Garden City, NY: Doubleday, 1970), 57–63.

48. See Eric M. Meyers, "Judaic Studies and Archaeology: The Rochaeology: The Legacy of Michael Avi-Yonah," *EI* 19 (1987): 21–27.

of Archaeology (now the Institute of Archaeology) was founded at Hebrew University in Jerusalem in 1934.

The number of excavations in Palestine mushroomed during this period. Major projects included the digs at Samaria (1931–35, under the supervision of J. W. Crowfoot), Jericho (directed by John Garstang, 1930–36), Tell en-Nasbeh (directed by W. F. Bade for five seasons between 1926 and 1935), and Bethel (led by W. F. Albright in 1934). Major journals that are dedicated to the publication of archaeological materials from the region were founded during this phase: for example, the *Bulletin of the American Schools of Oriental Research* (1919) and the *Biblical Archaeologist* (1938) came into being.

PHASE 6: DEVELOPMENT OF SYSTEMATIC EXCAVATION (1948–67)

Between 1940 and 1948, little archaeological work was done in Palestine because of World War II and the unrest that led to the partitioning of the land and the founding of the nation of Israel. This lull also marks a major change in archaeological methodology. Prior to 1940, the dominant excavation technique was the architectural method, which aimed at wide-scale exposure of complete buildings.[49] After the hiatus, new methods were introduced to the discipline that would affect archaeology from there on out.

The primary innovation came from the British archaeologist Kathleen Kenyon, who led the excavations at Jericho (1952–58) and at Jerusalem (1961–67). Kenyon introduced the methods of Mortimer Wheeler to the excavation of sites in Palestine. Wheeler had directed numerous excavations of Roman forts in Wales in the 1920s: Segontium, Y Gaer, and Isca Augusta, for example. There he developed what is known as the "Wheeler Method" of excavation, which focused on careful stratigraphic digging technique and detailed recording of excavation areas and finds. Applying this technique to Palestine, Kenyon "dug in smaller squares (usually 5 x 5 m) within a grid, leaving intervening catwalks, or 'balks,' which were then used to see the debris in section and to guide careful probing and stripping of the debris."[50]

In the archaeology of Palestine, this came to be known as the "Wheeler-Kenyon Method," and Kenyon's application of it stressed, to a great degree, the stratification of a site. The method had important consequences for digging: first, it gave a critical element of control and precision over an excavation area. Second, it provided a third dimension to an excavation field by leaving a balk around the individual areas. This allows the archaeologist to see what

---

49. David Ussishkin, "Where Is Israeli Archaeology Going?," *BA* 45 (1982): 93–95.
50. Dever, "Archaeological Method in Israel," 44.

has been excavated, and to view how the current level of excavation relates to what preceded it.

Many archaeologists working in Palestine during this period embraced the innovative techniques of Kenyon. For example, the Americans working at the site of Shechem (1956–66), under the direction of G. E. Wright, used Kenyon's methodology in conjunction with the attention that American archaeologists gave to detailed pottery analysis (based on Albright's work at Tell Beit Mirsim). These two techniques characterized American archaeological excavations for at least the next two generations.

Fig. 3.2. Professor Yigael Yadin

Israeli archaeologists became a major force in the discipline during this phase. Perhaps the greatest catalyst for this development was the work at Hazor (1955–58) and Masada (1963–65) under the direction of Yigael Yadin. These digs served as training ground for the next generation of Israeli archaeologists, including Yohanan Aharoni, Ruth Amiran, Amnon Ben-Tor, Moshe and Trude Dothan, David Ussishkin, and others. The methodology of the Israeli school of archaeology was primarily architectural in nature. Their aim was to expose large areas of architecture. However, this approach lost some stratigraphic control over the excavation areas. The differences between the Wheeler-Kenyon / American practices and those of the Israeli school became a dominant topic in the literature of the time. The solution to the problem would appear in the next phase of the archaeological history of Palestine.

PHASE 7: INFORMATION EXPLOSION (1967–)

A compromise has taken place between the two methodologies of excavation. Amihai Mazar correctly summarizes it as follows: "As much as possible of the area of the site is exposed with the intention of uncovering complete architectural units and studying their layout. Cross-examination of the occupational history is achieved by excavating at several different points. Analysis of the earth layers is not neglected: sections are examined and in many cases recorded by drawing and photography."[51] This is a good balance, in which stratigraphic control is kept while major areas of the site are exposed; the large picture and the small picture are both kept in view.

The major development during this period was the expansion of excavation staffs to include specialists from various disciplines, such as geologists, osteologists, botanists, ceramicists, zoologists, and others. This multidisciplinary approach has contributed greatly to the understanding of the material culture of a site. Although the approach was employed sparingly throughout the history of excavation, it really came to the fore during the American excavations at the site of Gezer (1964–73), under the direction of George E. Wright, William G. Dever, and Joe D. Seger. It became commonplace for excavations to take this approach, including the digs at Beersheba (1969–75), Tell el-Hesi (1970–83), Caesarea (1971–), Lachish (1972–), Ashkelon (1985–), Megiddo (1994–), and Heshbon in Transjordan (1968–). Beginning with the Gezer project, many of these excavations included field schools with the purpose of serving as an outdoor classroom for students.[52]

A second important development during this time was the formation of joint projects between archaeologists from different countries, and, in particular, the creation of university consortiums to investigate a site. For example, at the site of Bethsaida, the project team consists of a consortium of schools from Australia, Israel, and the United States. The chief archaeologist is Rami Arav, an Israeli who teaches at an American university. Israel Finkelstein directs current excavations at Megiddo under the auspices of Tel Aviv University, and there is a consortium of American and Israeli schools that contribute to the project.

In this phase, archaeology has become more regional and contextual. Archaeologists deem it vital not only to study the mound under investi-

---

51. Mazar, *Archaeology of the Land of the Bible*, 25.
52. For example, the author was initially trained at the field school held at the site of Tell Qasile for eight weeks during the summer of 1972 (under the direction of Amihai Mazar).

gation, but also to examine the environment surrounding the site. Such study provides a broad context for understanding the history of the tell. This regional approach perhaps began with the excavations of Yohanan Aharoni at Beersheba.[53]

Archaeology as a discipline has come a long way since Edward Robinson and others traversed the land in the mid-nineteenth century. They, with compass and thermometer in hand, traveled on horseback throughout Palestine to identify as many historical sites as possible. Today, archaeologists employ modern technology, such as computer analysis and data organization. The so-called New Archaeology has come to the fore, which includes a multidisciplinary approach that uses all of the sciences, both natural and social. William Dever says the excavators now "pay attention to floral and faunal remains, traces of past subsistence systems, evidence for environmental change, and indeed *all* data on material culture that by chance had been preserved in the archaeological record."[54] Thus, fields of study like ethnology, ecology, and general systems theory have become integral to excavation work in Palestine.[55]

KEY TERMS

balk
ceramic typology
New Archaeology
stratigraphy
Wheeler-Kenyon Method

DISCUSSION QUESTIONS

1. Why was the decipherment of Egyptian hieroglyphs so important for the study of the Old Testament? In your thinking and answering, consider the relationship that Israel had with Egypt in antiquity.

2. If you were to describe an archaeologist in the nineteenth century, how would that person differ from an archaeologist in the twenty-first century? What has happened that affected that change?

3. In 1923, William M. Flinders Petrie was knighted for his services to the study of archaeology and Egyptology. What archaeological practices of Petrie were so innovative that he has been called "the Father of Palestinian Archaeology"?

53. Ussishkin, "Where Is Israeli Archaeology Going?," 95.
54. William G. Dever, "Archaeology, Syro-Palestinian and Biblical," *ABD* 1 (1992): 355.
55. William G. Dever, "The Impact of the 'New Archaeology' on Syro-Palestinian Archaeology," *BASOR* 242 (1981): 15.

FOR FURTHER READING

Albright, William F. *The Archaeology of Palestine*. Gloucester, MA: Peter
     Smith, 1971. See chapter 2, pp. 23–28, titled "The Discovery of
     Ancient Palestine."

Currid, John D. *Doing Archaeology in the Land of the Bible*. Grand Rapids:
     Baker, 1999. See chapter 2, pp. 23–36, titled "A Brief History of Pal-
     estinian Archaeology."

Moorey, Peter R. S. *A Century of Biblical Archaeology*. Louisville: Westmin-
     ster / John Knox, 1992.

Silberman, Neil. *Digging for God and Country: Exploration, Archeology, and
     the Secret Struggle for the Holy Land, 1799–1917*. New York: Random
     House, 1982.

CHAPTER 4

Tell Excavation

"Archaeology and crime detection are similar because you have to clear away the debris to reveal shining truth."—Agatha Christie

I RECENTLY VISITED THE Shell Ring excavations on Hilton Head Island in South Carolina. This ancient site, dating to about 2000 B.C., consists of a circular shell ring about thirty-five meters in diameter and one meter high. The ring itself is comprised of multiple layers of shells, predominantly from mollusks. According to the excavator, the building of the ring occurred over a 300-year period. Its purpose is unknown; some thought it might have been a burial ground, but no graves have been found there. Excavations like this one—Indian sites or colonial towns in America—are normally small, and the tools of excavation are diminutive, including tools like the brush and dental pick. The sites are frequently one-period settlements. Consequently, the material remains at such a site tell the story of one group of people at one particular time in history.

Archaeology in the ancient Near East is much different. Rarely does the archaeologist deal with small, one-period sites; rather, one investigates settlements that have been occupied repeatedly over extended periods of time. For example, the town of Tel Beersheba, located in the Negev, was first settled in the Chalcolithic period (fourth millennium B.C.) and last inhabited during the Roman period (second through third centuries A.D.). During that 4,000-year history, there were many occupations, most notably during the Iron Age and the Persian period. And the site is large, comprising an area of 2.5 acres. As a further example, Tel Dan, which is located in northern Israel at the foot of Mount Hermon, is very large, encompassing an area of about 50 acres. Its earliest remains come from the Early Bronze II period (ca. 2800 B.C.); its final stage was its use as a military outpost with defensive trenches dating from the mid-twentieth century A.D. In between there were major settlements during the Middle Bronze, Late Bronze, and Iron Ages. So the question for us to answer is, what do these multilayered settlements look like? How do they differ from the sites that are found in the Americas?

THE TELL

What are the factors that would have drawn a group of people to settle a particular site in antiquity? There are several of these that need to be taken into consideration. The most important necessity, of course, was *a permanent water source*; without water and access to it, humans simply cannot survive. Before the discovery of means to control water supply, such as cisterns, aqueducts, and irrigation techniques, villages were founded next to perennial water sources, that is, wells, wadis, springs, and streams. In ancient Palestine, the earliest settlements were established in the Jordan River Valley and along the banks of the Sea of Galilee. For an overview of water management in ancient Palestine, see chapter 14 of this work.

Another critical condition for ancient settlement was *defense*. Many of the ancient sites were built on rocky outcrops because the elevation provided a good defensive posture.[1] The height gave people other military advantages, such as range of vision against approaching invaders and control of any thoroughfares that passed by the site. As early as the Neolithic period, settlers began erecting fortifications, and these outer walls, towers, and gates were built on top of the rocky outcrops. These man-made structures on top of a natural mound simply added to the stout military standing of a site. For a brief study of the fortifications of ancient Palestine, see chapter 15 of this work.

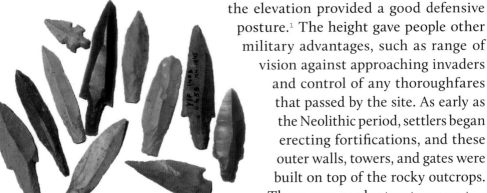

Fig. 4.1. Yiftahel Pre-Pottery Neolithic B Flint Arrowheads

With the transition of humanity from hunting and gathering to *agriculture* during the Neolithic period, the availability of rich agricultural land in close proximity to a settlement became paramount. Although local farming provided much of the sustenance needed by a settlement, many of the sites were located next to road systems that would provide access to commerce. Trade routes were valuable to emerging towns.

As mentioned, pioneers built their settlements on top of rocky outcrops. Availability of *building materials* was essential to this process. Ancient Palestinian towns were built with stone, mud-brick, or a combination of the two. Wood was used as well, but mainly in gate complexes. For further study of the materials used in architecture, see chapter 15 of this work.

1. Paul W. Lapp, *The Tale of the Tell* (Pittsburgh: Pickwick, 1975), 1–3.

All ancient towns, villages, and cities were either abandoned or destroyed. This termination came by various means. War, of course, was a primary cause of destruction. Natural disasters, such as famine, drought, earthquake, and fire, also took their toll. Sites were also abandoned because of plagues, pestilences, and diseases. Natural processes, such as torrential rains and erosion, could wreak havoc on a site and, consequently, rebuilding was a common practice. For whatever reason, all ancient sites were eventually destroyed and left unoccupied.

After the abandonment or destruction of a site, in the course of time, natural elements began to decay the human-built structures. William F. Albright defines one of these wasting processes: "During this period of abandonment, the rain, driven by the prevailing west wind, washed the debris of house walls and roofs off the site until further erosion was checked by the substructure of the fortifications, which remained standing under the debris of the superstructure."[2] Drifting winds also sped the decay and deposited sand and dirt in low-lying areas on top of the site. After decades and sometimes centuries of neglect, new settlers would discover the site and build on top of it. This second group chose the site for the same reasons as the original pioneers: water, defense, agriculture, and building resources. Unlike modern builders, the newcomers did not remove the ruins of the previous settlement; rather, they built directly on top of them. The rebuilding only enhanced the defensive posture of the site because it added to its elevation. According to Kathleen Kenyon, the depth of the debris on which new settlements were built ranged from a few inches to many feet.[3] Sometimes the new settlers would use some of the earlier building remains in their rebuilding, and at times they would use the earlier building foundations as the foundations for their structures. This act of "robbing" from earlier periods can be problematic for the investigator who tries to reconstruct the history of a site.[4]

This second occupation of the site met the same fate as the first settlement. It eventually was destroyed or abandoned. As time went on, successive occupations followed one another; the cycle of settlement, destruction, abandonment, resettlement occurred repeatedly at many sites. Large cities like Jericho, Lachish, and Megiddo all contained over twenty levels of occupation.

Archaeologists call each occupation layer at a site a *stratum* (pl. *strata*). The deposition of one stratum on top of another over time built up an arti-

---

2. William Foxwell Albright, *The Archaeology of Palestine* (Harmondsworth, UK: Penguin, 1949), 17.

3. Kathleen Kenyon, *Archaeology in the Holy Land*, 3rd ed. (New York: Praeger, 1970), 30.

4. An interesting example of this "robbing" appears at the site of Caesarea Maritima. The builders of the Crusader city there often used blocks of stone that were clearly from the time of Herod the Great in the first century B.C. to build gates and other fortifications.

ficial mound on top of a rocky outcrop that resembled "a low truncated cone, with flat top and sloping sides."[5] The shape of the mound is often compared to a cake that has many layers.

As one looks at a settlement mound today, there are two peculiar features. First, the mound is flat on top. This configuration developed after the last occupation ended: natural elements, over time, deposited debris on the top of the mound that was then held in place by the external walls of the ruined city. Through the centuries, the accumulation of debris gave a flat definition to the mound. Second, the sides of the mound are not vertical, but steeply sloped. This configuration was partially due to the erection of a glacis around the mound by ancient builders. A glacis was a long, sloping fortification that ran from the foot of the mound to the top of the defensive wall, and it normally surrounded the entire site. A glacis consisted of layers of rubble that acted much like a girdle: it held the mound together and limited erosion from the top of the mound. Consequently, the sides of a settlement mound were much steeper than a natural hill.[6] When archaeologist Joe Seger first visited the site of Tell Halif, which he would later excavate, he explained how he knew it was a settlement mound at first sight. He said, "The identifying configurations were the mound's sizeable flat surface on top and its regularly sloping sides. The flatness indicated successive building layers; the sloping sides, ancient fortification walls beneath the surface."[7]

Archaeologists call an occupation mound a *tell*, using an Arabic word meaning "hill" (pl. *tulul*). The modern Hebrew equivalent is *tel*, as in the city name Tel Aviv.[8] The origin of the word *tell* is unknown, although some scholars believe it may derive from the Akkadian *sillu* or Sumerian *dul*, which both mean "mound, heap of ruins, female breast." The Old Testament uses the Hebrew term *tel* to refer to a stratified mound with one city lying on top of another (see Josh. 11:13; Jer. 30:18).

There are thousands of tells that dot the landscape of the ancient Near East. As Mazar says,

> This phenomenon is fundamental to the archaeology of the Near East. Most of the pre-Hellenistic towns in Palestine are to be found in such *tells*. Their average area is 7–20 acres; the smallest known is half an acre, while the largest, Tel Hazor, measures 200 acres. Many *tells* were settled over a period of between one and two thousand years, and their accumulated

5. Albright, *The Archaeology of Palestine*, 16.
6. Oded Borowski, "How to Tell a Tell," *BAR* 7 (1981): 66–67.
7. Catharine Cole, "How a Dig Begins," *BAR* 3 (1977): 32–36.
8. Nineteenth-century Western publications often used the word *tall* for a stratified mound, but that designation has become obsolete.

debris may include more than twenty layers of ruined cities, each forming an archaeological stratum.[9]

The size of tells is not standardized or uniform. In fact, tells in Palestine are small in comparison to those of the rest of the ancient Near East. For example, Nippur, an important city in ancient Babylonia, consisted of three tells that covered almost 400 acres (almost twice the size of Hazor). The Assyrian city Nineveh was built on two tells that had a circumference of almost 8 miles.

DISCOVERY OF THE TELL

The nature of tell construction as described above is a recent revelation in the history of mankind. It was not until the second half of the nineteenth century that scholars began to understand the workings of tells. Prior to that time, stratigraphy was a mystery for the most part. Edward Robinson, a pioneer investigator of Palestine, commented on his visit to the site of Tell el-Hesi in the 1830s, saying

> The form of the Tell is singular, a truncated cone with a fine plain on the top. . . . From the information of our guides, and from the remarkable appearance of this isolated Tell, we had expected to find here traces of ruins. . . . Yet we could discover nothing whatever to mark the existence of any former town or structure.[10]

Things changed with the excavations at Troy, located at Hisarlik in modern-day Turkey, under the direction of Heinrich Schliemann (1822–90).[11]

The digging at Troy was the first excavation of a tell with the understanding that it was one ruined city on top of another. Stratigraphic analysis at the city, however, did not originate with Schliemann; in fact, his labors were often destructive and amateurish. The real pioneer of stratigraphic excavation at Troy was Wilhelm Dorpfeld (1853–1940), an architect who recognized and applied the method of dating layers of a site on the basis of objects and buildings found within the various layers. In fact, Arthur Evans, the excavator of Knossos, considers Schliemann's "greatest discovery" at Troy to be Wilhelm Dorpfeld![12] Although the excavators of Troy recognized

9. Amihai Mazar, *Archaeology of the Land of the Bible* (New York: Doubleday, 1990), 9.

10. Edward Robinson, *Biblical Researches in Palestine II* (London: J. Murray, 1841), 390, cited in Peter R. S. Moorey, *Excavation in Palestine* (Guildford, UK: Lutterworth, 1981), 21.

11. See Susan Heuck Allen, *Finding Walls at Troy: Frank Calvert and Heinrich Schliemann at Hisarlik* (Berkeley: University of California Press, 1999).

12. Arthur J. Evans, "Introduction," in Emil Ludwig, *Schliemann of Troy: The Story of a Goldseeker* (London: Putnam, 1931), 9–21.

that a mound represented layers of occupational debris, one settlement on top of another, "they paid little attention to the possibilities of pottery for dating purposes."[13]

Stratigraphic analysis came slowly to archaeological investigation in ancient Palestine. In 1890, a young Englishman named William M. Flinders Petrie (1853–1942) began excavating a 34-acre tell in the southern Shephelah called Tell el-Hesi. Petrie, an Egyptologist by trade, had spent over a decade doing archaeological work in Egypt and, most importantly, had employed pottery for dating purposes. He excavated Tell el-Hesi stratigraphically and noted that each level had its own characteristic pottery. Petrie then gave a rough chronology to the periods of the site by comparing its pottery to datable Egyptian ware. He concluded,

> I had six weeks of work there, including the whole month of Ramadan, when work is very difficult for the fasting and thirsty Muslims. But in that time, and without disturbing the crops, I succeeded in unravelling the history of the place, and obtaining a long series of pottery approximately dated.[14]

Frederick J. Bliss continued Petrie's work at the site from 1891 to 1893, and he was able to excavate a third of the acropolis area down to virgin soil. Bliss, partially based on Petrie's pioneering labors, was able to identify a total of eleven levels or "cities" during the history of Tell el-Hesi, which spanned almost 3,000 years. One city was built directly on top of another, and each city had its own distinctive ceramic.

The two elements of stratigraphy and ceramic analysis used in an elementary way at Tell el-Hesi are the very backbone of modern-day archaeological practice in Palestine. A tell is simply one ruined settlement on top of another, and the lowest layer of occupation must date earlier than the layers on top of it. The top layer of a tell is its latest occupation. It is important to understand that the archaeologist begins digging from the top down, and, therefore, is uncovering the deposition of the site in the reverse order from which it was laid down. For example, the top two strata of Tell el-Hesi consist of twentieth-century A.D. military trenching and a Muslim cemetery, and the lowest stratum is from the Early Bronze period. The occupation of Tell el-Hesi was a long one, although it was not a continuous occupation; in other words, various time periods between the Early Bronze period and modern military trenching were not in evidence at the site. Each tell has its own occupational history, and the task of the archaeologist is to uncover that particular history.

13. Albright, *The Archaeology of Palestine*, 29.
14. William M. Flinders Petrie, *Tell El Hesy (Lachish)* (London: Putnam, 1891), 10.

COMPLEXITIES OF A TELL

Although the concept of stratigraphy is simple and basic, the physical reality of how a tell was formed is quite complex. Every occupation layer at every site is distinctive; layers are not found laid out evenly across the mound, nor is the depth of layers the same. Each layer contains different pottery, building designs and remains, and small finds. The archaeologist is unaware of all the ins and outs of a site's occupational deposition prior to excavation. The irregularities of tell deposition are due to any number of factors, and we will consider a few of them here.

As the archaeologist excavates a site and attempts to determine the sequence of strata, a slew of depositional problems can obstruct the process. For example, the ancient builders of a settlement sometimes "robbed" material from earlier occupation layers. They dug pits or trenches into earlier strata, removed stones from earlier structures, and used them in their own building projects. The archaeologist, therefore, needs to be careful in dating a building solely on the basis of the type of masonry it has; some of the building may, in fact, have been built with reused stone.

Ancient builders also built various structures into earlier levels of occupation, such as cisterns, latrines, ovens, garbage containers, and facilities for compost. Perhaps most pitting activity on tells was for the purpose of grain storage.[15] At the outset of the Iron I period, grain pits were a dominating feature of tell architecture, such as at the sites of Shechem, Hazor, and Tell Ta'annek. Again, the archaeologist must be aware of pitting activity because it is intrusive and destructive of earlier material.

Burials on mounds pose a similar problem as pitting to the stratigrapher. Certain groups buried their dead on tells, intruding into earlier levels of habitation. The archaeologist must be careful to distinguish between the earlier strata and the later burials that abut those strata.

The excavator must also be aware of ancient rebuilding techniques that may affect proper stratigraphic analysis. For example, when builders decided to put up new buildings, they would often bring in debris to level an area for the new construction. Archaeologists call these various levels of debris *fills*. A fill can pose a major problem for stratigraphic analysis, especially if the debris was taken from another part of the mound predating the stratum in which it was being used. Occasionally, the opposite happened: ancient builders would remove occupational strata in order to level an area for construction. These practices could be quite disruptive to stratigraphic sequences and, therefore, the archaeologist must be on the lookout for them.

15. John D. Currid and Avi Navon, "Iron Age Pits and the Lahav (Tell Halif) Grain Storage Project," *BASOR* 273 (1989): 67–78.

The excavator must also be aware of natural forces that may affect the stratigraphy of a site. For example, torrential rains may be a destructive force that creates what are called wash layers. Pelting rain and flooding can move debris from one part of the tell to another. Consequently, pottery, debris, and other elements from different occupational levels become intermixed, and the archaeologist will have a difficult time unraveling the stratigraphy in the area. Most susceptible to this process are slopes on tells because they are easily eroded.

Each tell is unique and has its own occupational history and topography. Some tells have only one occupational level, and others have a few. Large sites, such as the tell at Beth Shean, contain a long and complex settlement history. It comprises over 70 feet of occupational debris and over twenty strata that span the periods of the Neolithic through the Byzantine. A common adage is that each tell tells its own tale. The job of the excavator is to unravel that tale and record it for history.

KEY TERMS

fill
glacis
mud-brick
robbing
stratum (*pl.* strata)
tell

DISCUSSION QUESTIONS

1. Imagine you are part of an ancient group of people in search of a place to build a permanent settlement. What would you be looking for? What would draw you to a particular place?
2. In modern building construction, engineers make sure that all previous structural remains have been removed from a site before they begin to put up a new building. Ancient builders did not do that, but built directly on top of preexisting levels of occupation. Why?
3. Imagine you are an archaeologist standing on top of an unexcavated tell, and you are preparing to dig it. What areas of the mound do you think would be important to excavate first?

FOR FURTHER READING

Borowski, Oded. "How to Tell a Tell." *BAR* 7 (1981): 66–67.

Cole, Catharine. "How a Dig Begins." *BAR* 3 (1977): 32–36.

Currid, John D. *Doing Archaeology in the Land of the Bible*. Grand Rapids: Baker, 1999.

Lance, H. Darrell. *The Old Testament and the Archaeologist*. Philadelphia: Fortress, 1981.

Lapp, Paul W. *The Tale of the Tell*. Pittsburgh: Pickwick, 1975.

CHAPTER 5

A Short History of the Lands of the Bible

"An archaeologist is the best husband a woman can have. The older she gets the more interested he is in her."—Agatha Christie (married to the archaeologist Max Mallowan)

A HISTORY OF THE ancient Near East deals with the peoples who settled in an area that resembles the shape of a one-humped camel, or dromedary.[1] This territory begins in the land of Egypt, it arches through Syria/Palestine, and ends at the Persian Gulf in the southeast. Human settlement developed early in the river valleys at the two ends of the hump, that is, the Nile River in Egypt and the Tigris and Euphrates Rivers in Mesopotamia. Wright concludes that this "is the region where the earliest development of agriculture took place, where the first towns were established (ca. 7000 B.C.), where methods of writing were invented (beginning ca. 3500 B.C.), and where the resources of those states were first used for empire-building."[2] The events that Wright listed—in particular, the invention of writing—are markers of the beginning of true historical studies in the ancient Near East. Because these discoveries were first made during the Neolithic period, it is there where we will begin our brief overview of the history of the ancient Near East.

NEOLITHIC PERIOD (CA. 8000–4000 B.C.)

Although writing was not invented in the ancient Near East until the fourth millennium B.C., the previous archaeological period, called the Neo-

---

1. James Henry Breasted coined the term "Fertile Crescent" to describe these ancient areas of settlement. He said, "This fertile crescent is approximately a semi-circle, with the open side toward the south, having the west end at the south-east corner of the Mediterranean, the center directly north of Arabia, and the east end at the north end of the Persian Gulf . . . The end of the western wing is Palestine; Assyria makes up a large part of the center; while the eastern wing is Babylonia" (*Ancient Times: A History of the Early World* [Boston: Ginn, 1916], 100–101).
2. George Ernest Wright, *Biblical Archaeology* (Philadelphia: Westminster Press, 1962), 27.

lithic, laid the foundations for its discovery. It was during this time that we witness the shift from hunting and gathering to the domestication of plants and animals. Food production was further enhanced by the appearance of village-farming communities. These communal settlements first appeared on the hilly flanks of mountain ranges in the ancient Near East, such as on the Zagros Mountains in Mesopotamia. Only later, during the eighth and seventh millennia B.C., did village settlement begin to emerge in the river valleys of Mesopotamia and Egypt. Humans thus began to construct year-round settlements that included permanent architecture, such as domestic dwellings and fortifications. In Palestine during the Pre-Pottery Neolithic (PPN, ca. 8000–6000 B.C.) period, the site of Jericho is an exceptional example of this development. Archaeologists uncovered there a 10-acre site with a domestic quarter, an outer city wall, and a massive tower that perhaps served as a military watchtower (for more detail, see chapter 15 on architecture). In addition, an irrigation system may have been found there that aided these early settlers in the cultivation of land. The remains at Jericho from this early period reflect the existence of a high level of social structure that resulted in the ability to build permanent settlements. As Mazar concludes, "This period was a crucial step forward in the history of human civilization in the ancient Near East."[3]

This long history of settled life is followed by the Pottery Neolithic period (PN, ca. 6000–4000 B.C.), in which pottery first appears in the village-farming communities. This innovation is one of the great marks of the transition from food gathering to a settled existence based on food production. The subsistence economy was actually not all that different than it was during the PPN period, but it was increasing and expanding during the PN period. Not only was agricultural practice more common, but herding was now predominating over hunting as a means to provide meat and other items. Population growth, greater density of population in settlements, and increasing trade characterized this period.

CHALCOLITHIC PERIOD (CA. 4000–3200 B.C.)

The term "Chalcolithic" derives from two Greek words: *chalkos* means "copper," and *lithos* means "stone."[4] This designation recognizes one of the major developments of the period, which was the discovery of how to make objects from copper—the first metal used by mankind. The period was also an extraordinary time of transition in the ancient Near East in regard to

3. Amihai Mazar, *Archaeology of the Land of the Bible* (New York: Doubleday, 1990), 44.
4. H. G. Liddell and R. Scott, *Greek-English Lexicon: Abridged Edition* (Oxford: Clarendon Press, 1994), 113, 776.

settlement patterns, the development of population centers, technology, trade, social structures, and many more things.

In Mesopotamia, this was the time of the Uruk period (beginning ca. 3500 B.C.), in which the Sumerians occupied lower Mesopotamia. Settlements were no longer merely agricultural villages; temple-cities were now being established. The city of Uruk, extensively excavated by the German Archaeological Institute beginning in 1912, was a huge site that included enormous temple complexes made of mud-brick. One of the temples was dedicated to the celestial deity Anu, and it was built on an artificial terrace that was a prototype of the later ziggurat.[5] Writing was invented by the Sumerians during this time, and it progressed from pictographic to ideographic and finally to syllabic.[6] It employed a cuneiform script that used a stylus to impress signs on clay tablets. Also during the Uruk period, copper smelting and the production of cylinder seals appear for the first time.

The fourth millennium coincided with the Predynastic period in Egypt that has been divided into two parts: Naqada I (ca. 4000–3500 B.C.) and Naqada II (ca. 3500–3000 B.C.). In the Naqada I period, Egypt had a small-scale village culture that was based on minimal social stratification. In addition, there was little foreign influence on the land. This scenario changed drastically with the dawning of the Naqada II period. As in Sumeria, we see the development of significant population centers, an increase in trade, an incipient copper technology, and new art forms (such as cylinder seals). At the close of Naqada II, writing appeared for the first time in Egypt, and it "defines the beginning of Egyptian history more than any other single change."[7]

In Palestine, the village settlements were larger than those of the Neolithic, and the patterns of settlement were also different. Now many of the settlements were located in the peripheral, semiarid regions of Palestine. Archaeologists are uncertain why there was this shift, although some believe it was due to climatic changes. These villages began to show craft specialization. In the Beersheba region of the Negev, for instance, the site of Abu Matar specialized in the smelting and processing of copper; the nearby site of Safadi was the only town in the area with an ivory craft. Specialization certainly was a factor in increased trade. Even so, the economy of the time was primarily one of herding. During this period, pottery manufacturing was in transition from handmade to slow wheel, which was an innovation that helped the potter to give symmetry and strength to a vessel, and the speed of manufacture would have increased.

5. Siegfried J. Schwantes, *A Short History of the Ancient Near East* (Grand Rapids: Baker, 1965), 21.

6. An ideogram is a written character symbolizing the idea of a thing without indicating its pronunciation; for example, numerals are ideograms.

7. John Baines and Jaromir Malek, *Atlas of Ancient Egypt* (New York: Facts on File, 1980), 198.

EARLY BRONZE AGE (CA. 3200–2350 B.C.)

During the third millennium B.C., formative and foundational changes occurred in the ancient Near East. This was a period when the two great civilizations of Egypt and Sumer developed and reached a high level of culture. In Mesopotamia, it was the Early Dynastic period when Sumerian civilization hit its zenith. Sumerian cities, following the model of Uruk, expanded greatly in size, and they contained monumental architecture. They all began to be fortified with external walls and towers. Cities flourished at this time, such as Nippur, Eridu, and Ur. Arts and crafts discovered in the royal tombs at Ur demonstrate a high level of technique and ornamentation.

The close of the fourth millennium B.C. marked the beginning of pharaonic civilization in Egypt. The Early Dynastic period included Dynasties I–III (ca. 3000–2575 B.C.). As with Sumer, this was a formative time in Egypt: writing became widespread, and major population centers, such as Memphis, were founded. Royal cemeteries have been discovered at Abydos and Saqqara from this early time. Djoser, a king during Dynasty III (ca. 2630–2611 B.C.), was the builder of the Step Pyramid at Saqqara, which "was the oldest stone building of its size in the world."[8] It served as a forerunner of the great pyramids built during the subsequent Old Kingdom (Dynasties IV–VI). Art, architecture, and technology showed great advances during the Early Dynastic period.

The Old Kingdom began with Dynasty IV (ca. 2575 B.C.), and it marked the culmination of pyramid building with the grand structures of Khufu, Khephren, and Menkaure at Giza. During the following Fifth and Sixth Dynasties (ca. 2465–2150 B.C.), the tomb-culture of ancient Egypt became quite elaborate. Painted scenes and detailed reliefs in the tombs provided clear and vivid representations of life at the time. In addition, important inscriptions called the Pyramid Texts first appeared then in the tomb of Wenis at Saqqara. It represents the first major corpus of Egyptian funerary literature. By all appearances, the Old Kingdom was a strong and prosperous time in Egypt, although it was not devoid of change and conflict. By the twenty-third century B.C., Egypt was in decline. It is not clear why this occurred, although some historians believe it was due to economic failure. There seem to have been several disastrous, low inundations of the Nile River that led to famine throughout the land.

In Palestine, the Early Bronze Age may be divided into four periods. The opening stage, called EB I (ca. 3200–2800 B.C.), continued the shift first seen in the Chalcolithic from a village-based society to an urban settlement pattern. Also, there was a great increase in the number of settlements. A brisk international trade was in evidence at this time, and it continued at least

8. Baines and Malek, *Atlas of Ancient Egypt*, 32.

into the next period (EB II). Egyptian contacts appear to have been strong: serekhs of Narmer, one of the earliest kings of Egypt (ca. 3000 B.C.) have been found in Palestine.[9] Contacts with Mesopotamia were more negligible, although some clay seals from there were found at the site of Arad in the Negev. EB I in Palestine maintained a flourishing ceramic industry in which the pottery wheel and kilns were in common use. The pottery also displayed a more consistent, standardized form than in any previous time. Finally, the inhabitants employed a full-fledged Mediterranean cropping method that included grains and fruits. Wine became an important product, and Palestine was a wine center that exported wines to Egypt.

The EB II period in Palestine (ca. 2800–2600 B.C.) witnessed a great increase in the size of settlements, such as the cities of Arad (22 acres) and Ai (27 acres). Ruth Amiran comments on Arad being called a city at this time, saying, "The designation 'city' is used here with good cause: The size of the settlement, selection of the location, water-supply system, well-planned and well-built fortifications, functional division of the city area into private dwelling quarters and a public-buildings center, all clearly indicate a developed conception of urbanization and planning."[10] Almost all the settlements were fortified, and this was a characteristic feature of the entire EB period in Palestine. These monumental fortifications included wide city walls, rectangular towers, and large city gates. The outer walls were often reinforced by an earthen glacis, which is "a long fortification slope running from the bottom of a mound to the defensive wall on the top."[11] This was also a period characterized by the development of temple architecture, and many temples were monumental "broad-room" structures.

The EB III period (ca. 2600–2350 B.C.) reflected a basic material continuity with the EB II period. Mazar rightly comments that "although some of the cities were destroyed and abandoned at the end of the EB II, others were rebuilt and continued to flourish in EB III. Typological changes in the pottery are the best criteria for distinguishing between EB II and EB III, yet even the pottery indicates cultural continuity rather than a break between these two subperiods."[12] So, for example, Khirbet Kerak ware appeared for the first time in Palestine during the EB III period, but it did not replace the common, traditional ceramic forms that developed from the EB II period. It was found alongside them. There was, therefore, no indication of a cultural shift based on the appearance of Khirbet Kerak ware.[13]

9. A serekh is a rectangular frame that contained the name of a pharaoh. See Yohanan Aharoni, *The Archaeology of the Land of Israel* (Philadelphia: Westminster Press, 1978), 60.

10. Ruth Amiran, "Arad," *EAEHL*, 1:75 (1975).

11. John D. Currid, *Doing Archaeology in the Land of the Bible* (Grand Rapids: Baker, 1999), 41.

12. Mazar, *Archaeology of the Land of the Bible*, 109–10.

13. Khirbet Kerak ware is identified as being handmade with a heavy slip, and it was highly burnished. The slip was black or dark red on the outside of the vessels and red on the inside. It was first

At the close of the EB III period, there was a great collapse of the culture in Palestine. Many of the EB III sites were either destroyed or abandoned. The reason for this devastation is unclear, although some scholars believe it was due to Egyptian military incursions at the end of the Old Kingdom era. Others argue that the land was perhaps ravaged by changes in the natural environment, such as drought, which could have led to insufficient resources to support an urban population. Perhaps several factors contributed to the demise of the cities.

EB IV–MB I TRANSITION (CA. 2350–2000 B.C.)

Archaeologists often combine the next two periods, and they call it the EB IV–MB I transitional age. It was a period in Palestine that was nonurban, in which the population was sparse and mostly consisted of village dwellers and seminomads. The shift to smaller and scattered sites was accompanied by minimal architecture, and fortifications were basically absent. One of the few sites with permanent architecture was Har Yeruham in the Negev, which contained thirty connected domestic structures built around a large central courtyard. The settlement had external walls, but they were weak and poorly constructed. Material finds from this period are limited, and much of it comes from single-burial tombs.

The collapse of the EB urban culture can be seen across the ancient Near East. In Egypt, the Old Kingdom had ended, and it was followed by the chaotic and disruptive First Intermediate Period (ca. 2135–2040 B.C.). There was no central political power in Egypt at this time, but power was divided among various cities and nomarchs. It was a period of general poverty, and this societal collapse may be attributed to severe drought conditions beginning in the twenty-second century B.C.[14] This century also saw the demise of the formidable Akkadian Empire in Mesopotamia. Schwantes describes it well, when he says, "This is a period of cultural stagnation and archaeological finds have not illuminated the age to any great extent."[15]

MIDDLE BRONZE II AGE (CA. 2000–1550 B.C.)

Throughout the ancient Near East, the beginning of the second millennium witnessed a recovery and renaissance in which various peoples attempted to revive their culture. The land had languished, but now there

---

identified by William F. Albright at the site of Beth Yerah; see his "The Jordan Valley in the Bronze Age," *AASOR* 6 (1926): 13–74.

14. Barbara Bell, "The Dark Ages in Ancient History. I. The First Dark Age of Egypt," *AJA* 75 (1971): 1–26.
15. Schwantes, *A Short History*, 29.

appeared a cultural resurgence. In Palestine, the MB II period was one of reurbanization. Major sites that had been abandoned during the EB IV–MB I transition were now resettled, such as the major cities of Hazor, Megiddo, and Shechem. Many new settlements were also established. These sites were spread across the Palestinian landscape in contrast to the previous period, in which many sites were located on the desert fringes. The catalyst for the resurgence is uncertain, although a good case can be made that its origin came from the Amorites who had captured much of Mesopotamia at this time and then made their way into Palestine. The MB II age was a period when peoples moved from one area to another. It fits well as the time in which the Hebrew patriarchs lived and traveled throughout the ancient Near East.

Sites at this time were heavily fortified, such as Tel Dan, Shechem, and Ashkelon. Hazor was the largest settlement in Palestine (180–200 acres), and it was fortified with huge outer walls (ca. 25 feet wide and 30 feet high). It had earthen ramparts that were foundational to the city walls, and they helped to raise the city high above the terrain of the surrounding area. The use of the glacis fortification was a common defensive technique of the day. Many of these strongly fortified settlements were destroyed at the end of the MB II period. Numerous scholars believe that this widescale devastation was at the hands of the Hyksos (see below).

Civilization in Mesopotamia was also on the rebound during the MB II period. After the collapse of the Akkadian Empire, a group called the Amorites invaded the land and subdued much of the southern regions of Mesopotamia. They dominated Mesopotamia for about 150 years (ca. 1950–1800 B.C.). Yet, under them, there was no real cultural, political, social, and economic unity. This did not come until the nineteenth century with the founding of the Babylonian Dynasty (ca. 1800–1595). At this time, the city of Babylon became the center of a kingdom that would contain much of central and southern Mesopotamia. The most important ruler of the dynasty was Hammurabi (ca. 1792–1750 B.C.) who united much of Mesopotamia under his rule through a series of extended wars. He, however, is perhaps most famous for his societal reforms, and a law code that bears his name. Hammurabi's successors were much weaker, and Babylonian power went into decline. Its demise came at the hands of the Hittite king Mursilis I, who invaded Babylon in 1595 B.C.

At the close of the nineteenth century B.C., the Hittites, who settled in the area of modern-day Turkey, began to unify as a nation. This was the beginning of the Old Kingdom period of Hittite history (ca. 1800–1450 B.C.). The Hittites became particularly strong under the rule of Hattusilis I (ca. 1650–1620 B.C.), who attempted to expand Hittite land holdings through conquest and diplomacy. He was unsuccessful for the most part, and he was thwarted in his attempt to capture Aleppo in Syria. His grandson, Mursilis I (ca. 1620–1590 B.C.) was able to conquer Aleppo and to attack faraway Babylon. Mursilis 1 was assassinated in a palace coup, and that event marked the beginning of the decline of Hittite power for the next century.

Egyptian culture began its recovery from the weak First Intermediate period at the start of the Twelfth Dynasty (ca. 1991–1783 B.C.). The first two kings, Amenemhat 1 (ca. 1991–1962 B.C.) and Senwosret 1 (ca. 1971–1926 B.C.) did much building in Egypt, and they expanded their borders especially with the conquest of Nubia. The outstanding pharaoh of this dynasty was Senwosret 111 (ca. 1878–1841). He centralized the power of Egypt in the monarchy, extended Egyptian influence into Palestine and beyond, and brought prosperity and stability to the land. The good economy appears to have remained durable throughout the following eighteenth century B.C., yet the power and influence of foreigners began to take hold in Egypt. By the middle of the seventeenth century, a foreign group called the Hyksos usurped much of the power in the land. This period of foreign rule in Egypt is called the Second Intermediate period (ca. 1640–1550 B.C.).

LATE BRONZE AGE (CA. 1550–1200 B.C.)

The Late Bronze Age is commonly divided into two periods: LB I (ca. 1550–1400 B.C.) and LB II (ca. 1400–1200 B.C.). The LB I period in Palestine

is characterized by a significant decrease in the number of settlements in comparison to the end of the MB period. There was a drop of about 40–50 percent in sites. Some archaeologists believe this reduction was due to Egyptian military incursions into Palestine. Yet many of the sites do not reflect destruction, but rather abandonment. The one region where site density increased was in the Negev. Most of these sites, however, can be accounted for as military stations associated with Egyptian traffic. The LB II period witnessed a resurgence of site settlement after the decline of the LB I period. Several sites that had been abandoned were repopulated, such as Tell Beit Mirsim, Jericho, Hazor, and Megiddo.

Fig. 5.1. El Amarna Tablet

During the LB II period, the land of Palestine/Canaan was divided into a series of city-states, each in control of a large region. We know this social structure from the discovery of cuneiform tablets at the site of el-Amarna in Egypt. These tablets contain diplomatic correspondence between the pharaohs of the fourteenth century B.C., Amenophis III (ca. 1391–1353 B.C.) and Amenophis IV (Akhenaten, ca. 1353–1335 B.C.), and kings of other lands and vassal states. These vassal states were, for the most part, located in Syria and Palestine. The Egyptian government administered these vassal states, and they established administrative centers in Palestine such as at Beth Shean, Gaza, and Joppa.

The LB Age coincided with the Egyptian Eighteenth (ca. 1550–1307 B.C.) and Nineteenth (ca. 1307–1196 B.C.) Dynasties. This was the time of the rise and prominence of the New Kingdom period in Egyptian history. The fortunes of Egypt were on the rise from the very beginning, in which Pharaoh Ahmose (ca. 1550–1525 B.C.) finished driving out the Hyksos from the land. He began a period of expansion as he campaigned in Palestine to the northeast and in Nubia to the south. His successors furthered the expansion of territory, especially under the rule of Pharaoh Thutmosis (ca. 1504–1492 B.C.), whose army reached the Euphrates River in the north and the fourth cataract of the Nile to the south. Many people groups in those extended territories, particularly in Syria and Canaan, became vassal states under the hegemony of Egypt. Egypt had a large standing army, and they kept a garrisoned presence in Canaan/Palestine.

After the unique reign of Amenophis IV (Akhenaton, ca. 1353–1335 B.C.), Egypt fell on hard times. However, when Haremhab came to the throne some sixteen years later (ca. 1319–1307 B.C.), he undid much of the religious revolution of Akhenaton and helped to restore order in the land. Seti I (ca. 1305–1290 B.C.) continued the restoration of Egypt, and he did this through a tireless building program and a series of military campaigns that retrieved much of Syria/Palestine that had been lost. Rameses II (ca. 1290–1224 B.C.) had a long reign, and by most standards it was the final high point in Egyptian history. His building activity outdid any other pharaoh in Egyptian history. Much of Rameses II's diplomatic and military activity was directed at the Hittite Empire that was particularly strong at this time. The succeeding king Merneptah (ca. 1224–1214 B.C.) had to deal with foreign aggression throughout his reign. The Libyans began to infiltrate the western Nile Delta, and they were allied with five groups of Sea Peoples, who likely came from the Aegean area. Merneptah defeated this alliance and drove out the Sea Peoples from Egypt. Some of these groups settled on the coastal plain of Palestine and came to be known as the Philistines. The people of Israel were first mentioned outside the Bible on a victory stele of Merneptah found at

Thebes. After Merneptah, Egypt again fell into chaos and disarray that ended up in civil war.

The LB II Age is the period of the New Empire of the Hittites. The greatest monarch of the New Empire was Suppiluliumas, who annexed much of Syria from the Egyptians during the confused reign of Pharaoh Akhnaten. He also subjugated all the lands of Asia Minor, and conquered the nation of Mitanni. By the close of his reign, the empire was at its greatest sociopolitical and economic height. His grandson, Mursilis II, continued the glory of the New Empire, although he fought many wars that began to take a toll on the nation. Mursilis II's son named Muwatallis struggled to keep the empire strong; he fought the Egyptians under Rameses II to a standstill at the battle of Kadesh in Syria (1296 B.C.). The Hittites were able to keep control of northern Syria, but Hittite power was beginning to wane due to the meteoric rise of the Assyrians to the east. At the close of the thirteenth century B.C., the Hittite kingdom fell because of invasions from the west; the Sea Peoples overran the land to the point that the Hittites ceased to exist.

In Mesopotamia, Babylon was conquered by the Hittites under Mursilis I at the beginning of the LB I period (ca. 1531 B.C.). After the sack of the city, a foreign group called the Kassites infiltrated and began to dominate the fortunes of Babylon. They ruled Babylon for almost the entire LB period (ca. 1531–1150 B.C.). Political weakness was a hallmark of the time in Babylon. For much of the LB II period, the Kassites were in a struggle with Assyria, which was now on the rise. In the thirteenth century B.C., the Assyrian kings Adad-nirari I and Shalmaneser I expanded their territorial holdings to the south and to the west. From this time onward, there was a gradual rise in the political, economic, and military influence of Assyria until it achieved supremacy over most of the ancient Near East during the early centuries of the first millennium B.C.

IRON I PERIOD (CA. 1200–1000 B.C.)

This period is one of major disruptions throughout the ancient Near East. During the Twentieth Dynasty in Egypt (ca. 1196–1070 B.C.), the Egyptians lost control of Palestine and Nubia. Baines and Malek describe Egypt itself as splitting "into a loose-knit, almost feudal society" during this time.[16] In fact, the entire eastern Mediterranean region entered a "twilight period," and Egypt lost its position of preeminence in the ancient Near East. The vacuum left in Canaan by the weakening of Egypt was filled in two ways: the Sea Peoples and Libyans invaded and settled on the southern coastal

16. Baines and Malek, *Atlas of Ancient Egypt*, 48.

plain of Palestine, and the Israelites escaped from Egypt and subsequently conquered Canaan/Palestine from the east.[17]

A primary area of settlement for the Israelites was the central hill country. Archaeological site surveys reveal that during the Iron I period there was a great increase in the number of settlements in the highlands of Palestine. In the Shephelah (foothills), Iron I site distribution was nearly 50 percent greater than the previous LB II period.[18] The analysis of the remains at some of these sites indicates a distinct cultural break from the LB II period. Many would argue that these new settlements were reflective of the Israelite conquest and settlement of the land. The Iron I Age in Israel would then be the time of the judges and the rise of the United Monarchy under Saul and David.

Further disruption is evident with the fall of the Hittite Empire at the close of the thirteenth century B.C. Its end was due to the invasion of the Sea Peoples from the west and the annexation of much Hittite land by the Assyrians from the east. Assyria's power and influence were rising at this time. In particular, the military might of Assyria came to be a force to reckon with under the rule of Tiglath-pileser I (ca. 1116–1078 B.C.). Siegfried Schwantes is correct in his assessment of this king when he says,

> His exploits were the inspiration of the Assyrian despots who caused the world to tremble from the ninth to the seventh century B.C. Under him the Assyrian army became a war machine which knew no mercy, whose cruelty spread terror over its enemies even before they engaged in battle. . . . Tiglathpileser I first directed his war effort against the Mushki in Asia Minor. . . . The Hittite state of Malatia submitted without fighting. . . . [He was] the first Assyrian king to set foot on the Phoenician coast . . . and Babylon [was] conquered.[19]

IRON II PERIOD (CA. 1000–586 B.C.)

At the dawn of the Iron II period in the tenth century B.C., Israel was at its height both socio-politically and militarily. This was the time of the kingship of Solomon (ca. 970–930 B.C.), which is described by the writer of 1 Kings as "King Solomon excelled all the kings of the earth in riches and in wisdom" (10:23). This high point was short-lived, however, because soon after Solomon's death Israel divided into two separate kingdoms (Judah in the south and Israel in the north). Due to that division, the Egyptians, who were on the rise under Shoshenk I (Shishak), saw a golden opportunity. They

---

17. Much has been written about the date of the exodus and conquest; see, e.g., Bruce Waltke, "Date of the Conquest," *WTJ* 52 (1990): 181–200.

18. John D. Currid, "The Deforestation of the Foothills of Palestine," *PEQ* (1984): 1–11.

19. Schwantes, *A Short History*, 115–16.

attacked both Israel and Judah, plundered them, and opened up trade routes to the east. For the remainder of the Third Intermediate Period (ca. 1070–712 B.C.), however, Egypt went into decline because of constant internal conflict that negatively affected the power of kingship in the land.

The real power in the ancient Near East during the tenth through seventh centuries B.C. was Assyria. This was the period of the New Assyrian Empire, which included a succession of able and strong monarchs that was unprecedented in the history of the ancient Near East. The restoration of Assyria's military and economic might began with Ashur-dan II (ca. 932–910 B.C.) and his immediate successors. These kings went on annual military campaigns to expand their territorial holdings or to subdue rebellious subjects. A good example of this activity was the military conquests of Ashurnasirpal III (ca. 883–859 B.C.). His armies subjugated the Arameans, and he vanquished the land of Phoenicia with its major Mediterranean coastal cities of Tyre and Sidon. The king's territorial expansion rivaled that of the former glory of Tiglath-pileser I from the twelfth century B.C. His successor, Shalmaneser III (ca. 858–824 B.C.), brought Syria and Israel under his sway as tributary states. After his death, Assyria went into a short period of decline, but it recovered with a vengeance under the rule of Tiglath-pileser III (ca. 745–727 B.C.).

Near the end of his reign, Tiglath-pileser III conquered Babylon and crowned himself king of Babylon. He assumed the following title: "king of the universe, king of Assyria, king of Babylon, king of Sumer and Akkad, king of the four quarters of the world." At the time of his death, Assyria stretched from the border of Egypt to the Caspian Sea in the northeast to the Persian Gulf in the southeast. Some serious rebellions, however, began to take place in the tributary states during the reign of his successors. One of these was the revolt of Israel during the reign of Hoshea (ca. 732–722 B.C.) against Shalmaneser V (ca. 726–722 B.C.). The Assyrian army promptly laid siege to Samaria for three years, until the nation of Israel fell in 722 B.C.

The last great king of Assyria was Ashurbanipal (ca. 668–631 B.C.). After his death, the disintegration of the empire quickly followed. In 612 B.C., a combined military force of Medes and Babylonians destroyed Nineveh and other major Assyrian cities. The Assyrian domination of the ancient Near East was over, and the establishment of the Neo-Babylonian Empire soon replaced it. The Babylonian monarch who took advantage of Assyrian weakness was Nabopolasser (ca. 625–605 B.C.). His troops participated in the conquest of Assyria in 612 B.C., and he began to flex his might throughout the remainder of the ancient Near East. He sent the crown prince Nebuchadnezzar to subdue the area of Syria/Palestine. In 605 B.C., he defeated the Egyptians at Carchemish and then quickly brought Syria/Palestine under Babylonian control.

Nebuchadnezzar succeeded his father to the throne of Babylon (ca. 605–562 B.C.). No doubt he was the greatest monarch of the Neo-Babylonian Empire. Both his building and his military exploits far surpassed that of anyone else at that time. He is perhaps most famous for having subdued Jerusalem in 597 B.C., setting up the puppet king Zedekiah over Judah, and then destroying rebellious Judah in 586 B.C. He then sent many of the Judeans into exile in Babylonia. After the reign of Nebuchadnezzar, Babylon went into decline rather quickly, and was soon conquered by the Persians under Cyrus in 539 B.C.

KEY TERMS

city-state
Sea Peoples
serekh

DISCUSSION QUESTIONS

1. Why was the invention of writing in the ancient Near East such an important development in the history of humanity?
2. Why was the shift from hunting/gathering to the domestication of plants and animals such a major development in human civilization?
3. Give some examples of how the knowledge of ancient Near Eastern history and culture helps us to understand the Old Testament better.

FOR FURTHER READING

Ahlstrom, Gosta W. *The History of Ancient Palestine*. Minneapolis: Fortress, 1993.

Baines, John, and Jaromir Malek. *Atlas of Ancient Egypt*. New York: Facts on File, 1980.

Kitchen, Kenneth A. *The Bible in Its World*. Downers Grove, IL: InterVarsity Press, 1977.

Roux, Georges. *Ancient Iraq*. 3rd ed. London: Penguin Books, 1993.

Schwantes, Siegfried J. *A Short History of the Ancient Near East*. Grand Rapids: Baker, 1965.

PART 2

A JOURNEY THROUGH THE LAND

THIS SECOND MAJOR section of our study looks briefly at many of the individual sites that have been excavated, and this is done according to region (see chapter 2). The reader should be aware that this is merely an overview and is not meant to be exhaustive. It is introductory, and it attempts to give the reader a taste of the rich material that is available. Only selected sites are discussed, but most of the major excavations have been included. Also, only the important finds from each site are surveyed. At the close of each overview, a few bibliographic references are given, so that the reader who wishes to dig deeper into the archaeology of a site may do so. The sites of each region are not dealt with in order of importance, but rather alphabetically.

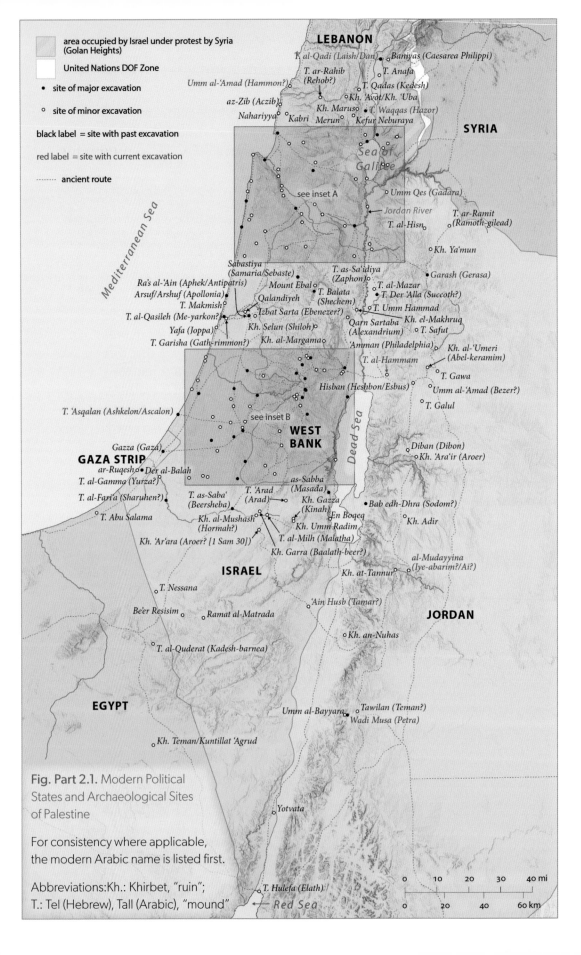

Fig. Part 2.1. Modern Political States and Archaeological Sites of Palestine

For consistency where applicable, the modern Arabic name is listed first.

Abbreviations: Kh.: Khirbet, "ruin"; T.: Tel (Hebrew), Tall (Arabic), "mound"

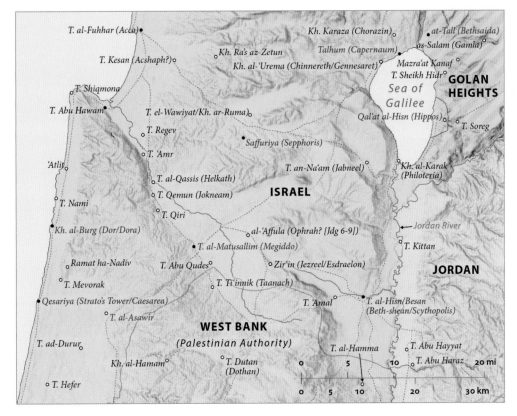

Fig. Part 2.2 Inset A

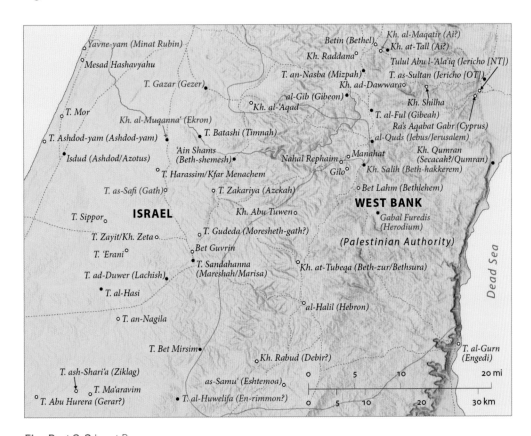

Fig. Part 2.3 Inset B

CHAPTER 6

Galilee / The Sea of Galilee Region

D UE TO ONGOING site surveys and excavations, the history of human settlement in the Galilee region is slowly emerging. For example, some important work has been done regarding the changes in settlement patterns from the LB Age to the Iron I period. During the LB Age, the Canaanite habitation of the region was sparse and poor. However, in the Iron I period, mostly during the twelfth through eleventh centuries B.C., many small settlements appeared in Galilee. In Lower Galilee, investigators estimate 22–25 new settlements emerged, and many of these were occupied for the first time.[1] There were similar settlement patterns in other areas of Palestine at this time.[2] It is tempting to attribute this influx of settlement to the Israelites after the conquest of the land.

ABEL BETH MAACAH

The biblical town of Abel Beth Maacah (Tell Abil-el-Qameh) is a 25-acre site located about 4.5 miles west of Tel Dan on modern-day Israel's northern border with Lebanon in Upper Galilee. The site is mentioned three times in the Bible. First, 2 Samuel 20 describes the rebellion of Sheba against Davidic rule during the early tenth century B.C., and how Sheba fled to Abel Beth Maacah from Joab and troops from David's army. The army "cast a mound against the city, and it stood against the rampart, and they were battering the wall to throw it down" (v. 15). A wise woman from within the town called to Joab, and said that he should not destroy the town because it is "a city that is a mother in Israel" (v. 19). The second passage refers to a war in the ninth century B.C. between Asa, king of Judah, and Baasha, king of Israel (1 Kings 15), in which both kings vied for the help of the Aramean

---

1. Zvi Gal, *Lower Galilee during the Iron Age* (Winona Lake, IN: Eisenbrauns, 1992), 84–87.
2. See, e.g., John D. Currid, "The Deforestation of the Foothills of Palestine," *PEQ* (1984): 1–11.

king Ben-Hadad. The latter came in on the side of Asa, and he "sent the commanders of his armies against the cities of Israel and conquered Ijon, Dan, Abel-beth-maacah, and all Chinneroth, with all the land of Naphtali" (v. 20). Finally, the town is listed among the sites that were captured by the Assyrian army under Tiglath-pileser III in the eighth century B.C. (2 Kings 15). The text says that "in the days of Pekah king of Israel, Tiglath-pileser king of Assyria came and captured Ijon, Abel-beth-maacah, Janoah, Kedesh, Hazor, Gilead, and Galilee, all the land of Naphtali, and he carried the people captive to Assyria" (v. 29).

The site consists of two mounds (upper and lower) with a saddle in between. Excavations began in 2013 with five areas under the shovel, three on the lower mound, one on the saddle, and one on the upper mound. The settlement history has been generally determined: the earliest architectural remains belong to the Middle Bronze II, and this is followed by substantial finds from the Late Bronze and Early Iron Ages. The archaeologists concluded that the lower mound was abandoned after that time, and that settlement then occurred only on the upper mound, where Iron Age II and following periods have been revealed. The hope is that these on-going excavations will shed light on, particularly, the transition from the Late Bronze Age to the Early Iron Age at the time of the conquest of the land by the Israelites, and the later relationships between Israelites and Arameans.

FOR FURTHER READING

Mullins, R. A., and N. Panitz-Cohen. "Looking for Arameans at Abel Beth Maacah." *BAR* 41/1 (2015): 28, 78.

Panitz-Cohen, N., R. A. Mullins, and R. Bonfil. "Northern Exposure: Launching Excavations at Tell Abil el-Qameh (Abel Beth Maacah)." *Strata: Bulletin of the Anglo-Israel Archaeological Society* 31 (2013): 27–42.

Panitz-Cohen, N., R. A. Mullins, and R. Bonfil. "Second Preliminary Report of the Excavations at Tell Abil el-Qameh (Abel Beth Maacah)." *Strata: Bulletin of the Anglo-Israel Archaeological Society* 33 (2015): 35–59.

BEISAMOUN

Beisamoun is a major PPNB site located close to the shore of the Hula Lake (drained) between two fresh water springs. It is the largest site in the region from that time period, perhaps covering more than 50 acres. Excavations began here in the 1950s, and renewed exploration began in 2007 and continues today. There are some remains from the PN and EB periods, but, by far, the primary ruins derive from the PPNB period. The site contains a large PPNB assemblage, and some of the houses in the domestic area have been excavated. Two plastered skulls were found in one of the buildings. Further work at the site may, in fact, be of great help in reconstructing a Neolithic village from this time.

FOR FURTHER READING

Bocquentin, Fanny, et al. "Renewed Excavation of the PPNB Site of Beisamoun, Hula Basin." *Neo-Lithics* 2 (2007):17–21.

Bocquentin, Fanny, et al. "The PPNB Site of Beisamoun (Hula Basin)." In *The State of the Stone Terminologies, Continuities and Contexts in Near Eastern Lithics*, edited by Elizabeth Healey, Stuart Campbell, and Osamu Maeda, 197–211. Berlin: *ex oriente*, 2011.

Khalaily, Hamoudi, et. al. "Beisamun: An Early Pottery Neolithic Site in the Hula Basin." *Atiqot* 82 (2015): 1–61.

TEL BETH YERAH

Tel Beth Yerah is a large Early Bronze Age town, covering about 80 acres, which lies on the southern end of the Sea of Galilee at the place where the Jordan River exits the sea. It was settled and occupied throughout the EB period (ca. 3200–2200 B.C.). Excavations began at the site in 1933, and they have taken place intermittently since then. The most recent excavations began in 2003 under the oversight of Raphael Greenberg of Tel Aviv University, in which further work was done on the monumental "granary" complex.

The EB town was an important settlement lying next to a strategic crossroads. Apparently it served as a major regional city. It contained a large external fortification system, and internally exhibited advanced urban planning: a city gate, domestic quarters, and streets reflect that planning. A particular type of bi-chrome pottery was discovered here, and it bears the name of the site: Khirbet Kerak ware (Albright 1924–25). It first appeared in the EB III period (ca. 2600–2350 B.C.), and was produced in large quantities at the site throughout the EB period.

Perhaps the most significant find of the EB III settlement was the so-called "granary" installation, which was a building of large proportions. It occupied the northern part of the mound, and it was separated from other buildings by a series of paved streets that isolated it. "The plan of the complex is roughly rectangular (angles at 88°), measuring 40 meters from east to west and 30 meters from north to south. It consists of a small central hall that is reached from the outside by a long corridor, surrounded by a massive, so-called foundational wall. On top of the wall at least nine large, stone circles were sunk 10 centimeters below the surface of the foundational wall or pavement. The average diameter of the circles is 8 meters, varying anywhere from 7 to 9 meters. These nine circles are the remnants of the bases of the circular-designed conical domes" (Currid 1986, 21). Scholars have suggested that the building served as a beehive granary complex, and that similar structures have been found throughout the ancient Near East during this period. The current excavators are unconvinced of this function, although they are uncertain of its purpose.

FOR FURTHER READING

Albright, William Foxwell. "The Jordan Valley in the Bronze Age." *AASOR* 6 (1924–25): 13–74.

Currid, John D. "The Beehive Buildings of Ancient Palestine." *BA* 49 (1986): 20–24.

Currid, John D. "The Beehive Granaries of Ancient Palestine." *ZDPV* 101 (1985): 151–64.

Greenberg, R., E. Eisenberg, S. Paz, and Y. Paz. *Bet Yerah—The Early Bronze Age Mound: Excavation Reports, 1933–86.* Jerusalem: Israel Antiquities Authority, 2006.

TEL DAN

Tel Dan is a 55-acre site located near the foot of Mount Hermon. It is frequently mentioned in the Bible, often as the northernmost point of the land of Israel: "from Dan to Beersheba" (e.g., Judg. 20:1; 1 Sam. 3:20). The city appears for the first time in the Old Testament in Genesis 14:14, in which Abraham travels there to rescue his nephew Lot. Since Abraham likely belongs to the MB period, one would expect some remains of that time at the site. At the close of the tenth century B.C., Jeroboam I (930–910 B.C.) set up a rogue cultic complex at Dan, which included high places, a golden calf, and a new priesthood (1 Kings 12:28–33). The golden calf remained standing at least until the time of Jehu (841–814 B.C.; 2 Kings 10:29). Dan was still operating as a cultic center in the eighth century B.C., according to the prophet Amos (8:14). It is likely that the Assyrian monarch Tiglath-pileser III destroyed this Israelite city in 732 B.C.

Major excavation work began in 1966 under the leadership of Avraham Biran, and excavations continue today. Tel Dan was an important site during the Neolithic period, had massive fortifications during the EB Age, and was a large site during the MB Age. During the Iron I period, it was an agrarian settlement that is to be identified with the Israelites. In Iron II, it became a major Israelite city. While several important finds were made here, we will consider only three of the most enlightening.

First, during the MB II period, there was a flourishing settlement at Dan, and it included some notable outer fortifications. In particular, the excavators uncovered a fully preserved mud-brick arched gateway dating to the nineteenth through eighteenth centuries B.C. Although mud-brick was used previously in the EB for fortifications, this gateway is the first found *in toto.* The arched mud-brick roof is an innovation for Palestine, and it had an advantage over the more common flat-roof designs supported by wooden timbers (that could be burned). A stepped stone pavement approached the gate complex from the outside; this was perhaps to deny access to enemy chariots. On the sides of the entrance pathway was a stone glacis that apparently ran from the gate alongside the entire length of the outer city wall. One of the main purposes of the glacis was to prevent a battering ram or other type of siege machine to approach and penetrate the city wall.

Fig. 6.1. Excavations at Tel Dan

On the southern end of the tell, the archaeologists unearthed a gate complex from the Israelite city of the ninth century B.C. It consisted of an outer and an inner gate with a stone-paved road as the entrance. Just outside the gate was a stone-paved plaza, and monumental walls surrounded the

city. The entire complex was built with massive stone boulders. Next to the
city wall within the outer gate, the excavators discovered a limestone bench
that was perhaps used by the elders of the city when they met (cf. Ruth 4:1–2).
Also, they found a structure here that may have been a foundation for either
a throne or a cult statue.

On the northern side of the mound, the archaeologists uncovered a
"high place" dating to the ninth century B.C. It was built with typical Israelite
masonry of the period, and it consisted of a three-tiered structure (which
has been restored). This complex is to be identified with the high place built
here by Jeroboam I for the worship of the golden calf (see 1 Kings 12:28–31).

FOR FURTHER READING

Biran, Avraham. *Biblical Dan*. Jerusalem: Israel Exploration Society and
    Hebrew Union College, 1994.
Biran, Avraham. *Dan: 25 Years of Excavations at Tel Dan* (Hebrew; English
    abstract). Tel Aviv: Hakibbutz Hameuchad, 1992, 251–56.
Biran, Avraham, et al. *Dan I-II*. Jerusalem: Nelson Glueck School of Biblical
    Archaeology and Hebrew Union College, 1996–2002.

TEL HADAR

Tel Hadar is a 4-acre site that is located on the eastern shore of the Sea
of Galilee, and it sits next to a major ancient highway that ran from the Mediterranean Sea to Syria, Bashan, and parts northeast. The site was inhabited
during three periods: Late Bronze I, Iron I, and Iron II, with six strata in all.
The most important finds come from the Iron I period, in which the site was
protected by two large, concentric defensive walls. The outer wall was over
12 feet thick, and it ran around the foot of the occupational mound. Inside
the walls, the excavators discovered a large public storage building from the
eleventh century B.C. that included a granary room. In room 3 of the building,
they found a huge pile of carbonized grain almost 2 feet high on the floor.
Near the close of the eleventh century B.C., the tell was destroyed by a huge
conflagration that left an ash layer in some of the rooms to a depth up to 7
feet. The archaeologists concluded that Tel Hadar was an important fortress
during the Iron I period, but it was likely not Israelite. Rather, like the Iron
Age occupations at Bethsaida, Tel Hadar was a Geshurite town.

The site was abandoned for at least a century, and then it was resettled
in the ninth century B.C. It was no longer a stronghold, but now it contained
numerous private dwellings. The settlers reused the Iron I outer wall for

defense, but they built houses right on top of the inner defensive wall of the Iron I period.

FOR FURTHER READING

Kochavi, Moshe. "The Land of Geshur Project: Regional Archaeology of the Southern Golan (1987–1988 Season)." *IEJ* 39 (1989): 1–17.

Kochavi, Moshe. "The Land of Geshur: History of a Region in the Biblical Period." *EI* 25 (1996): 184–201 (Heb.).

Kochavi, Moshe, et al. "The Land of Geshur." *BAR* 18 (1992): 30–44, 84–85.

TEL HAZOR

The importance of Hazor as a strategic site in antiquity is underscored by its sheer size. At its cultural height as a Canaanite city during the LB Age, it covered 190 acres, which included upper and lower cities. It is the largest tell in Palestine and, arguably, it was the most important city in Galilee. In fact, when Joshua led the Israelite army on an invasion of the north, Hazor "was the head of all those kingdoms" (Josh. 11:10). Its strategic importance is further enhanced by its location on the northern extension of the Great Trunk Road, which served as a vital commercial and military highway between Egypt and Mesopotamia.

The mound of Hazor contains over twenty layers of settlements built one on top of another. The first major occupation began about 2800 B.C., and the habitation was limited to the upper mound. By the eighteenth century B.C., the upper mound could not contain the population, so the people spread to the lower city in the north. The lower city obviously did not have a height advantage for defense, so the Canaanite populace built a moat around it and then added a glacis (an artificial sloping revetment) to the lower mound for defensive purposes. Documents from the Mesopotamian city of Mari from the MB II period indicate that Hazor was a major commercial and trade center in the ancient Near East. During the following LB period, Hazor became a significant Canaanite city-state.

In the northern campaign of Joshua, the Israelite army captured Hazor, placed it under the ban, and burned it with fire (Josh. 11:10–13). The archaeologist Yigael Yadin exposed a huge destruction layer at Hazor that he dates to the thirteenth century B.C. and attributes to Israel's conquest of the city. During the subsequent period of the judges in the Iron I period, Hazor reverted to Canaanite rule under "Jabin king of Canaan, who reigned in Hazor" (Judg. 4:2). Solomon, in the tenth century B.C., rebuilt Hazor and made it into a core fortress of his kingdom (1 Kings 9:15). Its final destruction occurred in 732 B.C. at the hands of Tiglath-pileser III (2 Kings 15:29).

John Garstang was the first to excavate Hazor (1928), although it was merely a series of probes that yielded few results. In the 1950s and 1960s, the site underwent major excavation under the direction of Yigael Yadin (five seasons in all). Since 1990, archaeological work has continued to the present day, supervised by Amnon Ben-Tor. Much material has been uncovered at the site, and I refer the reader to the select bibliography for further study.

During the LB Age of the fourteenth century B.C., Hazor was a major Canaanite city. Excavators found a large "Ceremonial Palace" on the acropolis that dates to this time and was built with mud-brick on a basalt stone foundation. It consisted of a courtyard, a porch, and the structure itself. In the courtyard, a *bamah* (raised cultic platform) was discovered with lots of bones and ash. This has led some scholars to believe that the structure was actually a temple, not a palace. A massive fire destroyed this building and much of the Canaanite city; this conflagration was likely due to the invading Israelite army.

Hazor became an important, major Israelite city during the reign of Solomon in the tenth century B.C. In confirmation of that reality, the excavators uncovered a Solomonic six-chambered gateway connected to an outer fortification wall of the casemate design. Yigael Yadin has correctly identified this same defensive system at the sites of Megiddo and Gezer from Solomon's time (1 Kings 9:15).

Hazor continued to flourish during the subsequent Omride Dynasty of the ninth century B.C. It appears that Ahab (ca. 874–853 B.C.) expanded the city and added new types of construction. For example, tripartite pillared buildings first appear at the site. There has been much debate regarding their purpose, although the evidence suggests their use for storage. Ahab also constructed a palace/citadel on the west side of the upper mound.

The two most vulnerable areas when a city came under attack were the gates and water tunnels (see 2 Sam. 5:8). At Hazor, Ahab's builders solved the second problem by digging a 19-meter-deep rectangular shaft through the bedrock inside the upper city. They hit the natural water level of the mound, and thus created a pool at the bottom of the shaft. A typical Israelite four-room building that led to steps down the shaft controlled the entrance to the water system. Hazor during the Iron II period was one of the most impressive Israelite cities.

FOR FURTHER READING

See the six volumes of excavation reports: *Hazor I–VI*. Jerusalem: Israel Exploration Society, 1958–2012.

Currid, John D. "Puzzling Public Buildings." *BAR* 18 (1992): 52–61.

Yadin, Yigael. *Hazor: The Schweich Lectures of the British Academy, 1970.* London: Oxford University Press, 1972.

Yadin, Yigael. *Hazor: The Rediscovery of a Great Citadel of the Bible.* London: Weidenfeld and Nicholson, 1975.

TEL KEDESH

The biblical town of Kedesh is a 20–25 acre site located about 6 miles north-northwest of Hazor in the rural interior of Upper Galilee. The site was established during the Early Bronze Age and became a large Canaanite city in the Middle Bronze II period. Kedesh is mentioned in the Egyptian Execration Texts of the ninth century B.C. According to the book of Joshua, the Israelites defeated the "king of Kedesh" during the northern campaign of the conquest (Josh. 12:22), and it was named a "fortified city" that was given by lot to the tribe of Naphtali (Josh. 19:32–37). Its importance to the Israelites was underscored by its designation as a city of refuge (Josh. 20:7) and as a Levitical city (Josh. 21:32). The military leader Barak, from the time of Judges, was an inhabitant of Kedesh (Judg. 4:6). Kedesh is specifically mentioned as one of the sites captured by Tiglath-pileser III of Assyria in the eighth century B.C. (2 Kings 15:29).

Tel Kedesh is a large site, measuring more than a half mile from north to south. It consists of two mounds: an upper tell that was founded in the Early Bronze Age, and a lower tell constructed first in the Middle Bronze Age. The tell remained unexcavated until 1997, and the surrounding region was mostly unexplored. Excavation of the site began that year and concluded in 2012. The excavations focused primarily on the Persian and Hellenistic remains of the site, but there is hope that future work will explore the early remains.

FOR FURTHER READING

Berlin, Andrea, and Sharon Herbert. "Life and Death on the Israel-Lebanon Border." *BAR* 31 (2005): 34–43.

Erlich, Adi. "Happily Ever After? A Hellenistic Hoard from Tel Kedesh in Israel." *AJA* 121 (2017): 39–59.

TEL KINROT

Tel Kinrot is a large site, about 25 acres, that is located on the north-western shore of the Sea of Galilee, 6 miles north of modern Tiberias. The early investigators, Dalman (1921) and Albright (1923), identified the mound with the biblical town of Kinneret, which is mentioned in the Old Testament as a "fortified city" inherited by the tribe of Naphtali (Josh. 19:35). Tel Kinrot is the only settlement in the region that could fit the description as fortified during the LB–Iron I periods, and thus it appears to be a solid identification. The town of Kinneret is also mentioned in extrabiblical literature from the Late Bronze Age, such as in the conquest lists of Thutmosis III (ca. 1479–1425 B.C.) at Karnak.

Although some preliminary excavation work took place in the 1930s, it was not until the 1980s that systematic and thorough work occurred. The digging continued until 2008, and now is in its publishing stage. Early and sporadic remains have been uncovered here from the Pottery Neolithic, Chalcolithic, and Early Bronze periods. More substantial finds, however, were made from the late Middle Bronze period and the early Late Bronze Age. At this time, there was an impressive defensive system at the site. Perhaps the most important ruins came from the Iron I period of the eleventh century B.C. The excavators did major work in the domestic quarter of the period, and found that the site was carefully planned and basically had an urban layout. They believe that an earthquake destroyed that settlement. Later, the site contained a strong fortress during the Iron II period that was probably destroyed by the Assyrians in 734–733 B.C. Minimal and meager settlement occurred on the mound after that.

FOR FURTHER READING

Fritz, Volkmar. "Kinneret: Excavations at Tell el-Oreimeh (Tel Kinrot). Preliminary Report on the 1994–1997 Seasons." *Tel Aviv* 26 (1999): 92–115.
Munger, Stefan. "Kinneret—An Urban Center at the Crossroads: Excavations on Iron IB Tel Kinrot at the Lake of Galilee." *NEA* 74 (2011): 68–90.

SHA'AR HAGOLAN

Sha'ar Hagolan is a Neolithic site located just south of the Sea of Galilee in the central Jordan Valley on the northern bank of the Yarmouk River. The settlement of the site dates to about 6000 B.C., at the beginning of the

PN period. Its size is about 50 acres, making it one of the largest settlements during the PN period. Excavations took place here under the direction of Moshe Stekelis (1949–52) and Yosef Garfinkel (1989–90, 1996–2004).

The site is important because Stekelis identified, for the first time, the Yarmukian culture, which was present throughout parts of Israel during the PN period. Some of the earliest pottery in the history of Palestine was manufactured here; it was a chevron-incised ceramic with painted rims, and it came in various forms and sizes. Over 300 pieces of art have been discovered, and many of them are religious figurines of a goddess made of stone or fired clay.

The sixth millennium B.C. site is an impressive Neolithic village that reflects advanced town planning. The most recent excavations discovered a series of large courtyard houses that were separated by streets. Their walls were strong, constructed of field stones with loaf-shaped mud-bricks on top. There was a main street that ran through the middle of town, about 10 feet wide. At the center of the village was a large public building, although its function is uncertain. Archaeologists even discovered a well that had been dug in order to reach the water table at about 14 feet. Sha'ar Hagolan was a permanent settlement. This is critical, because for a long time scholars have assumed that the PN period was primarily inhabited by nomadic peoples who lived in temporary settlements.

FOR FURTHER READING

Garfinkel, Yosef. *The Goddess of Sha'ar Hagolan: Excavations at a Neolithic Site in Israel.* Jerusalem: Israel Exploration Society, 2004.
Stekelis, Moshe. *The Yarmukian Culture.* Jerusalem: Magnes Press, 1972.

TEL SOREG

Tel Soreg is a small site, less than 1 acre in size, that sits on a hill overlooking the valley of the En Gev River about 3 miles east of the Sea of Galilee. Moshe Kochavi and Pirhiya Beck excavated the site in the years 1987–88. It was first inhabited at the beginning of the Middle Bronze Age (2200–2000 B.C.), and one of the reasons to settle there was nearby springs. The first settlers dug shallow pits and built huts on top that served as domestic quarters. Late Bronze pottery has been found, but there are few architectural remains. Collared-rim storage jars are in evidence, and these are indicators of Iron I remains. A small fort was uncovered from the ninth or eighth centuries B.C., and it included an Iron Age casemate wall system.

Many agricultural artifacts were found, such as silos, mortars, pestles, and grinding stones. Some argue that it was a site devoted to agriculture, although that is uncertain. Tel Soreg was under the control of the Arameans at this time, and it was destroyed in the late ninth or early eighth centuries B.C. "The destruction can be attributed either to the Assyrian invasions of 838–837 B.C.E. or 796 B.C.E., or to Joash of Israel in the early eighth century B.C.E." (Hasegawa 2012, 72).

Some scholars have identified Tel Soreg with Aphek in the Bible (1 Kings 20:26–30; 2 Kings 13:17, 24–25). The archaeologists deny this identification because the site is so small.

FOR FURTHER READING

Kochavi, Moshe, et al. "The Land of Geshur." *BAR* 18 (1992): 30–44, 84–85.
Hasegawa, Shuichi. *Aram and Israel during the Jehuite Dynasty*, 92. Berlin: de Gruyter, 2012.

ET-TEL

The site of et-Tel is located a little more than a mile north of the Sea of Galilee near the spot where the northern Jordan River flows into the sea. The mound covers about 20 acres. Excavations began there in 1988 under the supervision of Rami Arav, and they continue today. The earliest level at et-Tel belongs to the Early Bronze Age, and there appears to have been uninterrupted occupation from EB I (3200–2800 B.C.) through EB II (2800–2600 B.C.). A thick wall made of huge boulders fortified the town, and some remaining portions of it have been exposed to a height of over 4 feet.

The major finds date to the Iron II period. Settlement first occurred during the tenth century B.C., and it was separated into two parts: a lower precinct that extended over much of the mound, and an acropolis located on the higher, northeastern part of the tell. Excavations of the acropolis revealed that a large, fortified wall with a monumental gateway complex surrounded it. The gate consisted of two parts: an outer gate of two massive towers that bracketed the passage into the city, and an inner gateway that was a typical four-room complex of the Iron II period. The gateway area was adorned with cultic representations and installations, such as a *bamah* (altar) and a stylized pillar with a warrior-bull chiseled on it.

Inside the gateway on the acropolis was found a wide plaza, and on its northern side sat a large public building that excavators believe was a palace.

These finds led the archaeologists to conclude that et-Tel at this time was perhaps the capital city of the land of Geshur mentioned in biblical literature (e.g., 2 Sam. 3:3; 14:32). The city was likely destroyed at the hands of the Assyrian monarch Tiglath-pileser III during his invasion of the area in 734 B.C. The site was abandoned for the most part until the Hellenistic-Roman periods. The excavators identify it as the New Testament site of Bethsaida, the home of three of Jesus's disciples.

FOR FURTHER READING

Arav, Rami, and Richard Freund, eds. *Bethsaida: A City by the North Shore of the Sea of Galilee*. 4 vols. Kirksville, MO: Thomas Jefferson University Press, 1995–2009.

Savage, Carl E. *Biblical Bethsaida: An Archaeological Study of the First Century*. Lanham, MD: Lexington Books, 2011.

CHAPTER 7

The Jezreel Valley

THE JEZREEL VALLEY separates the Galilee region in the north from the central highlands in the south. It spans much of the country from east to west, and it served as a vital means of travel and communication between the Mediterranean coast and regions inland. Major fortified cities were built here in antiquity in order to guard these highways. Some of the great invasions and battles of history took place in the Jezreel Valley, such as the invasions of Thutmosis III in the fifteenth century B.C. and Shishak in the tenth century B.C. Important battles in biblical history occurred in the valley, including Israelite troops under Barak against the forces of the king of Hazor (Judg. 4–5), Saul's army against the Philistines (1 Sam. 29–31), and Josiah's troops against Pharaoh Necho's army (2 Kings 23). The Assyrians under Tiglath-pileser III destroyed many sites in the valley in about 734 B.C. The valley was also critically important throughout history because it served as the breadbasket of Palestine in antiquity.

BETH SHEAN

Beth Shean was located at the junction of two major passes in antiquity: (1) the thoroughfare that ran from the Jezreel Valley eastward, and (2) the roadway that traversed the length of the Jordan Valley from north to south. Beth Shean was strategically located to guard both passes.

The site was occupied almost continuously from the late Neolithic (ca. 4000 B.C.) to the Early Arab period (ca. A.D. 600). It was first mentioned in extrabiblical texts in the annals of Thutmosis III at Karnak (fifteenth century B.C.); this was followed by its appearance in the topographical lists of Seti I (ca. 1306–1290 B.C.) and Rameses II (ca. 1290–1224 B.C.). In fact, excavations at Beth Shean uncovered two commemorative stelae that belonged to those two pharaohs (*ANET*, 255). The site was clearly under the control of the Egyptians during much of the Late Bronze Age. It was not conquered by the invading Israelites, although it had been allotted to the tribe of Manasseh

(Josh. 17:11–12). The Philistines perhaps settled there during the Iron I period (e.g., 1 Sam. 31:8–10). By the time of Solomon's kingship, Beth Shean had come under Israelite hegemony (1 Kings 4). As an aside, the city was a major textile center during the Roman period called Scythopolis. Major excavations and reconstruction of the Roman settlement have taken place.

The tell is huge. It stands about 260 feet high, and it contains 18 superimposed strata. Excavation was first done in 1921–33 by the University of Pennsylvania under the direction of C. S. Fisher, A. Rowe, and G. M. Fitzgerald. Yigael Yadin and Shulamit Geva conducted a brief season of work there in 1983 to explore the Iron I strata (Yadin and Geva 1986). Major excavation work continued under Amihai Mazar of Hebrew University from 1989 to 1996.

Based on these excavations, the first sizeable settlement at Beth Shean occurred in the EB I period. A large public building was found made of mud-brick. Fourteen wooden posts standing on flat stone would have held up its roof, and mud-brick benches lined the inside walls of the building. A huge fire destroyed it. Few remains were discovered from the EB II period, but a "dense settlement" was uncovered in the EB III period (Mazar 1997, 65). The EB IV–MB I transition period left sparse remains.

There was an occupation gap during the twentieth through eighteenth centuries B.C. (MB IIA). This was followed by a small settlement in the seventeenth through sixteenth centuries B.C. that was unfortified. Excavators uncovered the domestic quarter from this time, and a series of child pit burials and child jar burials were found here.

The LB Age at Beth Shean was dominated by Egyptian presence. The site served as an outpost or garrison for the Eighteenth through Twentieth Dynasties of Egypt. Mazar concludes, "Beth-Shean served only as the headquarters of Egyptian rule, containing administrative buildings, temples, and dwelling quarters of the Egyptian officials and the soldiers serving in the Egyptian garrison" (Mazar 1997, 67). It was from this period that the archaeologists uncovered some impressive Egyptian monuments, including two stelae from the reign of Seti I. Sometime during the twelfth century B.C., the site was violently destroyed and the Egyptian presence ended. It is not clear who destroyed the site, although during the early monarchic period of Israel the city was in the hands of the Philistines. It did not become part of Israel's kingdom until the reigns of David and Solomon.

From the tenth century B.C. during the time of Solomon, archaeologists found a citadel and several other public buildings on the summit of the tell. These were destroyed by fire, perhaps due to the invasion of Pharaoh Shishak after the death of Solomon (site number 16 on Shishak's inscription on the Bubastite Portal at Karnak; Currid 1997, 191). In the subsequent Iron

II period, Beth Shean was unfortified, although the buildings from this time were well planned and large. Tiglath-pileser III and the Assyrians probably destroyed the settlement in about 734 B.C.

FOR FURTHER READING

Currid, John D. *Ancient Egypt and the Old Testament*. Grand Rapids: Baker, 1997.

Mazar, Amihai, et al. *Excavations at Tel Beth-Shean, 1989–1996*. Vols. I–IV. Jerusalem: Institute of Archaeology, Hebrew University, 2006–2012.

Mazar, Amihai. "Four Thousand Years of History at Tel Beth-Shean: An Account of the Renewed Excavations." *BA* 60 (1997): 62–76.

Yadin, Yigael, and Shulamit Geva. *Investigations at Beth Shean: The Early Iron Age Strata*. Jerusalem: Institute of Archaeology, Hebrew University, 1986.

MEGIDDO (TELL EL-MUTSELLIM)

Megiddo sits strategically in the Jezreel Valley and controls a major pass along the Via Maris. Due to its location, the site was one of the great theaters of history. Its name first appeared on the Temple of Karnak, in which Thutmosis III carved a detailed record of a battle he fought at Megiddo in about 1468 B.C. Later, in Joshua 12:21, the "king of Megiddo" is listed as one of the monarchs defeated by the invading Israelite army. Megiddo was then apportioned to the tribe of Manasseh, but they were unable to dislodge the Canaanites from the city and its immediate surroundings. Judges 1:27 says, "Manasseh did not drive out . . . the inhabitants of Megiddo and its villages, for the Canaanites persisted in dwelling in that land." The next biblical reference we have of Megiddo is that the city was part of a northern administrative district under Solomonic rule (1 Kings 4:12). About 150 years elapsed between those two accounts; it is not clear who brought Megiddo under Israelite hegemony, although perhaps it was David (Currid 1991, 31). Under Solomon's regime, Megiddo gained increasing importance, as is suggested by 1 Kings 9:15, "And this is the account of the forced labor that King Solomon drafted to build the house of the LORD and his own house and the Millo and the wall of Jerusalem and Hazor and Megiddo and Gezer." After the death of Solomon, Pharaoh Shishak invaded Israel in about 918 B.C. Not only is Megiddo mentioned as one of the cities captured by Shishak on the Karnak inscription, but an unstratified piece of the Shishak stele was found on the mound of Megiddo (Fisher 1929, 16 and figs. 7–9). During the period of the divided monarchy, Megiddo and its environs continued

Fig. 7.1. Excavations at Megiddo

to be strategic, as evidenced by several biblical references to the area (see, e.g., 2 Kings 9:27; 23:29–30; 2 Chron. 35:22).

Megiddo has been one of the most intensely and extensively excavated sites in Palestine. The initial work took place in the years 1903–5 under the direction of Gottlieb Schumacher on behalf of the Deutscher Palästina-Verein. The value of his work is difficult to assess because the techniques of excavation were in their infancy. From 1925 to 1939, the University of Chicago did major excavation work at the site under the direction of various archaeologists: C. S. Fisher, P. L. O. Guy, and G. Loud. It was truly the first scientific excavation in Palestine in which careful excavation, recording, and analyses were applied to the dig. The Israeli archaeologist Yigael Yadin excavated Megiddo for six seasons, from 1960 to 1971, and he mainly tried to determine the precise stratigraphy of the Iron Age levels. Beginning in 1994, the Institute of Archaeology of Tel Aviv University has conducted a long-term excavation project at Megiddo with the goal of uncovering unknown parts of the site and answering some of the questions remaining from previous excavations (Finkelstein 2006 and 2013).

The University of Chicago excavations were able to identify twenty major layers at the site from the Neolithic period to the Persian period. Pottery sherds indicate the presence of a Neolithic settlement; there are no structures uncovered from this time (stratum XX). In the subsequent

Chalcolithic period, dwellings, pits, ovens, and mud-brick walls were discovered. The Early Bronze Age strata revealed a major settlement. A sacred area was found that included a sequence of superimposed temples that were in use all the way into the Iron I period. A huge circular stone *bamah*, an altar or high place, was unearthed. A great city wall, about 25 feet thick surrounded the site, "which was the largest and strongest wall ever built on the mound" (Yadin 1977, 834).

A large city wall, supported by a glacis and entered through a monumental gateway, surrounded the MB Age city. The sacred area continued in use, and three new temples were erected in the vicinity of the EB high place. Investigation also revealed several palatial buildings from the MB period. Megiddo during the LB period was a major Canaanite city. Its significance was shown by the discovery of the Megiddo ivories. This hoard was found in the LB palace; it included 382 objects demonstrating a wide range of ancient Near Eastern influences.

The Old Testament does not describe how Megiddo fell into the hands of the Israelites, but by the tenth century B.C. it had become an important city in Solomon's kingdom; Baana served as a district governor residing at Megiddo (1 Kings 4:12). Solomon, in fact, spent much time and effort in building Megiddo (1 Kings 9:15), and it became a city of grandeur. Several large palaces from his time (designated stratum VA-IVB) have been unearthed, and they were constructed of ashlar masonry. Typical of the time, ashlar masonry may be defined as finely dressed blocks that have been cut rectangularly, and the blocks were often arranged in a header-stretcher fashion (i.e., courses of stones whose shorter ends were exposed alternated with courses whose longer ends were exposed). Yadin discovered a monumental six-chambered city gate from Solomon's time, although more recent work suggests that the Solomonic gate was below that one. In addition, two sets of structures were found by the Chicago expedition that were interpreted as the stables of Solomon (1 Kings 9:19). The use of these "tripartite pillared" buildings is a matter of debate. Some argue they were stables, others storehouses, and others barracks or markets. What is clear about them is that they do not belong to Solomon's time, but rather to the ninth century B.C. (perhaps the time of Ahab).

Perhaps the most significant find from the ninth century B.C. was a major water system (see chapter 14 for more detail). The city remained in Israelite hands until the last half of the eighth century B.C., when the Assyrians under Tiglath-pileser III captured Megiddo and made it the capital of an Assyrian province (ca. 734 B.C.). Near the city gate, excavators found two impressive buildings that were characteristic of Assyrian administrative structures of the time.

FOR FURTHER READING

Currid, John D. "The Re-Stratification of Megiddo during the United Mon-
    archy." *ZDPV* 107 (1991): 28–38.
Finkelstein, Israel, et al. *Megiddo IV: The 1998–2002 Seasons*. Tel Aviv: Tel
    Aviv University, 2006.
Finkelstein, Israel, et al. *Megiddo V: The 2004–2008 Seasons*. Tel Aviv: Tel
    Aviv University, 2013.
Fisher, C. S. *The Excavation of Armageddon*. Chicago: University of Chi-
    cago Press, 1929.
Yadin, Yigael. "Megiddo." *EAEHL*, 3:830–56 (1977).

TAANACH

The mound of Taanach lies about 5 miles southeast of Megiddo; it does
not sit at the juncture of a major pass, but is next to the southern branch of
the Via Maris. Taanach is an 11-acre mound, and it rises above the Jezreel
Valley about 130 feet. Taanach is first mentioned in the ancient sources in the
fifteenth century B.C., in which Thutmosis III describes his forces mustering
there during the battle of Megiddo (ca. 1468 B.C.). Later, Pharaoh Shishak
names the site in a list of towns on his invasion route through Palestine in
the last quarter of the tenth century B.C. It is site number 14 on Shishak's
relief on the Bubastite Portal at Karnak (Currid 1997, 191). In Joshua 12:21, the
king of Taanach is listed as one of the monarchs that Joshua defeated. The
city and its surroundings were allotted to the tribe of Manasseh (Josh. 17:11;
1 Chron. 7:29). It was also designated as a Levitical city (Josh. 21:25). According
to the book of Judges, the Manassites were unable to displace the Canaanite
inhabitants of Taanach (Judg. 1:27). In the days of the Israelite judge Deborah,
there was a battle at Taanach between the Canaanites and the Israelites.

Ernst Sellin first excavated Taanach in 1902–4 (see Wilson 1904, 388–91).
The results are of limited value because techniques of excavation were in
a primitive stage. There were three major excavation seasons in 1963, 1966,
and 1968 under the auspices of the American Schools of Oriental Research
and the direction of Paul Lapp. Four areas were excavated in the western
and southwestern quadrants of the tell. The investigators discovered that
the earliest city dates to the EB II–III periods. Four phases of fortifications
belong to that time, and they include a large city wall (almost 14 feet thick)
with several towers in the early phases. In the later phases, a large glacis and
several retaining walls were added.

A 700-year gap in occupation followed, and then a small campsite appeared on the mound during the MB II period. This was followed by a more extensive MB II–LB I settlement. Much building activity took place at this time, although it was "poorly constructed domestic architecture and fortifications" (Glock 1978, 1143). It is likely that Thutmosis III destroyed this city in about 1468 B.C. No significant settlement occurred at the site until the late thirteenth century B.C.

Taanach became a larger town in the twelfth century B.C., with a substantial domestic quarter, numerous public buildings, and some defenses. It was destroyed in the last quarter of that century, about 1125 B.C. There was a minimal occupation in the eleventh century B.C., but that was followed by a larger tenth-century settlement. An important structure was found from this period that related to cultic practices at the site, and a 2-foot-high cult stand was found in an associated cistern. Pharaoh Shishak destroyed this town in about 918 B.C.

FOR FURTHER READING

Currid, John D. *Ancient Egypt and the Old Testament.* Grand Rapids: Baker, 1997.

Glock, A. E. "Taanach." *EAEHL,* 4:1138–47 (1978).

Lapp, Paul W. "The 1963 Excavation at Tell Ta'annek." *BASOR* 173 (1964): 4–44.

Lapp, Paul W. "The 1966 Excavation at Tell Ta'annek." *BASOR* 185 (1967): 2–39.

Lapp, Paul W. "The 1968 Excavation at Tell Ta'annek." *BASOR* 195 (1969): 2–49.

Wilson, Charles. "Austrian Excavations at Taanach." *PEQ* 36 (1904): 388–91.

TEL 'AFULA

Located about 6 miles directly east of Megiddo in the central plains of Jezreel, Tel 'Afula is perhaps to be identified with the biblical site of Ophrah. There Gideon performed his first act of deliverance by cutting down a pagan Asherah pole and replacing it with an altar to the Lord (Judg. 6:25–32). The mound itself covers an area of about 6 acres, although other remains, such as tombs, are distributed over a wider area. Early excavation work was done at the site under the supervision of E. L. Sukenik (1926, 1931, 1948), I. Ben-Dor (1950–51), and Moshe Dothan (1951). Several small-scale excavations were carried out during the 1990s and the first decade of the 2000s. The various excavations demonstrate that the site was inhabited in the Chalcolithic period and then in every major archaeological period until the Late Byzantine period.

A prominent period of habitation was during the MB Age. A pottery workshop was discovered in MB I, which included three kilns next to a building. The subsequent MB II settlement was more elaborate; it was carefully planned with town streets and buildings with courtyards on both sides of the streets. Another pottery workshop was found in this level and it was for the making of Tell el-Yehudiyah ware. The next significant habitation was during the Iron I period. It included granaries, a large four-room building, and kilns. The appearance of Philistine pottery and Cypriote ware indicates that the town was involved in foreign trade. The archaeologists believe the site was destroyed in the second half of the eleventh century B.C., perhaps during the kingship of Saul.

FOR FURTHER READING

Dothan, Moshe. "Afula." *EAEHL*, 1:32–36 (1975).
Dothan, Moshe. "The Excavations at 'Afula." *Atiqot* 1 (1956): 19–70.
Feig, Nurit. "Tel 'Afula." *Hadoshot Arkheologiyot* (2012): 124.
Sukenik, E. L. "Archaeological Investigations at 'Affula." *JPOS* 21 (1948): 1–78.

TEL KASSIS

Approximately 3 miles north of Tel Yokneam on the banks of the Kishon River lies the site of Tel Kassis. It has been identified by some scholars, such as Y. Aharoni, as the biblical settlement of Helkath. According to the book of Joshua, Helkath belonged to the tribe of Asher (19:25), and it served as a Levitical city belonging to the Gershonite clan (21:31). A salvage excavation took place at the site in 2010 because of the installation of a gas pipeline in the area. The probes indicate that the site was inhabited during both the EB and the MB periods. However, the height of the city was during the LB Age. At the close of the period, the city was destroyed by a huge conflagration. Other sites in the region, including Tel Yokneam, were also razed at this time. It is tempting to identify these destructions with the invading Israelites under the leadership of Joshua.

During the salvage excavation, archaeologists uncovered a cache of more than one hundred "cultic" vessels in a natural hollow in bedrock. They belonged to the Canaanite LB habitation at the site. Among the objects found were an incense stand and a ritual goblet with a sculpted woman's face on it.

Some vessels were imported from the Aegean area, and this is evidence for trade relations with the coast at this time. One theory regarding this cache is that the cultic vessels were buried for safekeeping at the end of the LB Age because of threatened invasion. In reality, the horde is more likely an example of a favissa, which is a pit used for burying obsolete cult objects. Favissae have been found from the LB period—for example, in the Fosse Temple at Lachish—and at an Iron I temple at Tell Qasile. Because the objects were ritually set apart, they were buried in a special place, rather than simply discarded.

FOR FURTHER READING

See the preliminary reports of the Israel Antiquities Authorities Publications (for the 2010 excavations).

TEL REGEV

Located next to the Kishon River, Tel Regev (el Harbaj) sits at a crossing point of the ancient Via Maris. It is one of the sites that controlled the western entrance to the Jezreel Valley, which was the primary east-west thoroughfare in Palestine. The area is quite fertile, and it served as an important region for trade between coastal and inland peoples. The tell was probed by John Garstang in the 1930s, but the major excavation work occurred in the years 2011–14 as part of the Southern Plain of Akko Project. This study has focused on the Late Bronze and Iron Ages at the site with the aim of learning more about the trade, society, and culture of these periods in the region. We still await the final reports on the excavation work.

Surveys of sites in the Jezreel Valley near the Kishon River indicate that settlements in the plains were of large size during the Late Bronze Age. In the subsequent Iron I period, these sites decreased in size. In addition, numerous new settlements appeared in the adjacent highlands, which coincide with the tribal allotment of Asher (Lehmann 2001, 87–90). It is likely that these new villages were founded by the incursion of the Israelites. The surveys also found monochrome and bichrome pottery in the sites of the plain, and these are indicators of the presence of the Sea Peoples. Some believe there was a mixture of them with Canaanites and Israelites living in the area. On the other hand, it may simply indicate trade from the coastal regions. Remains from the Iron II period reflect a movement of population away from the highlands and back into the plains, where new settlements appear. Publication of the recent excavations at Tel Regev will help in defining these population movements.

FOR FURTHER READING

Horovich, Z., and D. Lipkunsky. "A Salvage Excavation near Tel Regev."
    'Atiqot 62 (2010): 1–13.
Lehmann, Gunnar. "Phoenicians in Western Galilee: First Results of an
    Archaeological Survey in the Hinterland of Acco." In *Studies in the
    Archaeology of the Iron Age in Israel and Jordan*, edited by A. Mazar,
    65–112. *JSOT* Supp. 331. Sheffield: Sheffield Academic Press, 2001.

TEL YOKNEAM

Tel Yokneam is located at the western extreme of the Valley of Jezreel about 7 miles northwest of Megiddo. It is strategically placed, as it stands at the entrance of a pass that goes through the Mount Carmel range toward the southwest to the Mediterranean Sea. Yokneam was an important Canaanite site during the Late Bronze Age; confirmation comes from the conquest lists of Pharaoh Thutmosis III, which mention the capture of the city (1468 B.C.). According to Joshua 12:22, the invading Israelite forces defeated numerous local kings, and one of them was "the king of Jokneam in Carmel." The city was part of the inheritance of the tribe of Manasseh, and it was located next to the allotment of the Zebulunites at the Kishon River (Josh. 19:10–11). Yokneam served as a Levitical city in Israel (Josh. 21:34).

Significant excavation work took place at the site under the direction of Amnon Ben Tor from 1977 to 1988. According to the excavators, Yokneam was more or less continually inhabited from the Early Bronze Age to the time of the Mamluks. The first period containing architectural remains was the MB II period; an impressive fortification system was unearthed from this time that included a 10-foot-wide outer wall with a tower. The wall was built directly on bedrock and had a stone base with a mud-brick superstructure. A glacis was built abutting the wall on the outside.

In contrast, the LB settlement contained no fortification system, "which suggests that the site was unfortified throughout the Late Bronze Age" (Ben Tor 1993, 809). Architectural remains consist of houses on the slopes of the mound. Yokneam was destroyed at the end of the LB; the ash layer was more than 3 feet deep. This conflagration occurred near the end of the thirteenth century B.C. and, therefore, may have been a result of the Israelite conquest under Joshua (see Josh. 12:22).

After a gap in occupation, the site was resettled near the close of the twelfth century B.C. Like its LB predecessor, the town was unfortified during the Iron I period. The most significant architectural find is what the excavators called the "Oil Maker's House," which was given that name because of evidence for olive oil production in the building. It consisted of a central courtyard surrounded by several domestic units. In the courtyard, the archaeologists uncovered circular installations carved from bedrock with many olive pits and stone weights. The structure, and the entire settlement for that matter, was destroyed by a large fire which the investigators believed was due to David's conquests in the area.

The major remains from the site date to the Iron II period, primarily to the tenth through eighth centuries B.C. There were two fortification systems during the period; the earlier one consisted of a large outer wall casemate system. A double city wall replaced this outer wall, perhaps by the beginning of the ninth century B.C. The excavators concluded that the "plan of this fortification system is different from all other Iron Age defense systems in Israel. A peripheral street, which ran along the inner side of the wall, separated it from the residential structures" (Ben Tor 1993, 807).

FOR FURTHER READING

Avissar, Miriam. *Tel Yoqne'am Excavations on the Acropolis.* Jerusalem: Israel Antiquities Authority, 2005.

Ben Tor, Amnon. "Jokneam." In *NEAEH,* 3:805–10 (1993).

Ben Tor, Amnon, et al. *Yokne'am II: The Iron Age and the Persian Period.* Qedem Reports 6. Jerusalem: Institute of Archaeology, Hebrew University, 2005.

Ben Tor, Amnon, et al. *Yokne'am III: The Middle and Late Bronze Ages.* Qedem Reports 7. Jerusalem: Institute of Archaeology, Hebrew University, 2005.

CHAPTER 8

The Negev

THE TERM *NEGEV* in Hebrew means "south" (BDB, 616), and over time it came to denote the region directly south of the Judean highlands. Because of its rugged terrain and climate, the Negev was sparsely populated in antiquity, and it had little economic importance for Palestine. The first permanent settlements were founded during the Chalcolithic period (see the discussion of the Beersheba group below). Few remains of the EB period have been uncovered, except for the major site of Arad, but more settlements appeared during the MB time. The MB Age was the period in which the Hebrew patriarchs were sojourning in the Negev. At the beginning of the Iron II period, the Israelites, probably under David and Solomon, constructed a line of fortresses in the Negev (e.g., Arad and Kadesh-Barnea) as defense against Egyptian aggression. In about 925 B.C., after the death of Solomon, Pharaoh Shishak (Shoshenq I) led a military campaign against Israel and Judah, and many of the sites subjugated by him were located in the Negev (tiers 6–10 on the Bubastite Portal).[1] During the following ninth through eighth centuries B.C., some sites, such as Beersheba, became important cities in the nation of Judah.

ARAD

Tel 'Arad is located in the Negev about 17 miles east of Beersheba and about 14 miles west of the Dead Sea within the dry-steppe climatic zone. It has two primary levels of occupation: the EB period (twenty-ninth through twenty-seventh centuries B.C.) and the Iron II period (tenth through seventh centuries B.C.). Excavations at the site were conducted under the direction of Yohanan Aharoni and Ruth Amiran in the 1960s and 1970s. It is perhaps the best restored and preserved EB site in all of Palestine. Arad is first mentioned in extrabiblical literature on the list of cities that Pharaoh Shishak had inscribed on the Bubastite Portal at Karnak. Signs 108–9 on that inscription are a compound name that means "Great Arad." Shishak's invasion of

1. John D. Currid, *Ancient Egypt and the Old Testament* (Grand Rapids: Baker, 1997), 196–202.

Palestine is described in 1 Kings 14:25–26 and 2 Chron. 12:1–9. Arad is first mentioned in the Bible in Numbers 21:1, in which the king of Arad prevented the Israelites from entering the Judaean hill country. The king of Arad is listed as one who was defeated by Joshua during the conquest (Josh. 12:14), and the city was part of the tribal inheritance of the tribe of Judah. The Kenites later settled in that area (Judg. 1:16).

The excavations at Arad revealed that there was an upper city and a lower city. The lower city was occupied during the EB period, and its shape was saddle-like. The rock upon which the city was built, in contrast to the surrounding environment, was impervious to water. The shape and form of the site made it a natural catchment area for winter rains. The layout of the city demonstrated deliberate town planning. Its city wall, originally over 8 feet thick, surrounded the entire site, and it extended for two-thirds of a mile and enclosed 22 acres. It was constructed entirely of stone. At intervals of 65–80 feet, semicircular towers appeared, and these measured 10–12 feet in diameter as they projected out from the city wall. The towers were entered through ground-level doorways in the wall.

Fig. 8.1. EB Lower City, Arad

The EB town layout contained public buildings in the center of the site and housing on the periphery near the city wall. The houses were of the broad-room style, which is rectangular with the entrance in one of the long sides; this was typical of the EB period. Stone benches ran inside the houses on all four sides, and there were no windows. A main, central pillar resting on a stone base supported the roof.

The occupation of Arad came to an abrupt end about 2700 B.C., and it was not resettled until the eleventh century B.C. At this time, the Israelites placed a military outpost on the highest point of the site (upper city). The settlement reached its cultural and architectural apex during the ninth through eighth centuries B.C. One entered the fortress through a large gate that consisted of two towers on either side of the entrance that projected about 6 feet out from the fortress wall. These projections presumably gave the defenders greater firepower at the gate area. The fortress walls were 13 feet thick, and they were constructed using the offsets/insets technique.

On the inside of the fortress, the archaeologists discovered a ninth-century temple. Its form was broad-room, and it included a holy of holies at its western back end. In the courtyard, the excavators found

Fig. 8.2. Arad Sanctuary

an altar for burnt offerings. Three steps led up into the holy of holies that was flanked by two incense altars. Inside the holy of holies was a paved platform containing a stone pillar. This temple had several features that reflected the form of the earlier Solomonic temple in Jerusalem. The Arad temple was destroyed near the beginning of the seventh century B.C., and that destruction may have been a result of Hezekiah's reform (2 Kings 18:1–4).

FOR FURTHER READING

Aharoni, Yohanan. "Arad." *EAEHL* 1:74–89 (1975).
Aharoni, Yohanan. *Arad Inscriptions*. Jerusalem: Israel Exploration Society, 1981.

BEERSHEBA

Tel Beersheba is located in the central Negev next to the Besor Brook to the east of the modern city of Beersheba. The site measures about 2.5

acres in area. The initial excavations took place from 1969 to 1976 under the direction of Yohanan Aharoni and Zeev Herzog (1976). Herzog later returned to work specifically on the Iron II water system at the site in 1993–95. The excavation and restoration of Tel Beersheba is one of the finest archaeological projects in Israel. It was an important biblical site, particularly during the time of the patriarchs. It received its name, literally, "well of the oath," because of incidents involving the Hebrew patriarch Abraham (Gen. 21:25–33). The Lord met with Isaac at Beersheba (Gen. 26:23–25). And it was here that Jacob received a vision to lead his family to Egypt (Gen. 46:1–7). Throughout Old Testament history, Beersheba served as a geographical symbol of the southern border of the land of Israel in the phrase "from Dan to Beersheba" (Judg. 20:1; 1 Sam. 3:20; etc.).

The excavations at Tel Beersheba contribute mostly to the understanding of Israel during the monarchic periods. Although there is disagreement among scholars, it is likely that David built a fortress here at the close of the eleventh century B.C. On the summit, houses were built close to one another in a circular fashion that formed a defensive wall. The entrances to the houses opened inward to a central courtyard. In the mid-tenth century B.C., the city increased in size, was heavily fortified, and perhaps served as an administrative center during Solomon's reign. It was a well-planned town that contained a solid outer wall with stone foundations and upper courses of mud-brick. The city was destroyed, probably at the hands of Pharaoh Shishak, about 925 B.C.

In the ninth through eighth centuries B.C., Beersheba became a significant city in the nation of Judah. Excavations have uncovered an example of remarkable town planning. The outer city wall was now a casemate system composed of two parallel walls with space between them for living and storage areas. For the domestic quarter, the casemate room served as the rear room of the common Israelite four-room house. From the outer wall down the slope of the tell, the builders erected a glacis (sloping revetment) that surrounded the mound for fortification purposes. On the southeast side of the town was the gate complex, consisting of an outer and an inner gateway. The inner gateway had four chambers and was constructed in the tenth century B.C., perhaps during the reign of David.

Inside the gate was a square from which radiated circular streets that coursed along the outer city wall, and a main street that went through the heart of the town. To the northwest of the square was the domestic quarter, and to the east of it stood three tripartite-pillared structures that probably served as public storehouses. In the northeast sector of the town, the builders constructed an impressive water system within the city walls that descended down to a water chamber.

A large, horned altar of cut stones was discovered at the site from the Iron II period. It does not conform to biblical law, which says, "You shall wield no iron tool on them; you shall build an altar to the LORD your God of uncut stones" (Deut. 27:5–6). There was probably a rogue cult center at Beersheba, and Amos prophesied against it (Amos 5:4–5; 8:14). The altar was dismantled and later used as building material during the religious reform of Hezekiah (2 Kings 18:3–4).

The ninth- through eighth-century town of Beersheba was destroyed at the hands of Sennacherib, king of Assyria, in 701 B.C.

FOR FURTHER READING

Aharoni, Yohanan, ed. *Beer-Sheba I: Excavations at Tel Beer-Sheba, 1969–1971 Seasons*. Tel Aviv: Tel Aviv Institute of Archaeology, 1973.

Herzog, Zeev. "Beer-Sheba of the Patriarchs." *BAR* 6 (1980): 12–28.

Herzog, Zeev, ed. *Beer-Sheba II: The Early Iron Age Settlements*. Tel Avi: Tel Aviv Institute of Archaeology, 1985.

Singer-Avitz, Lily, and Zeev Herzog, eds. *Beer-Sheba III: The Early Iron IIA Enclosed Settlement and the Late Iron IIA–Iron IIB Cities*. Tel Aviv: Tel Aviv Institute of Archaeology, 2016.

THE BEERSHEBA GROUP

During the Chalcolithic period (ca. 4000–3200 B.C.), the population of Palestine settled in more arid regions. The reason(s) for this population shift is unknown, although some researchers believe it was due to some type of climatic upheaval. One central area of settlement was in the Negev on the Nahal (River) Beersheba near the ancient tell of Beersheba. Three Chalcolithic villages were founded close together, and they are known as the Beersheba group: Tell Abu Matar, Horvat Batar, and Safadi. The three villages sustained a combined population of 700–1000 people. The villages specialized in crafts. For instance, Tell Abu Matar specialized in metalworking. Remains of this industry included "copper ore (malachite) brought from Wadi Punon that descends to the Arabah, rock anvils for breaking up the ore, fireplaces with dross, fragments of crucibles, and smelting tools" (Gophna 1975, 154). Safadi, on the other hand, was centered on an ivory industry, and a workshop for ivory objects was found there.

Unique to these settlements was a subterranean architecture. Mazar comments that the "Chalcolithic settlers took advantage of the soft loess soil to carve out a series of burrows and subterranean dwellings, storage and work rooms" (Mazar 1990, 66). At Tell Abu Matar, there were four basic levels of settlement; the first three phases were under ground, and the last phase was above ground. The underground village contained clusters of five to seven rooms that were connected by galleries. Some of the rooms had paved flooring. These underground installations reflect the ability of the population to adapt to the physical environment of the area.

FOR FURTHER READING

Gilead, Isaac, et al. "Excavations at Tell Abu-Matar (the Hatzerim Neighborhood), Beer Sheva." *Israel Prehistoric Society* 24 (1991): 173–79.

Gophna, Ram. "Beersheba." *EAEHL*, 1:152–59 (1975).

Mazar, Amihai. *Archaeology of the Land of the Bible*. New York: Doubleday, 1990.

Perrot, Jean. "Structures d'habitat, mode de vie et environnement: Les villages souterrains des pasteurs de Beershéva." *Paleorient* 10 (1984): 75–96.

Perrot, Jean. "The Excavations at Tell Abu Matar, near Beersheba." *IEJ* 5 (1955): 17–40.

KADESH-BARNEA

The site of Kadesh-Barnea is generally recognized today to be located at Tell 'Ain el-Qudeirat, which sits next to an abundant spring on the way from Sinai into the Negev. The area of the mound is about three-fourths of an acre. Exploration of the tell began with the investigators Leonard Woolley and T. E. Lawrence in 1914. As part of their survey for the Palestine Exploration Fund, they examined the site and drew plans of the remains there. This was followed by an exploratory excavation under the direction of Moshe Dothan in 1956, and further work by Rudolph Cohen in 1976–82.

Kadesh-Barnea was an important site in the Old Testament, and it was mentioned frequently in regard to the wilderness wanderings of Israel. It was from this site that Moses sent the twelve spies to reconnoiter the land of Canaan (Num. 13:17). They returned to Kadesh-Barnea with a weak-kneed majority report. God condemned the people for their fear and disobedience (Num. 14:20–35). The Israelites responded by attacking the highlands of Canaan despite God's judgment, and they were soundly defeated by the inhabitants (Num. 14:39–45). They returned to Kadesh-Barnea, where they began forty years of wandering.

Three main settlement phases were found on the mound, each containing a fortress complex. The archaeologists uncovered minimal architectural remains from the earliest level: two casemate rooms that had curved outer walls. Cohen has suggested that this earliest fortress was oval-shaped. The pottery from the two rooms indicates that the fortress belonged to the tenth through ninth centuries B.C. The second fortress was a rectangular structure with a solid outer wall that measured about 13 feet wide. Square towers projected from the outer wall at each corner of the fortress and in the middle of each side, for a total of eight towers. No gate complex has been found. The pottery from this period was mostly wheel-made, and that dates the structure to the eighth through seventh centuries B.C. The latest fortress was built with a design similar to the previous one, although the outer wall was casemate rather than solid. It also included eight project-ing towers that were attached to those of the previous structure. This last occupation was rich in pottery finds, and these date to the seventh through sixth centuries B.C.

There is no evidence at the site of remains prior to the tenth century B.C. Some commentators, consequently, have asked the question, Where then are the physical remains from the time of Israel's wilderness wanderings? In reality, the Israelites were a nomadic people at that time, and the physical remains of a wandering group are difficult to discern (see Rosen 1988). It is also possible that the earlier remains at the site or in the area have not been discovered yet.

FOR FURTHER READING

Cohen, Rudolph, and Hannah Bernick-Greenberg, eds. *Excavations at Kadesh Barnea (Tell el-Qudeirat) 1976–1982: Part I: Text.* Jerusalem: Israel Antiquities Authority, 2007.

Dothan, Moshe. "The Fortress at Kadesh-Barnea." *IEJ* 15 (1965): 134–51.

Rosen, Steven A. "Finding Evidence of Ancient Nomads." *BAR* 14 (1988): 46–53, 58–59.

Woolley, Leonard, and T. E. Lawrence. "The Wilderness of Zin." *APEF* 3 (1914–15): 62–71.

SHIQMIM

Approximately 6 miles due west of Beersheba, on the northern bank of the Nahal Beersheba, lies the site of Shiqmim. It is a large (ca. 24 acres), single-period site dating to the Chalcolithic period (ca. 4000–3200 B.C.). Its size indicates that perhaps it served as a regional center for several smaller sites that surrounded it. Survey work of Shiqmim and its surroundings was begun in 1977 by Levy and Alon (Levy and Alon 1985, 71), and excavation work followed in 1979–84 and 1987–93.

Survey and excavation work revealed that Shiqmim consisted of three main components: an upper village, a lower village, and a mortuary complex. The site contained four or perhaps five strata from the Chalcolithic period. The habitation displayed both aboveground and belowground installations, much like that which appeared in the Beersheba group. The purpose of the underground tunnels and rooms is a matter of scholarly debate; they may have been used for storage, for primary burials (secondary burials would then be in the mortuary precinct), or for hiding when attacked. Aboveground architecture included typical Chalcolithic structures, including rectilinear domestic buildings, courtyards, and storage areas.

Adjacent to the village, excavators uncovered cemeteries containing Chalcolithic cist burials and aboveground interment circle burials. The bodies had received an extensive degree of treatment. This mortuary precinct is the most important find for revealing burial practices during the Chalcolithic period.

FOR FURTHER READING

Levy, T. E., and D. Alon. "Shiqmim: A Chalcolithic Village and Mortuary Center in the Northern Negev." *Paleorient* 11 (1985): 71–83.
Levy, T. E., ed. *Shiqmim I*. Oxford: BAR, 1987.

TELL ESH-SHARI'A (TELL SERA')

The mound of esh-Shari'a is located midway between Beersheba and Gaza, overlooking the Nahal Gerar. It is about 12 miles northwest of Beersheba in the northern Negev. The summit of the tell measures about 5 acres, is shaped like a horseshoe, and has steep slopes on all sides except the west. Excavations took place under the direction of Eliezer Oren for six seasons in the 1970s.

The site was inhabited from the late MB II period (seventeenth century B.C.) until the Byzantine period in the fourth through sixth centuries A.D. The first major and extensive settlement occurred in the LB Age, especially during the thirteenth through twelfth centuries B.C. A large structure was discovered from that time that perhaps served as a fortress. Within one room, excavators found a number of ostraca inscribed with Egyptian hieratic texts from the time of Rameses III (ca. 1194–1163 B.C.). Perhaps invading Philistines from the west destroyed the building in the middle of the twelfth century B.C. The tell was uninhabited until the eleventh century B.C.

The excavators described the Iron I settlement of the eleventh century B.C. as Philistine, primarily because of the preponderance of Philistine pottery on the floors of the buildings. Four-room houses were discovered at this level, and so the archaeologists suggested that this architectural tradition originally belonged to the Philistines and was later adopted by the Israelites. Not all commentators agree with that assessment.

The Iron II levels of the tenth through ninth centuries B.C. contained well-planned public and private architecture. Oren describes one such building that "consists of long narrow halls surrounded by a massive wall. The bricks were laid in two rows, in a fashion somewhat similar to the header-and-stretcher technique characteristic of Israelite architecture. The floors were beaten earth with a pebbled surface. The plan and contents of this building suggest that it served as a public storehouse" (Oren 1978, 1063).

Tell esh-Shari'a has been identified with the biblical site of Ziklag, which is mentioned 15 times in the Bible. It was part of the tribal allotment of Simeon (Josh. 19:5), which was in the northern part of the Negev (cf. 1 Sam. 30:1, 14). The city was located in an area disputed by Israel and Philistia, and Achish, king of Gath, gave David possession of the city (1 Sam. 27:5–7). According to 1 Samuel 27:6, Ziklag belonged to the kings of Judah "to this day."

FOR FURTHER READING

Oren, Eliezer. "Tell esh-Shari'a." *EAEHL*, 4:1059–69 (1978).

Oren, Eliezer. *Tell esh-Shari'a (Tell Sera'): A Biblical City on the Edge of the Negev*. Beersheba: Ben Gurion University, 1972.

Oren, Eliezer. "Ziklag—A Biblical City on the Edge of the Negev." *BA* 45 (1982): 155–66.

CHAPTER 9

The Shephelah

THE TERM *SHEPHELAH* in Hebrew means "lowland," and it is used as a technical definition for a strip of foothills to the west of the Judean Mountains and east of the southern coastal plain. Its location is of utmost importance, particularly for the Iron Age, because it served as the buffer zone and often the area of conflict between the mountainous Israelites and the coastal Philistines. The patterns of human settlement in the Shephelah are beginning to emerge. The earliest settlements were in or next to alluvial plains, and many of these small occupations appeared during the Chalcolithic period. While there were a few major settlements during the EB Age, such as at Tell el-Hesi, most mounds were not heavily fortified until the MB II period; these include sites such as Gezer, Lachish, Beth-Shemesh, and Tel Batash. The subsequent Late Bronze Age was dominated by large cities in the alluvial areas, and some of these sites served as Canaanite royal centers, such as Lachish. Many of these city-state centers were destroyed in the thirteenth century B.C.; historians identify various enemies as possible perpetrators, such as the Philistines, the Egyptians, and the Israelites. In regard to the following Iron I period, I state elsewhere:

> The first evidence of man settling and presumably cultivating the non-alluvial areas of the Shephelah is at the beginning of the Iron I period, *ca.* 1200 B.C. At this time, the density of settlement became more intense than that of the Late Bronze Age. As a matter of fact, the Iron I site distribution is almost 50% greater than that of the earlier period. Moreover, no longer are sites merely limited to areas adjacent to or on the banks of major *nahal* systems, but settlement has penetrated into all parts of the hilly regions.[1]

In my opinion, many of these sites were settled by the incoming Israelites. During the Iron II period, many of the major cities were resettled and became formidable Israelite towns.

---

1. John D. Currid, "The Deforestation of the Foothills of Palestine," PEQ (1984): 7.

BETH-SHEMESH

Tel Beth-Shemesh was an important biblical site that is located in the northeastern Shephelah, about 12 miles west of Jerusalem and 8 miles east of Gath. It is a mound that covers about 7 acres, and it overlooks the Sorek Valley. The town is first mentioned in the Old Testament as a border city for the allotment of the tribe of Judah (Josh. 15:10), and it was designated a Levitical city in that tribal area (Josh. 21:16). Beth-Shemesh was clearly under full Israelite control by the end of the period of the judges, when the ark was returned from Philistia (1 Sam. 6:1–21). It continued to be an Israelite city within one of Solomon's administrative districts (1 Kings 4:9). A battle took place here during the divided monarchy between Joash of Israel and Amaziah of Judah (2 Kings 14:11–14; 2 Chron. 25:21–24). During the reign of Ahaz (ca. 732–716 B.C.), the Philistines captured the city from Judah and "settled there" (2 Chron. 28:18).

Duncan Mackenzie first excavated Beth-Shemesh in 1911–12 for the Palestine Exploration Fund. This was followed by five seasons of exploration by Haverford College under the direction of Elihu Grant in 1928–33. G. E. Wright prepared some of the important reports for that excavation (Grant and Wright, 1938–39). Recent excavations began in 1990, initiated by Shlomo Bunimovitz and Zvi Lederman on behalf of the Institute of Archaeology of Tel Aviv University. These excavations continue today; their primary purpose is to expose remains from the Iron Age and the lower levels from the Canaanite occupation.

The earliest occupation of the site was during the MB Age. In the MB II period, the town had a strong city wall, about 7.5 feet wide. The construction was typical of the time: the lowest course was made of large stones, and the upper courses consisted of mud-brick. Three towers were exposed from the period, and a city gate. This level was destroyed at the beginning of the LB period, about 1500 B.C. According to Wright, "A most prosperous period in the city's history was that of stratum IV in the Late Bronze Age" (Wright 1975, 251). A large building was uncovered that contained two brick smelting furnaces with flues in their sides. Also, a tablet was found in Ugaritic script and an ostracon with letters in an early Canaanite alphabetic script. This city was destroyed at the end of the thirteenth century B.C.

In the following Iron I period, the excavators discovered a large, two-storied building that they called the "Patrician House." It had a few spacious rooms, one with a paved floor of river pebbles. Next to it were houses built in a more common, pedestrian fashion. Wooden columns set on stone basins held up some of the ceilings.

During the tenth century B.C., Beth-Shemesh was under Israelite hegemony, and it was transformed into an administrative center for the region.

The town was surrounded by strong fortifications, including a massive city wall and a large retaining tower. An iron workshop was found in the southern part of the site. By the eighth century B.C., olive oil production was in evidence at the site. Sennacherib and the Assyrians destroyed Beth-Shemesh, like many other towns in the Shephelah, in 701 B.C.

FOR FURTHER READING

Bunimovitz, Shlomo, and Zvi Lederman. "Beth-Shemesh: Culture Conflict on Judah's Frontier." *BAR* 23 (1997): 42–49, 75–77.

Bunimovitz, Shlomo, and Zvi Lederman. "Iron Age Fortifications of Tel Beth-Shemesh." *IEJ* 51 (2001): 121–48.

Grant, Elihu, and G. E. Wright. *Ain Shems Excavations*, vols. 4–5. Haverford: Haverford College, 1938–1939.

Wright, G. E. "Beth-Shemesh." *EAEHL*, 1:248–53 (1975).

GEZER

The archaeological site of Tel Gezer is located at the point where the slopes of the Judean Mountains end and the northern Shephelah begins. The mound covers about 30 acres and lies about 8 miles north-northwest of Beth-Shemesh. The site has a strategic location as it overlooked various ancient highways that branch off from the Via Maris that led from Egypt to parts east. Gezer is first mentioned in the Old Testament in the account of Joshua's campaign in southern Canaan: Horam, the king of Gezer, and his army attempted to give military aid to the city of Lachish, but they were soundly defeated by the Israelites (Josh. 10:33; 12:12). Gezer was allotted to the tribe of Ephraim, but "they did not drive out the Canaanites who lived in Gezer" (Josh. 16:10; Judg. 1:29). Gezer was also designated a Levitical city given to the clan of the Kohathites (Josh. 21:21). According to 1 Kings 9:16, the Egyptians captured Gezer and destroyed the Canaanite inhabitants. Pharaoh then gave the city as a dowry to Solomon, who married the daughter of the Egyptian king. Subsequently, Solomon fortified the city along with Jerusalem, Hazor, and Megiddo (1 Kings 9:15).

The importance of Gezer in antiquity is indicated by numerous extra-biblical references to the site. Its first mention was on the military invasion list of Thutmosis III against Canaan in the fifteenth century B.C. In the Amarna Letters of the fourteenth century B.C., there were ten letters written by three different kings of Gezer. The Merneptah Stele from about 1220 B.C., which mentions the name of "Israel" for the first time, also states that Gezer was seized by the forces of Merneptah (*ANET*, 378). Some historians identify Gezer as the twelfth site on the first tier of Shishak's invasion itinerary from the late tenth century B.C., although not all scholars agree (Currid 1997, 190).

Tel Gezer has been excavated several times. R. A. S. Macalister for the PEF led the first dig in 1902–9. The value of the remains for today's scholars is minimal. William Dever comments, "The tragedy of Macalister's excavation at Gezer was that a mass of rich material was torn from context and published in such a way as to make it virtually useless for reconstructing the history of the site" (Dever 1976, 434). A. Rowe led a limited excavation in 1934, but it was soon abandoned. G. E. Wright and others then excavated Gezer from 1964 to 1976 under the auspices of Hebrew Union College and the Harvard Semitic Museum. Excavations from 1984 to 1990 were led by William Dever for the University of Arizona. The HUC-Harvard expedition held the first field school for students to learn the art of archaeology. Since 2006, excavations have continued at the site under the sponsorship of the Tandy Institute for Archaeology at Southwestern Baptist Theological Seminary, led by S. Ortiz and S. Wolff.

Gezer was occupied almost continuously from the Chalcolithic period through to the Roman/Byzantine period. It was first fortified during the MB II period, when there was a large inner wall with a glacis about 25 feet high surrounding the city. Macalister found what he called a "high place," consisting of ten standing stones, which perhaps served as a ritual site for a covenant treaty among various tribes. Later scholars determined that the structure dated to the MB II period. The major finds of the following LB Age included a strong outer wall fortification and a huge palace that dated to the fourteenth century B.C. and contained many Egyptian small finds. It is likely that this level was destroyed by Pharaoh Merneptah, as mentioned in the so-called Merneptah Stele during the late thirteenth century B.C.

The major finds from the Iron Age probably date to the time of Solomon in the tenth century B.C. These include a six-chambered city gate and a casemate-style city wall. Yigael Yadin saw that parallel fortifications appeared at both Megiddo and Hazor from Solomon's time (Yadin 1970, 65–96), and it reflected Solomon's building program as described in 1 Kings 9:15. Other scholars disagree and date these structures to later kings in the ninth through eighth centuries B.C. The current excavators of Gezer are in agreement with Yadin's original assessment.

FOR FURTHER READING

Currid, John D. *Ancient Egypt and the Old Testament*. Grand Rapids: Baker, 1997.

Dever, William G. "Gezer." *EAEHL*, 2:428–43 (1976).

Dever, William G., and G. E. Wright. *Gezer I: Preliminary Report of the 1964–1966 Seasons, Vol. I.* Jerusalem: Hebrew Union College, 1970.

Ortiz, Steven, and Samuel Wolff. "Guarding the Borders to Jerusalem: The Iron Age City of Gezer." *NEA* 75 (2012): 4–19.

Yadin, Yigael. "Megiddo of the Kings of Israel." *BA* 33 (1970): 65–96.

LACHISH (TELL ED-DUWEIR)

Tell ed-Duweir is located in the southern Shephelah on the border of Philistia, about 9 miles directly south of Gath, which was one of the Philistine capital cities. Archaeologists generally accept the identification of Tell ed-Duweir with the important ancient site of Lachish. The mound was occupied from the Chalcolithic period until the Persian period with several occupational gaps. Lachish was a Canaanite royal city during the Late Bronze Age, in which it was first mentioned in the Amarna Letters of the fourteenth century B.C. It was captured by the invading Israelites during Joshua's military campaign in the Shephelah (Josh. 10:31–32). The city remained in ruins until it was fortified by the Judaean king Rehoboam (ca. 930–913 B.C.). It served as the southernmost fort in a line of defense protecting his kingdom (2 Chron. 11:5–12).

Fig. 9.1. Conquest of Lachish

One of Rehoboam's successors in the southern kingdom rebuilt the city on a monumental, grandiose scale. It was heavily fortified with a double line of fortification walls surrounding the town. Inside the city, a large, raised podium was constructed that probably had a palace on top of it. Highlighting its formidable military character was the incident of King Amaziah's (ca. 796–776 B.C.) flight to Lachish for protection from palace intrigue in Jerusalem (2 Kings 14:19).

During the reign of Hezekiah (ca. 716–687 B.C.), the Assyrian ruler Sennacherib invaded Judah, conquered Lachish, and made the city his base of operations. The battle at Lachish (701 B.C.) was considered so important to the Assyrian king that he had carved reliefs made of the battle and placed them on the walls of his palace in Nineveh. The Judaeans rebuilt the city during the seventh century B.C., and the Babylonians under Nebuchadnezzar destroyed it in 587/586 B.C. Lachish and Azekah were the last cities conquered in this campaign before Jerusalem (Jer. 34:7). In the destruction layer of the gateway at Lachish, archaeologists uncovered a series of letters (ostraca) that gave some details of the march of the advancing Babylonian army.

Lachish is one of the largest and most prominent mounds in ancient Judah. It measures about 16 acres, with a flat top and steep slopes due to the presence of massive ancient fortifications. Four archaeological expeditions have been mounted in order to investigate the remains. The first was a British expedition under the direction of J. L. Starkey in 1932–38. In two seasons, 1966 and 1968, Y. Aharoni focused his work particularly on the so-called Solar Shrine. The third expedition was a major excavation under D. Ussishkin from 1973 to 1994. Recently (2017) a fourth dig began at the site, led by Y. Garfinkel, M. Hasel, and M. Klingbeil, which aims to study in more depth the Iron I settlement. The remains recovered are massive, and so we will give a mere overview of them.

The first settlers came to the site during the Neolithic period, and by the close of the EB Age Lachish was a fully settled site. During the MB II period, it became a major settlement in the Shephelah that included enormous fortifications: the defensive system included a significant glacis that gave form to the site and a moat/fosse at the bottom of the glacis that surrounded the site. Lachish was destroyed at the end of the MB II.

The Canaanite city of the LB Age was large and prosperous. Excavation uncovered the Fosse Temple, which was located in the moat that had become obsolete. Another sanctuary from this time was discovered on the mound itself, and it is called the Acropolis Temple. Many rich small finds have come from this period, including ivories and cult figurines from the Fosse Temple. Lachish had an important political and trade connection with Egypt, as shown by the many scarabs with the names of Egyptian kings. The city was completely destroyed during the thirteenth century B.C.. Some scholars want to identify this destruction with the invading Sea Peoples, although it most likely was due to the military campaign of the Israelites under Joshua.

Lachish lay abandoned until the kingship of Rehoboam at the end of the tenth century B.C. He constructed a fortress there that later became a major city in Judah. The later site included a monumental defensive system including a double city wall and a large city-gate complex. The gateway had two gates, and both are depicted in the Assyrian relief on Sennacherib's palace at Nineveh. In the middle of the settlement was a large palace complex, and it probably served to house the governor of the city. Most impressive from its destruction in 701 B.C. are the remains of an Assyrian siege ramp that

Sennacherib employed to conquer the city. Also found by the excavators was a counter-siege ramp that the Judaeans used to defend the same area. After this destruction, Lachish was resettled by Judaeans, but it was a poorer and weaker fortress. The Babylonians destroyed it in 587/586 B.C.

FOR FURTHER READING

Aharoni, Yohanan. *Investigations at Lachish: The Sanctuary and the Residency (Lachish V)*. Tel Aviv: Gateway Publishers, 1975.

Tufnell, Olga. *Lachish II: The Fosse Temple*. London: Oxford University Press, 1940.

Tufnell, Olga. *Lachish III: The Iron Age*. London: Oxford University Press, 1953.

Tufnell, Olga. *Lachish IV: The Bronze Age*. London: Oxford University Press, 1958.

Ussishkin, David. *The Renewed Archaeological Excavations at Lachish (1973–1994)*, vols. I–V. Tel Aviv: Institute of Archaeology, 2004.

TEL BATASH (TIMNAH)

Tel Batash is a site of about 10 acres located on the south bank of the Sorek Valley in the northern Shephelah. It was excavated under the direction of George Kelm and Amihai Mazar from 1977 to 1989. Many scholars agree that Tel Batash is to be identified with the biblical site of Timnah. It was at Timnah that Judah kept his sheep for shearing, and on the road to Timnah he was lured by his daughter-in-law Tamar (Gen. 38:12–14). Timnah was on the boundary of the inheritance of the tribe of Judah in the allotment given to them by Joshua (Josh. 15:10). During the period of the judges, Timnah appears to have been in Philistine hands, as Samson married a Philistine woman from that city (Judg. 14:1–5).

Excavation has revealed that Tel Batash was first fortified in the MB II period. Earthen ramparts were constructed on the flat plain that surrounded the tell, and they formed an exact square oriented to the four points of the compass. A moat perhaps existed outside the ramparts for further defensive measures. This city was destroyed at the close of the MB II Age. The subsequent LB period contained five occupational levels that covered the time from about 1550 to 1200 B.C. In contrast to the heavily fortified MB II city, there were no city walls during the LB period. Excavators found large patrician houses, some that were built to the very edge of the mound. They were rectangular in form, had stairs to a second floor, and contained storage rooms. Two rows of pillars held up a roof, and this design was perhaps a forerunner of the so-called Israelite four-room house (Mazar 1997, 340). The LB settlement was destroyed at the close of the thirteenth century B.C., and this may have been done by the Philistines.

In the Iron I period (i.e., the time of the judges in Israel), excavations have uncovered a town that was probably in the hands of the Philistines (stratum V). The town had a fortification system, was densely built, and included much Philistine painted pottery. The material remains of the architecture consisted of mud-brick walls on stone foundations.

During the Iron II period of the united monarchy (tenth century B.C.), Timnah was unfortified and it appears to have been under Israelite control. Pharaoh Shishak perhaps destroyed this stratum IV city at the end of the tenth century B.C. The mound was not re-occupied until the eighth century B.C., and evidence of Judaean occupation was provided by the discovery of *lmlk* seals at the site (stratum III). Sennacherib conquered this settlement in 701 B.C. Timnah was rebuilt in the seventh century, and it was a well-planned, prosperous site. It appears to have been destroyed by the Babylonians around 600 B.C.

FOR FURTHER READING

Kelm, George L., and Amihai Mazar. *Timnah: A Biblical City in the Sorek Valley.* Winona Lake, IN: Eisenbrauns, 1995.
Mazar, Amihai. *Timnah (Tel Batash) I: Stratigraphy and Architecture.* Jerusalem: Institute of Archaeology, 1997.
Panitz-Cohen, N., and A. Mazar. *Timnah (Tel Batash) III: The Finds from the Second Millennium B.C.E.* Jerusalem: Institute of Archaeology, 2006.

TELL BEIT MIRSIM

The mound of Tell Beit Mirsim is located in the southern Shephelah on the edge of the Negev, about 8 miles southeast of Lachish. It is a tell that measures about 7.5 acres. W. F. Albright conducted excavations here for four campaigns, which took place in 1926, 1928, 1930, and 1932. M. Ein Gedy directed a small salvage dig in 2004, although much of the remains were from an early church at the site. The identification of the site is unknown. Albright argued it was the biblical city of Debir, but many scholars today locate Debir at Khirbet Rabud (Albright 1975, 171–72). The Tell Beit Mirsim excavations are important, not because of the site's biblical importance, but rather because the basic ceramic chronology of ancient Palestine was determined here for the first time. For the most part, this chronology has stood the test of time, although it has been tweaked over the decades by further excavation work in Palestine.

Tell Beit Mirsim was first occupied in the EB III period, although it was a slight and slim habitation. A small city was built during the MB I period that contained a city wall with a rampart extending around it. Toward the end of the MB II period, the city was rebuilt, and it was surrounded by stronger fortifications, including high outer walls, a moat, and a glacis. It was a formidable city at that time, although it was destroyed in the early decades of the LB Age in the sixteenth century B.C. During the LB Age, the city grew in size and flourished. It apparently had an outer fortification wall about 8 feet thick that is in evidence next to the east gate complex. According to Albright, this Canaanite settlement was destroyed in the thirteenth century B.C. during "the critical phase of the conquest of the Shephelah by the Israelites" (Albright 1975, 177).

A small occupation followed in the Iron I time that was characterized by numerous grain pits, the exposure of some house walls (stratum B), and a casemate wall surrounding the town. This appears to have been an early settlement of the Israelites. Pharaoh Shishak likely destroyed it in the late tenth century B.C. The Iron II city was characterized by numerous dye vat installations that included vats, channels, tanks, and loom weights. The excavators concluded that during the time of the Judean kingdom, Tell Beit Mirsim served as a town with a guild of weavers and dyers. The final destruction of the site was originally dated by Albright to the invasion of the Babylonians in 589–587 B.C. Further analysis by later archaeologists, however, has determined that this final conflagration occurred at the hands of the Assyrians under Sennacherib in 701 B.C.

FOR FURTHER READING

Albright, W. F. "The Excavation of Tell Beit Mirsim." *AASOR* 2 (1943): 21–22.
Albright, W. F. "The Fourth Joint Campaign of Excavation at Tell Beit Mirsim." *BASOR* 47 (1932): 3–17.
Albright, W. F. "Tell Beit Mirsim." *EAEHL*, 1:171–78 (1975).
Ein Gedy, Miki, and Karni Golan. "Tell Beit Mirsim." *Hadeshot Arkheologiyot* (2007): 119.

TELL ʿEITUN

The mound of Tell ʿEitun sits in the southeastern part of the Shephelah, about 7 miles east-southeast of Lachish and about 10.5 miles to the west of Hebron. Its location on the ancient road between these two cities is an important clue as to the identity of the tell. According to Joshua 10:34–36, the town of Eglon was located between the cities of Lachish and Hebron. Many scholars today agree with this identification. Joshua and the Israelites conquered Eglon after they had destroyed Lachish and before they captured Hebron. Eglon was part of the allotment of the tribe of Judah (Josh. 15:39). The site is fairly large, measuring about 15 acres.

Investigation of the site began in 2006 with mapping and survey work. Excavation has continued on an intermittent schedule under the direction of Avraham Faust of Bar Ilan University. Survey work has indicated that the mound was first occupied during the EB period, and that there was some settlement in the MB period. Excavation has uncovered remains from the LB Age through the Iron II period of the eighth century B.C. Tell ʿEitun appears to have been a significant site in the Shephelah during the eighth century B.C. The most important architectural find from this period was discovered in Area A, the highest point of the tell, which was a large building containing Iron II pottery. The excavators provisionally called it a "Governor's Residency." Apparently this level was violently destroyed by the Assyrians under Sennacherib in 701 B.C. It was not rebuilt as a city after that time.

FOR FURTHER READING

Faust, Avraham. "Canaanites and Israelites in the Southern Shephelah: The Results of 10 Seasons of Excavations at Tel ʿEton." *Qadmoniot* 152 (2016): 82–91.

Faust, Avraham, and Hayah Katz. "A Canaanite Town, a Judahite Center, and a Persian Period Fort: Excavating Over Two Thousand Years of History at Tel ʿEton." *NEA* 78 (2015): 88–102.

TELL HALIF

Tell Halif is a 7-acre site that lies in the southern Shephelah, about 10 miles north of Beersheba. It overlooks the coastal plain to the west. Its identification is uncertain, although the archaeologists suggest it is the site of biblical Rimmon. According to Joshua 19:7, Rimmon was allocated to the tribe of Simeon after the Israelite conquest, although eventually it was considered part of the inheritance of Judah (Josh. 15:32). The reason for this ambiguity is stated in Joshua 19:9, "The inheritance of the people of Simeon formed part of the territory of the people of Judah. Because the portion of the people of Judah was too large for them, the people of Simeon obtained an inheritance in the midst of their inheritance." The site was occupied from Chalcolithic times to the Iron II period with some gaps, and it contains 19 strata.

Excavations began on the mound in 1976 as part of the Lahav Research Project, and they have been conducted in four phases. The first two phases were under the direction of J. D. Seger from 1976 to 1989. These included eight seasons in the field that defined the general stratigraphy of the site and focused on the EB and LB occupational strata. P. F. Jacobs and O. Borowski directed the next phase of three seasons (1992–99), which looked specifically at the Iron Age remains. The final phase continues today and Borowski directs it. Its aim is to understand the eighth century B.C. settlement in order to reconstruct the daily life of the Judaean population.

During the Chalcolithic period, Tell Halif was a hamlet. After its demise, the site was abandoned for three centuries until the beginning of the EB III period (ca. 2500 B.C.). This settlement contained large fortifications, including a glacis, an outer defensive wall about 11 feet wide, and a tower that was about 24 feet wide. This level was violently destroyed; it was soon rebuilt, but it lacked major fortifications.

Following a hiatus of some seven centuries, the tell was resettled at the beginning of the LB Age. A prominent architectural feature from this level was the "Egyptian residency" building, which contained a central courtyard with rooms on all sides of it. The excavators determined that this structure was related to the Egyptian rule of Canaan during the LB period.

The principal remains exposed through excavation belonged to the Iron II period of the Judaean kingdom. Large numbers of tools and loom weights led the archaeologists to conclude that the major industry of the site was textile production; in fact, a large textile workshop was uncovered. This settlement underwent a huge conflagration that the excavators identified with the assault of the Assyrians under Sennacherib in 701 B.C.

FOR FURTHER READING

Borowski, Oded. "The Biblical Identity of Tel Halif." *BA* 51 (1988): 21–27.

Borowski, Oded. "Tell Halif: In the Path of Sennacherib." *BAR* 31 (2005): 24–35.

Borowski, Oded. "Tel Halif." *IEJ* 58 (2008): 100–103.

TELL EL-HESI

The settlement area of Tell el-Hesi is about 25 acres, and it is located about 3 miles to the west of Lachish in the southern Shephelah. It was first occupied in the Pre-Pottery Neolithic period and was settled until the Hellenistic period, although not continuously. The first excavation work was under the direction of W. Flinders Petrie in 1890 and F. J. Bliss in 1891–92. The work here was critical for the future of archaeology because Petrie discovered that the mound was man-made through an accumulation of strata over time. He also determined that each stratum contained its own distinctive pottery style, and this was crucial for the formulation of a basic chronology for the history of ancient Palestine. A second series of excavations began in 1970 and lasted for eight seasons in the field until 1983. This project, under the supervision of various archaeologists, concentrated on exposing the acropolis and the EB III wall system of the lower city. The identification of the site is uncertain. Petrie said it was Lachish, and W. F. Albright thought it was Eglon. Many scholars do not accept either identification today.

Tell el-Hesi was a major fortified city in the Shephelah during the EB II–III periods. Significant fortifications have been unearthed here, including a glacis that was built to strengthen the foundation of the mound against erosion and against military attack. The site was abandoned until the LB Age. Some historians interpret a large building at the site from this period as a fortress that perhaps served as an Egyptian military outpost. The site was occupied during the Iron II period, beginning in the eighth century B.C. It is likely that it served as a Judaean outpost to guard against possible Egyptian incursions into the land. Its military nature at this time is witnessed by a series of walled chambers with fill that raised the height of the tell for defensive purposes.

FOR FURTHER READING

F. J. Bliss. *A Mound of Many Cities*. London: Palestine Exploration Fund, 1894.

Doermann, Ralph W., and Valerie Fargo. "Tell el-Hesi, 1983." *PEQ* 117 (1985): 1–24.

Fargo, Valerie, and Kevin G. O'Connell. "Five Seasons of Excavation at Tell el-Hesi (1970–1977)." *BA* 41 (1978): 165–82.

CHAPTER 10

The Jordan River Valley

THROUGHOUT ANCIENT TIMES, the lower Jordan Valley, between the Sea of Galilee and the Dead Sea, was not an area of dense population. It is true that some of the earliest settlements in the history of mankind in Palestine have been discovered here, such as Ubeidiya and Sha'ar Hagolan. Early settlers were drawn to the area because of the perennial water sources of the sea and the river. The valley itself is entirely below sea level, and it is fairly rugged territory with minimal rainfall especially south of Beth Shean. Thus, certain periods were almost devoid of population centers in the region. For example, the area was almost completely uninhabited during the LB period.[1] However, site survey work by Adam Zertal has found over 60 sites in the valley with sherds dating to the Iron I period; most of these sites were first inhabited at this time. Zertal and others associate these many new sites with the early Israelites who came across the Jordan River and settled in the land of Canaan.

EIN GEDI

While surveying the region of the Ein Gedi spring in 1956, Yohanan Aharoni discovered an ancient structure that lay on a scarp above the oasis on the western shore of the Dead Sea. The following year, Joseph Naveh conducted a trial excavation at the site, and he dated the structure to the Chalcolithic period, based on pottery remains. The site was fully excavated in 1962, in part with the main excavation at Tel Goren under the direction of Benjamin Mazar of Hebrew University; his graduate student David Ussishkin supervised the Ein Gedi part of the dig, and subsequently published the results (Ussishkin 1980, 1–44).

What the archaeologists uncovered was a sacred shrine complex that consisted of four structures connected by a stone outer wall that dated to the

---

1. Adam Zertal and Shay Bar, *The Manasseh Hill Country Survey: From Nahal Bezeq to the Sartaba*, vol. 4 (Leiden: Brill, 2017), 58. Cited in Ralph K. Hawkins and David Ben-Shlomo, "Khirbet el-Mastarah: An Early Israelite Settlement?," *BAR* 44 (2018): 40–46, 68.

Chalcolithic period. The complex was entered through the first structure, which was a double gateway that had benches along its walls. On the other side of the complex was another gate structure, but it was a single entrance. The third structure was a small auxiliary room near the single-entry gate. Its purpose is unknown, since no small finds appeared in the room to help determine its function. The final building was large (ca. 64 by 18 feet), with an entrance in its long wall facing the courtyard. It served as the central sanctuary of the complex. The archaeologists found an altar in the sanctuary that "was filled with ashes, some animal bones, and a clay figurine of a bull laden with two churns" (Ussishkin 2014, 17).

There was no evidence of a domestic quarter at the site, so the complex probably served as a religious center for seminomadic pastoralists. About 6.5 miles to the south of the temple, archaeologists found what is called the Nahal Mishmor cave, which contained a hoard of 422 objects. Most of them were made of copper and were not tools or objects of everyday life. They were likely used in religious rituals. It is reasonable to assume, as do the excavators of Ein Gedi, that the hoard was associated with the temple complex.

FOR FURTHER READING

Bar-Adon, Pesach. *The Cave of the Treasure: The Finds from the Cave in Nahal Mishmar.* Jerusalem: Israel Exploration Society, 1980.

Ussishkin, David. "The Chalcolithic Temple in Ein Gedi: Fifty Years after Its Discovery." *Near East Archaeology* 77 (2014): 15–26.

Ussishkin, David. "The Ghassulian Shrine at En-Gedi." *Tel Aviv* 7 (1980): 1–44.

JERICHO

The biblical site of Jericho is located at Tell es-Sultan, a mound in the Jordan Rift Valley about 5 miles northwest of the Dead Sea. It is one of the oldest continuously inhabited towns in the history of the ancient Near East, and it is one of the lowest cities on earth (ca. 850 feet below sea level). Jericho is mentioned over sixty times in the Old Testament, most prominently as the first city west of the Jordan River that was captured by the Israelites during the conquest (Josh. 6). Jericho was abandoned after that destruction for a few centuries until Hiel the Bethelite established a new settlement in the ninth century B.C. (1 Kings 16:34).

Four major excavations have taken place at Jericho. The first was in the years 1907–9 and 1911, under the direction of Ernst Sellin and Carl Watzinger.

Fig. 10.1. Jordan River Valley, Israel, Seen from the Golan Heights

This Austro-German excavation provided mixed results: the building plans of the excavators were significant and detailed, and can be used to a limited extent today. Ceramic chronology, however, which was still in its infancy, was not used, and therefore their dating of the site's history was faulty and cannot be trusted. The next excavations, supervised by John Garstang, ran from 1930 to 1936. Ceramic dating had begun to take center stage in archaeology at this time, but the lack of detailed stratigraphic analysis hampered the findings of Garstang. Much of Garstang's dating of occupation layers has proved to be inaccurate. Kathleen Kenyon, on behalf of the British School of Archaeology in Jerusalem, carried out excavations at Jericho from 1952 to 1958. She employed advanced excavation techniques, including detailed stratification methods (called the Wheeler-Kenyon method) and ceramic analysis for dating purposes. Finally, an Italian team led by Lorenzo Nigro has been excavating the site since the late 1990s (1997–2000, 2009–present).

Jericho was first settled about 10,000 B.C. By the Pre-Pottery Neolithic period (ca. 8000–6000 B.C.), it had become a large, fortified town about 6 acres in size. It had a city wall, some 4.5 feet wide, attached to a monumental stone tower about 26 feet high. These are some of the earliest fortifications known to mankind. After a hiatus during the Chalcolithic period, Jericho was reoccupied as a major city during the EB Age with a huge mud-brick city wall, a central palace, and a temple. During the following MB period, the city continued to be well fortified, and it was closely connected to Egypt at this time. At the close of that period, Jericho experienced a major destruction (ca. 1550 B.C.).

Little evidence has been produced through excavation regarding the Canaanite occupation of Jericho during the LB period. However, there appears to have been a destruction of the site in the thirteenth century B.C. Kenyon remarks, "It is very possible that this destruction is truly remembered in the Book of Joshua, although archaeology cannot provide the proof" (Kenyon

1976, 564). After this time, Jericho was abandoned until the time of the divided monarchy.

FOR FURTHER READING

Garstang, John, and J. B. E. Garstang. *The Story of Jericho*. London: Marshall, Morgan and Scott, 1948.

Kenyon, Kathleen. *The Bible and Recent Archaeology*. Atlanta: John Knox, 1978.

Kenyon, Kathleen. *Digging Up Jericho*. London: Ernst Benn, 1957.

Kenyon, Kathleen. "Jericho." *EAEHL*, 2:550–64 (1976).

KHIRBET EL-MASTARAH

This mound is a 2.5 acre site that is located on a wadi (a seasonal stream) in the desert north of Jericho. Excavations were conducted there in 2017 under the supervision of Ralph K. Hawkins and David Ben-Shlomo for the Jordan Valley Excavation Project. Based on pottery found through survey and excavation, the occupation of the site began during the MB II period, but the height of settlement occurred during the Iron I–II periods.

Some structures were uncovered that were small-rounded, large-rounded, or rectilinear roomed. They were built with fieldstones. The date and purpose of the enclosures is uncertain because of the paucity of finds within them.

Site survey and excavation work have demonstrated that Khirbet el-Mastarah was merely one site of many founded in the Jordan Valley during the Iron I period. The Jordan Valley was basically uninhabited during the preceding LB Age. What was the catalyst for this settlement and population increase? The excavators conclude that "the rise in settlements in the Jordan Valley was clearly part of a settlement phenomenon that spanned both sides of the Jordan River during the transition from the Late Bronze Age to the Iron Age—a phenomenon that was probably connected with the tribes of Israel" (Hawkins and Ben-Shlomo 2018, 44).

FOR FURTHER READING

Ben-Shlomo, David, and Ralph K. Hawkins. "Excavations at Khirbet el-Mastarah, the Jordan Valley, 2017." *Judea and Samaria Research Studies* 1/26 (2017): 49–82.

Hawkins, Ralph K., and David Ben-Shlomo. "Khirbet el-Mastarah: An Early Israelite Settlement?" *BAR* 44 (2018): 40–46, 68.

MUNHATA (HORVAT MINHA)

Munhata is a small site, about one-half acre in area, which lies about 7 miles south of the Sea of Galilee in the Jordan Valley. It was excavated by Jean Perrot in 1962–63 on behalf of the French Archaeological Mission and the Department of Antiquities. Renewed excavations took place in 1993 and 1995 (Commenge 1996, 43). Perrot's excavations determined that there were six occupation levels at the site (stratum 6 being the earliest). They extended from the Pre-Pottery Neolithic B period through the Pottery Neolithic period.

Strata 6–4 "resemble the Pre-Pottery Neolithic B at Jericho and have analogies in their flint industry and architecture" (Perrot and Zori 1977, 874). Stratum 6 was a primitive settlement with paved areas for huts, and the excavators found unbaked animal figurines near them. In the next level (stratum 5), a large platform was found, made of basalt stones, with associated hearths, basins, and floors. The function of the installation is unknown, although it perhaps served as a threshing floor. The following stratum 4 contained a rectangular house with mud-brick walls and plastered floors. Numerous clay figurines appeared in this level, and they were predominately female figurines called "mother-goddess" types.

In strata 3–2, pottery first appears, and it was of the Yarmukian style that was painted brown and had chevron designs. The living quarters were semi-subterranean huts, and there were hearths, benches, storage pits, and many tools. These small finds indicate that the population was probably sedentary.

FOR FURTHER READING

Commenge, C. "Horvat Minha (el-Munhata)." *Excavations and Surveys in Israel* 15 (1996): 43.

Perrot, Jean. "Les deux premières campagnes de fouilles à Munhata (1962–1963). Premiers résultats." *Syria* 41 (1964): 323–45.

Perrot, Jean. "La troisième campagne de fouilles à Munhata (1964)." *Syria* 43 (1966): 49–63.

Perrot, Jean, and N. Zori. "Horvat Minha." *EAEHL*, 3:871–74 (1977).

PELLA

Pella is a large tell, about 25 acres in size, that is located about 18 miles south of the Sea of Galilee in the northern Jordan Valley. It sits on the east side of the Jordan River, about 7 miles south-southeast of Beth Shean. The attraction for settlement here was threefold: there was a perennial spring at the base of the mound, abundant land for agriculture surrounded the site, and nearby highways, both north-south and east-west, served commerce and trade. Pella was first settled in the Early Neolithic period, perhaps as early as 7500 B.C., and it was occupied almost continuously after that. Pella was mentioned in the Egyptian Execration Texts of the nineteenth through eighteenth centuries B.C. It then appeared in the Amarna Letters of the fourteenth century B.C. Pella is not, however, mentioned in the Old Testament.

The first archaeological exploration of Pella took place in 1887, led by Gottlieb Schumacher for the Palestine Exploration Fund, and he was able to identify numerous Byzantine remains, including a number of churches. Excavations began in earnest in 1967 under the direction of Robert Houston Smith. Since the mid-1980s, excavation work has been carried out by the University of Sydney, first under the supervision of J. Basil Hennessy (until 1990) and then under Stephen Bourke (to the present).

Important finds for the various periods of occupation have been uncovered at Pella. Housing has been exposed from the Neolithic period, and storage complexes from the Chalcolithic. Large fortifications have been revealed from both the EB and the MB periods; the former had strong stone defensive platforms from the EB I period, and the latter had large mud-brick city walls. Remains from the MB and LB Ages are perhaps the most impressive. Temples and palatial residences have been uncovered through excavation. For example, the archaeologists spent ten years digging the stone Migdol (Fortress) Temple that went through three building phases extending from the MB Age (about 1800 B.C.) through the Iron II period (ca. 800 B.C.). Small finds in the complex were splendid, including several painted cult stands, gold jewelry, stone figurines, and much more.

FOR FURTHER READING

Bourke, Stephen. "The Christian Flight to Pella: True or Tale?" *BAR* 39 (2013): 30–39, 70.

Schumacher, Gottlieb. *Pella*. Cambridge: Cambridge University Press, 1888; reprint, 2010.

Smith, Robert Houston. *Pella of the Decapolis I: The 1967 Season of the College of Wooster Expedition to Pella.* Wooster, Ohio: College of Wooster, 1973.

TELEILAT GHASSUL

The site of Teleilat Ghassul is located about 1.5 miles northeast of the Dead Sea in the Jordan Valley. It is a large site that consists of over ten mounds, spreading out over about 60 acres. Located on the edge of the Wadi Ghassul, the site sits about 900 feet below sea level. The area, however, has good underground water sources, including two springs and numerous wells. The settlement has undergone some large-scale excavation work, starting out under the direction of Alexis Mallon and Robert Koeppel for the Pontifical Biblical Institute from 1929 to 1938, and Robert North in 1960. J. Basil Hennessy led a team to the site for the University of Sydney (1967, 1975–77). Another group, directed by Stephen Bourke, worked at the site from 1994 to 1999, also under the auspices of the University of Sydney.

The occupation of the site began in the Late Neolithic period, and its most extensive occupation occurred during the Chalcolithic period. Semi-subterranean, circular, single-room dwellings characterized the Late Neolithic settlement. Numerous storage pits were also found from this period, reflecting a sedentary existence. In the following Chalcolithic period, the housing form changed to rectilinear, mud-brick structures built on stone foundations. They were mostly single-room dwellings with one entrance and a beaten earth floor. Some of the walls were plastered with painted designs. The wall paintings were the most impressive discovery: the "best known example is the eight-pointed Star of Ghassul which combines the geometric form with 'spook' masks and imaginary creatures" (Lee 1978, 1212).

FOR FURTHER READING

Hennessy, J. Basil. "Preliminary Report on a First Season of Excavations at Teleilat Ghassul." *Levant* 1 (1967): 1–24.
Hennessy, J. Basil. "Teleilat Ghassul: Its Place in the Archaeology of Jordan." In *Studies in the History and Archaeology of Jordan*, ed. Adnan Hadidi, 1:55–58. Amman: Department of Antiquities, 1982.
Lee, J. R. "Tuleilat el-Ghassul." *EAEHL*, 4:1204–13 (1978).

TELL DEIR ʿALLA

This tell sits in the Jordan Valley about 3 miles east of the Jordan River and about 1 mile west of the Jabbok River as it enters the land of Gilead. The junction of those two rivers lies about 7 miles to the south-southwest of Tell Deir ʿAlla. The site appears to have been first occupied during the Chalcolithic period as a small village, but was then abandoned until the MB Age. Major occupation followed during the LB and Iron Ages. Identification of the mound has been a matter of dispute. Many early investigators believed it to be the biblical town of Succoth (Gen. 33:17; Josh. 13:27; Judg. 8:4–17; 1 Kings 7:47), and some still hold to that identification (Mazar 1990, 358; Currid 2017, 60). Others, such as William Shea, identify it with the biblical site of Pethor (Shea 1989, 97–119), mentioned in Numbers 22:5.

The first excavations on the mound took place for five seasons beginning in 1960 under H. J. Franken of Leiden University. Franken's primary goal was to determine the archaeological chronology of the settlement based on careful stratigraphic excavation and detailed ceramic typology. Fieldwork resumed in 1976 for six seasons (until 1987) as a joint venture of Leiden University and the Jordanian Department of Antiquities/Yarmouk University, directed by M. Ibrahim and G. van der Kooij. A third series of excavations began in 1994 under the same auspices.

One of the more important discoveries at the site was an LB sanctuary. "The oldest stage was constructed on an artificial mound so that the cella of the temple rose about one meter above the surrounding buildings" (Franken 1975, 322). There was no defensive wall around the site, which indicates it was an open sanctuary settlement; it may have been used as a ritual center for pastoralists. The shrine was repeatedly rebuilt during the LB Age until it was destroyed about 1200 B.C. Some archaeologists argue that this destruction was due to an earthquake, while others say it was the result of military invasion, perhaps by the invading Israelites. After the conflagration, remains were found of a series of silo pits from the Iron I period. Such remains reflected the life in Canaan during this time, and perhaps indicated the presence of the Israelites.

The excavation is best known for its discovery of a painted text from the ninth century B.C. containing a prophecy of Balaam, a pagan prophet and the main character in Numbers 22–24. The Tell Deir ʿAlla Inscription begins with the words, "Warnings from the book of Balaam the son of Beor. He was a seer of the gods." The text then describes various visions that Balaam had in regard to a coming destruction.

FOR FURTHER READING

Currid, John D. "Succoth / Tell Deir Alla." *ESV Archaeology Study Bible*, 60. Wheaton, IL: Crossway, 2017.

Franken, H. J. "Tell Deir 'Alla." *EAEHL*, 1:321–24 (1975).

Franken, H. J. *Excavations at Tell Deir 'Allā*. Leiden: Brill, 1969.

Mazar, Amihai. *Archaeology of the Land of the Bible, 10,000–586 B.C.E.* New York: Doubleday, 1990.

Shea, William H. "The Inscribed Tablets from Tell Deir 'Alla, Part II." *Andrews University Seminary Studies* 27 (1989): 97–119.

TELL ES-SA'IDIYEH

The mound of Tell es-Sa'idiyeh lies about 1 mile east of the Jordan River, approximately halfway between the Sea of Galilee and the Dead Sea, in the heart of the Jordan Valley. It is strategically located at the crossroads of two major ancient highways. The area is rich in both water sources and agriculturally productive land. William F. Albright identified Tell es-Sa'idiyeh as the biblical site of Zaphon (based on Judg. 12:1), but others, such as Nelson Glueck, believed it was biblical Zarethan (see Josh. 3:16 and 1 Kings 7:46) (Pritchard 1978, 1028). Many scholars, including the current excavators of the site, agree with Glueck's proposal.

Excavation of the site began with preliminary soundings by Henri de Contenson in 1953. Major excavation work did not begin until 1964–67 by the University Museum of the University of Pennsylvania under the direction of James B. Pritchard (1964–66) and J. E. Huesman (1967). Since 1985, excavations have continued under the supervision of Jonathan N. Tubb of the British Museum.

The earliest settlement at the site was a small village without city walls that dated to the fifth millennium B.C. (PN period). By the end of the EB I period, the site had become a major prosperous city. The town layout demonstrated highly evolved city planning, and the architecture was sophisticated for the time. The most impressive building was found on the lower mound, and it was a palatial manufacturing complex for winemaking, textile production, and olive oil processing. These industries strongly suggest that an important trade network existed with other areas of the ancient Near East.

The Iron I remains are also important because they verify that Tell es-Sa'idiyeh was, like Beth Shean, a central, major outpost for Egyptian hegemony over Canaan. The excavators discovered public buildings that reflect Egyptian form, and they uncovered a cemetery with numerous graves (well over 400 have been excavated) of Egyptian style with Egyptian grave goods. An important water system has also been exposed from this time period.

FOR FURTHER READING

Pritchard, James B. "Tell es-Sa'idiyeh." *EAEHL*, 4:1028–32 (1978).

Pritchard, James B. *Tell es-Sa'idiyeh: Excavations on the Tell, 1964–1966.* Philadelphia: University Museum of the University of Pennsylvania, 1985.

Tubb, Jonathan N. *Canaanites: Peoples of the Past.* London: British Museum, 1998.

CHAPTER 11

The Southern Coastal Plain

T HIS AREA, OFTEN called Philistia, extends from the Yarkon River in the north to the Besor Brook south of Gaza. Its coastline along the Mediterranean Sea is about 50 miles long, yet it contains few natural harbors. Few port cities existed in antiquity in this region. It is mostly grassy flatland with little forestation. As such, it was an area of transit throughout ancient history. The Great Trunk Road (often called the Via Maris, "way of the sea") ran from Egypt along the Mediterranean coast to Gaza and Ashdod, and then northward. The Old Testament refers to this route as "the way of the land of the Philistines" (Ex. 13:17), and the Egyptians called it "the way of Horus."

The southern coastal plain is principally known as the area where the Philistines settled. In 1220 B.C., the Egyptian pharaoh Merneptah defeated a coalition of Libyans and five groups of "Sea Peoples" who were likely of Aegean origin. Merneptah drove them out of Egypt. Some of these defeated groups ended up settling in the southern coastal plain and came to be known as the Philistines. Directly to the east of Philistia is the geographical zone of the Shephelah. This region served as a buffer between the Philistines and the Israelites, who mainly lived in the central highlands of Palestine. Much of the fighting between Israel and Philistia took place in the Shephelah.

ASHDOD

Tel Ashdod is located in the southern coastal plain on the Via Maris that extends from Egypt to points northeast. It is about 2.5 miles east of the Mediterranean Sea and about 9 miles northeast of the coastal city of Ashkelon. It lies on the same latitude as the town of Beth-Shemesh in the Shephelah to the east. Ashdod is a large site with an acropolis covering about 20 acres and a lower city of approximately 70 acres. Although surface sherds were found at the site that date to the Chalcolithic and EB periods, the first evidence of a town came from the MB II period (seventeenth century B.C.). It was occupied during most periods until the Early Roman period (first century A.D.).

Ashdod is mentioned in several extrabiblical texts, such as the Ugaritic Texts from Ras Shamra during the LB II period. "Ashdod is further mentioned in the list of place-names composed by the Egyptian Amenopete in the eleventh century B.C. (number 263)" (Dothan 1975, 103). The Old Testament refers to the city several times; in the conquest account, it is allotted to the tribe of Judah (Josh. 15:47). There is no evidence, however, that the Judahites conquered and occupied the city. Ashdod was a city in the Philistine Pentapolis (Josh. 13:3). In fact, when the Philistines captured the Hebrew ark of the covenant, they took it first to the city of Ashdod and set it up in their temple to Dagon (1 Sam. 5:1–2). During the eighth century B.C., the Judahite king Hezekiah (767–740 B.C.) attacked and breached the wall of Ashdod, and then built cities in its territory (2 Chron. 26:6). The prophets Amos and Isaiah referred to the destruction of Ashdod at the hands of the Assyrians at the end of the eighth century B.C., and the later prophets Jeremiah, Zechariah, and Zephaniah mentioned its destruction by the Babylonians in the early sixth century B.C.

Major excavations at the site took place in 1962–72 under the direction of Moshe Dothan as a joint project of the Israel Department of Antiquities, Pittsburgh Theological Seminary, and the Pittsburgh Carnegie Museum. Salvage excavations were carried out in 2002–4 for the Israel Antiquities Authority; the major find, under the supervision of Elena Kogan-Zahavi and Pirhiya Nahshoni, was an Assyrian administrative palace located about 650 feet north of the tell.

The first major settlement of the site was during the MB II period, in which only the acropolis was occupied. A large brick wall with a glacis and a fosse/moat surrounded it. Part of a huge mud-brick gate was excavated as well. The site appears to have been mostly abandoned during the following LB I period, although some pottery has been found from the period. Ashdod was refortified and rebuilt during the LB II period. Strong mud-brick fortifications and public buildings were found. The final stratum of the LB II period was destroyed and covered by a huge ash layer; this destruction was likely due to an attack by the Philistines.

The subsequent Iron I period (beginning with stratum XIII), contained clear evidence of Philistine occupation, as did strata XII–X (twelfth through eleventh centuries B.C.). The town grew in size, and it now included the lower city. A large gate with two towers was uncovered in stratum X, but it was destroyed during the tenth century B.C., perhaps at the hands of David. The Iron II city was located almost completely in the lower city, and it included a large gateway, a city wall, and a small temple. It was destroyed at the close of the eighth century B.C., perhaps by the Assyrian king Sargon II.

FOR FURTHER READING

Dothan, Moshe. "Ashdod." *EAEHL*, 1:103–19 (1975).

Dothan, Moshe. *Ashdod II–III: The Second and Third Seasons of Excavations, 1963, 1965*. Jerusalem: Department of Antiquities, Atiqot, 1971.

Dothan, Moshe, and David N. Freedman. *Ashdod I*. Jerusalem: Department of Antiquities, Atiqot, 1967.

ASHKELON

The tell of ancient Ashkelon sits directly on the shore of the Mediterranean Sea. Ashkelon was the only city of the Philistine Pentapolis situated directly on the seacoast. It is located about 12.5 miles north-northwest of Gaza and about 9 miles southwest of Ashdod. The site was of utmost strategic value in antiquity because it stood on the edge of the Via Maris, an international highway that led from Egypt to points north. The importance of the city in Old Testament times is highlighted by the frequency of its name appearing in extrabiblical literature, such as the Egyptian Execration Texts (nineteenth century B.C.), the Amarna Letters (fourteenth century B.C.), and Merneptah's "Israel" Stele (thirteenth century B.C.). In the Old Testament, Ashkelon was located in the land allotted to the tribe of Judah, and that tribe captured it during the conquest (Judg. 1:18). It was soon retaken by the Philistines, and it became a major city of that people (1 Sam. 6:17; 2 Sam. 1:20).

Lady Hester Lucy Stanhope did some excavating at the site in 1815; some have considered it the first truly stratigraphic excavation in Palestine (Silberman 1984, 68–75). In 1920–21, John Garstang and W. J. Phythian-Adams dug at the site, and they found mainly ruins from the Hellenistic period onward. They also dropped a trench in the seafront scarp of the tell in order to discover the basic stratigraphy of the site. Major excavations, beginning in 1985, were done by the Leon Levy Expedition under the sponsorship of the Semitic Museum at Harvard University. Seventeen consecutive seasons of excavation, until the year 2000, were directed by Lawrence Stager. A second phase, under the field directorship of Daniel Master, began in 2007 and concluded in 2016. The archaeologists are actively publishing a series of final reports of the finds.

Ashkelon was first settled in the Chalcolithic period, although it did not become a major city until the beginning of the MB II period. The Canaanite

Fig. 11.1. Ashkelon Calf

city at this time covered about 150 acres, and a monumental rampart surrounded it. A city gate was unearthed from this period that still stands two stories high, and it is the oldest arched city gate from antiquity. Perhaps the most famous artifact from Ashkelon was found at the base of the rampart just outside the gateway: a small bronze calf inside a ceramic shrine, identified by the excavators as a representation of the Canaanite god Baal Zaphon.

Ashkelon was settled by the Philistines during the early twelfth century B.C. and was a thriving city after that. Of particular note is the recent discovery of a Philistine cemetery, which dates to the tenth through ninth centuries B.C. and is the only one of its kind in Palestine. Excavations of the cemetery from 2013 to 2016 have revealed burial methods that included primary ones and some cremation burials. Limited amounts of grave goods were found in the graves. The Philistine city was destroyed by Nebuchadnezzar in 604 B.C.

FOR FURTHER READING

Silberman, Neil Asher. "Restoring the Reputation of Lady Hester Lucy Stanhope: A Little-Known Episode in the Beginnings of Archaeology in the Holy Land." *BAR* 10 (1984): 68–75.

Stager, Lawrence, et al. *Ashkelon 1: Introduction and Overview (1985–2006)*. Winona Lake, IN: Harvard Semitic Museum/Eisenbrauns, 2008.

Stager, Lawrence, et al. *Ashkelon 3: The Seventh Century B.C.* Winona Lake, IN: Harvard Semitic Museum/Eisenbrauns, 2011.

DEIR EL-BALACH

The site of Deir el-Balach is located in the dune lands of the Gaza Strip. It was a unique Egyptian border settlement near the Mediterranean Sea that dates to the LB II / Iron I periods (fourteenth through twelfth centuries B.C.). It is not mentioned in the Old Testament, but its remains provide an interesting glimpse into the life and culture on the Canaanite-Egyptian frontier at this time. Excavations took place here between 1972 and 1982 under the direction of Trude Dothan for the Institute of Archaeology of the Hebrew University in Jerusalem.

Fig. 11.2. Excavating Anthropoid Clay Coffin

Dothan's team began excavations in a cemetery that was buried deep in the sand dunes. They were able to uncover several intact anthropoid clay coffins that were the earliest known from ancient Palestine; later ones have been found at Beth Shean, Lachish, and Tell el-Farah (South). Spectacular small finds were found in the coffins, such as jewelry in Tomb 118 (the so-called "Romeo and Juliet" coffin, in which a male and a female were buried together). Included in that burial were gold hoop and drop-shaped earrings, a seal ring of gold, and a necklace of carnelian beads. Amulets of various deities, such as Bast and Bes, along with numerous scarabs, also appeared in the coffins.

Dothan reasoned that there must have been a settlement accompanying the cemetery hidden under the dunes. She oversaw the removal of thousands of tons of dune sand and found settlements:

> Subsequent excavation revealed six settlement strata crucial to understanding the site. Dothan traces the development of the settlement strata from an Amarna-age (c. fourteenth century B.C.E.) Egyptian-style settlement with an elite residency, to a fortress with pool that she identifies as the terminal

military bastion along the way of Horus (the military road between Egypt and Canaan) contemporary with Seti I, to a final Ramesside-era artisan's village contemporaneous with the cemetery that produced coffins and grave goods for the burials. (Redmount 2010, 5)

FOR FURTHER READING

Dothan, Trude. *Deir el-Balah: Excavations in 1977–1982 in the Cemetery and Settlement*, vol. 1, *Stratigraphy and Architecture*. Qedem 49. Jerusalem: Institute of Archaeology, Hebrew University, 2010.

Dothan, Trude. *Deir el-Balah: Uncovering an Egyptian Outpost in Canaan from the Time of the Exodus*. Jerusalem: Israel Museum, 2008.

Dothan, Trude, and Baruch Brandl. *Deir el-Balah: Excavations in 1977–1982 in the Cemetery and Settlement*, vol. 2, *The Finds*. Qedem 50. Jerusalem: Institute of Archaeology, Hebrew University, 2010.

Redmount, Carol A. Review of Trude Dothan's *Deir el-Balah: Uncovering an Egyptian Outpost in Canaan from the Time of the Exodus*. *BAR* 36 (2010): 5.

GATH

The mound of Tell es-Safi, identified with the biblical Philistine city of Gath, is located just west of the Shephelah, about 5 miles directly south of the city of Ekron. Gath plays a prominent role in the Old Testament narratives, especially at the time of David. It is mentioned in the Old Testament more than any other Philistine city. Gath was part of the inheritance of the tribe of Judah, although there is no evidence that it was captured by the Israelites during the conquest. It is first mentioned in the Old Testament as a place where the Anakim still resided during Joshua's time; they were a race of giants that remained in the land from the earlier Canaanite populace (Josh. 11:22). One of these giants was perhaps the Philistine Goliath, whom David defeated in his rise to power (1 Sam. 17). Later, when David was king, he captured Gath (1 Chron. 18:1), and his grandson Rehoboam fortified it for the defense of his kingdom (2 Chron. 11:5–10). At some point, Gath reverted to Philistine control (Amos 6:2), and it remained in Philistine hands until the Assyrian king Sargon II destroyed it at the end of the eighth century B.C.

Tell es-Safi was first excavated by F. J. Bliss and R. A. S. Macalister in 1899, but it was only a brief, two-week excavation. For the most part, the site was left alone until 1996, when a team from Bar-Ilan University began large-scale excavations that continue until the present time. The chief archaeologist is

Aren M. Maeir. Excavations have revealed a long history for the site, beginning in the PN period, about 5000 B.C., and it has been continually settled, more or less, until the modern day.

Although major fortification systems have been found in both the EB and the MB periods, the most impressive finds thus far have come from the Iron II period. In the primary excavation area, the archaeologists found a huge destruction layer that dated to the ninth century B.C. Sealed beneath the ash, the diggers uncovered ruined houses that contained hundreds of pottery vessels and some weapons and jewelry. The level dated to the ninth century B.C., soon after the division of Israel into two kingdoms.

A unique find from the Iron II period was a man-made trench that surrounded the settlement on three sides. It was about 1.5 miles in length, 25 feet wide, and 16 feet deep. The excavators concluded that it served as part of a siege system in order to keep people from escaping from the city. They speculate that it may reflect the siege of Gath by the Arameans (see 2 Kings 12:17) at the close of the ninth century B.C.

Perhaps the most famous small find came from the middle of the tenth century B.C. It is the earliest Philistine inscription known to date, and it mentions two names that may be related to the original form of the name Goliath. This is important because its date is close to the time of David's exploits.

FOR FURTHER READING

Maeir, Aren M. "Zafit." *NEAEHL*, 5:2079–81 (2008).

Maeir, Aren M., and C. S. Ehrlich. "Archaeology in Israel: Tell es-Safi." *AJA* 102 (1998): 785–86.

Maeir, Aren M., and C. S. Ehrlich. "Excavating Philistine Gath: Have We Found Goliath's Hometown?" *BAR* 27 (2001): 22–31.

TELL JEMMEH

Tell Jemmeh is located in the southern coastal plain at the confluence of the Besor and Gerar Brooks. It sits on the southern bank of the Besor, and is about 6 miles south of Gaza. The site was first settled in the MB II period and was inhabited almost continuously into the Persian period. Early investigators, such as W. F. Petrie, identified the mound with biblical Gerar (Gen. 20:1–2; 26:1, 6, 17, 20, 26). It is more likely that Tell Jemmeh should be identified with the city of Yurza, which is mentioned on some Egyptian topographical lists (Mazar 1957, 65). The town of Yurza is not mentioned in the Old Testament.

The first excavation of the site involved a sounding or a trial trench under the direction of W. J. Phythian-Adams in 1922 (Phythian-Adams 1923, 140–46). W. F. Petrie did more intense digging in 1926–27, and excavated in the western part of the site for six months. From 1970 to 1990, Gus Van Beek led an expedition to Tell Jemmeh under the auspices of the Smithsonian Institution.

The most significant findings of the excavation include, first of all, a well-preserved pottery kiln from the twelfth century B.C. for the production of local ceramics. It is the only Philistine pottery kiln found to date. Second, the excavators unearthed a complex of administrative buildings dating to the seventh century B.C. They were made of mud-brick, and their form and style were Assyrian; they had vaulted ceilings and the floors were covered with Assyrian palace ware. These finds indicate an important Assyrian administrative and military presence at the site in the late Iron Age. Located on the Great Trunk Road from Egypt, the fortress of Tell Jemmeh served as an Assyrian guard post against any Egyptian incursions.

Both Petrie and Van Beek discovered several round granary facilities that belonged to the Persian period. These were exceptional finds, although there is some scholarly disagreement regarding the exact form and shape of the granaries (Currid 1986, 21–22; Van Beek 1986, 245–47).

FOR FURTHER READING

Ben-Shlomo, David, and Gus W. Van Beek. *The Smithsonian Excavation at Tell Jemmeh, Israel, 1970–1990.* Washington: Smithsonian Institution Scholarly Press, 2014.

Currid, John D. "The Beehive Buildings of Ancient Palestine." *BA* 49 (1986): 20–24.

Mazar, Benjamin. "The Campaign of Pharaoh Shishak to Palestine." *VTS* 4 (1957): 57–66.

Phythian-Adams, W. J. "Report on Soundings at Tell Jemmeh." *PEF Quarterly Statement* 55 (1923): 140–46.

Van Beek, Gus W. "Are There Beehive Granaries at Tell Jemmeh? A Rejoinder." *BA* 49 (1986): 245–47.

TEL MICHAL

Tel Michal is a site located on the Mediterranean coast about 4 miles north of the Yarkon River. It sits on a kurkar (sandstone) ridge overlooking the sea, and its remains are scattered across five hills. The highest hill, which was the core of the settlement, measures about three-fourths of an acre. Jacob Ory (1940) and R. W. Hamilton (1944) did some preliminary investigations of the site. The most extensive work occurred during four excavation seasons from 1977 to 1980 under the direction of Ze'ev Herzog and James Muhly, primarily on behalf of Tel Aviv University. Herzog conducted a salvage operation in 1982 that uncovered four Iron Age wine presses.

Excavations revealed that the site was first settled in the MB II period. The settlers built a raised platform on the highest hill that was supported by a glacis and a retaining wall. It is assumed that buildings existed on top of the platform, although none of them have survived. Various foreign objects, such as Egyptian pottery and scarabs, were discovered in this level. This led the investigators to believe the site was a trading post or fort with deep connections to ancient Egypt.

After the site was destroyed, it was resettled in the LB I period. It appears to have been a trading post, as in the earlier time period. Several houses were excavated just south of the fort. This level was also destroyed and then resettled during the LB II period. The new settlers also reused the fort, and they strengthened its foundations by extending its rampart and adding a new retaining wall at its base. The site was abandoned at the end of the LB period and remained uninhabited until the tenth century B.C.

The Iron II settlement was found on the high hill and on three of the lower hills. Typical Iron Age housing was discovered, and several one-room cultic structures emerged through excavation. Four wine presses were also found from this period. The site was quickly abandoned in the tenth century B.C., and then resettled briefly during the eighth century B.C.

FOR FURTHER READING

Herzog, Ze'ev. "Excavations at Tel Michal 1978–1979." *Tel Aviv* 7 (1980): 111–51.

Herzog, Ze'ev. "Tel Michal." *NEAEHL*, 3:1036–41 (1993).

Herzog, Ze'ev, Ora Negbi, and Shmuel Moshkovitz. "Excavations at Tel Michal 1977." *Tel Aviv* 5 (1978): 99–130.

TEL MIQNE-EKRON

Ekron, in the Philistine Pentapolis, is located at the site of Tel Miqne in the eastern coastal plain near the Shephelah that separates Philistia from Judah. It lies about 7 miles to the west of Beth-Shemesh and about 5 miles north of Gath. It is one of the largest sites in ancient Palestine, including a

10-acre acropolis and a 40-acre lower city (that increased to 65 acres during the Iron II period). Ekron is mentioned over twenty times in the Old Testament. After the Israelite conquest, the city was allotted to the tribe of Judah (Josh. 15:45). The Israelites captured the city at that time, but there is no evidence of any lasting presence. Ekron later played an important role in the ark episode (1 Sam. 5:10–12; 6:17).

Ekron was excavated for fourteen seasons between 1981 and 1996 as a joint expedition of Hebrew University and the Albright Institute of Archaeological Research. The senior archaeologists were Trude Dothan and Seymour Gitin. The project is currently in the publication phase. Pottery remains reflect human presence at the site as early as the Chalcolithic period, and it was continually occupied until the close of the Iron II period around 600 B.C.

The first fortified site was from the MB II period. The excavators uncovered monumental platforms that served as part of the defensive ramparts of the town. But the subsequent LB settlement was unfortified, and only the acropolis was occupied. Numerous remains from foreign areas, such as Cypriote, Mycenaean, and Anatolian pottery, reflect a brisk international trade. This settlement met a violent end about 1200 B.C., evidenced by a large ash layer on top of an LB storehouse. The destruction was likely at the hands of the invading Sea Peoples (Philistines).

In the following Iron I period, the settlement was again fortified, and a mud-brick city wall was found surrounding both the upper and lower cities. The earliest Iron I level, stratum VII, displayed a new material culture that was introduced by the Philistines. This included typical Philistine pottery that was influenced by Aegean ware. The Iron I occupation was destroyed in the early tenth century B.C., perhaps by David.

The city was resettled in the first half of the eighth century B.C., but only the upper city was refortified with a mud-brick outer wall and a tower. The Assyrians under Sennacherib conquered this settlement in 701 B.C. In the seventh century B.C., Ekron was reoccupied, including the lower city; the prominent feature was an olive oil industrial complex. This city met its end at the hands of the Babylonian monarch Nebuchadnezzar in about 604 B.C.

FOR FURTHER READING

There are seven preliminary excavation reports that have been published in the Tel Miqne-Ekron Limited Edition Series (ELES). The final reports have begun to appear, and the series will include seven more volumes. The first of the final reports is:

Meehl, Mark W., Trude Dothan, and Seymour Gitin. *Tel-Miqne-Ekron Excavations, 1995–1996. Field INE East Slope: Iron Age I (Early Philistine Period).* Jerusalem: W. F. Albright Institute of Archaeological Research and the Hebrew University, 2006.

TELL QASILE

Tell Qasile is an ancient inland port near the Mediterranean Sea on the northern bank of the Yarkon River. It lies within the confines of the modern city of Tel Aviv, and is located about 9 miles directly west of ancient Aphek. At its cultural apex, Tell Qasile covered approximately 4 acres and lay a mere 500 feet from the river. The site is not mentioned in the Old Testament, although the excavators make the case that it served as a port where the cedars of Lebanon were unloaded for the building of the temple in Jerusalem (2 Chron. 2:16; Ezra 3:7).

The first excavations at the site were under the auspices of the Israel Exploration Society and ran for three seasons, 1948–50. Benjamin Mazar directed them. Amihai Mazar for the Hebrew University resumed them in 1971–74, and led some short seasons between 1982 and 1989. Although a few sherds were found from the MB I period, perhaps reflecting a small, short-lived occupation, the earliest remains from the mound were from the Iron I period (the twelfth century B.C.). The Philistines were the founders and builders of this early settlement.

Excavations revealed three distinct strata of the Philistine settlement (strata XII–X). Perhaps the most significant find from this time was a Philistine sacred complex that existed in all three occupation levels. In the earliest level (XII), the archaeologists uncovered a small temple that consisted of a single room made of mud-brick with plastered walls. A *bamah* (raised platform) was discovered at the west end of the building. A second temple was built on the ruins of the first one in stratum XI; it was larger than the first one, although it consisted of only one room as well. Benches were built along its walls. A small enclosure next to the temple contained a variety of vessels, some of which appear to have been cultic in nature. A courtyard next to the sanctuary was excavated, and in it the excavators found a favissa (a ritual pit) that contained other cultic vessels. In the final stratum (X), the temple was enlarged again, using some of the walls of the previous structure. At its entrance, archaeologists discovered two stone bases upon which columns would have rested to support a roof. On one side of the sanctuary was a small storage room, and abutting its wall was a *bamah*. Along the walls of this temple were a series of benches.

The city was at its zenith in the eleventh century B.C. The Philistines built it with precise urban planning: streets divided the settlement into three basic areas—a sacred complex, living quarters, and an industrial area. David probably destroyed this city in the first quarter of the tenth century B.C.

FOR FURTHER READING

Mazar, Amihai. *Excavations at Tell Qasile. Part One: The Philistine Sanctuary: Architecture and Cult Objects.* Qedem 12. Jerusalem: Institute of Archaeology, Hebrew University, 1980.

Mazar, Amihai. *Excavations at Tell Qasile. Part Two: The Philistine Sanctuary: Various Finds, the Pottery, Conclusions, Appendixes.* Qedem 20. Jerusalem: Institute of Archaeology, Hebrew University, 1985.

Mazar, Amihai. "Excavations at Tell Qasile, 1982–1986." *IEJ* 36 (1986): 1–15.

CHAPTER 12

The Central Highlands

D UE TO THE terrain, the central hill country was a difficult region for ancient pioneers to settle. Growing crops on hillsides, soil erosion, and storing water were only three major obstacles to settlement. Thus, for much of antiquity, much of the population was located in the valleys of the highlands, where water and good soil were readily available, and agriculture and horticulture could easily be practiced. For example, during the LB Age, the Canaanites were mainly urbanized, with their population living mostly in large towns or city-states; few sites have been found on the slopes of the highlands from this time. However, beginning with the Iron I period, there was a great increase of settlement in all parts of the hilly regions. The settlers of these sites used such things as terracing and lime-plastered cisterns in order to overcome the obstacles of the terrain. Many scholars identify this influx of immigrants into the highlands with the Israelites. The central hill country was the main area of occupation for Israel throughout its history, and its two main capitals, Jerusalem and Samaria, were both in the heart of the highlands.

BETHEL

Many scholars place biblical Bethel at the modern site of Beitin, about 11 miles due north of Jerusalem. A few investigators locate it at el-Bireh, a few miles southwest of Beitin, or at Beit El, about a mile north of Beitin. The latter views have gotten little traction in the archaeological community. Excavations were undertaken at Beitin in the years 1934, 1954, 1957, and 1960 under the auspices of ASOR and Pittsburgh-Xenia Seminary. William F. Albright directed the first campaign, and James L. Kelso led the later excavations. Since 2012, further work has been undertaken jointly by the Ministry of Tourism and Antiquities of Palestine and Keio University in Japan.

Bethel appears often in the Old Testament. It was a place where the patriarchs often stayed. Jacob, for instance, had a dream at Bethel in which God gave to him covenantal promises, as he saw angels ascending and descending on a ladder from heaven (Gen. 28:10–17). God later blessed Jacob and changed his name to Israel at Bethel (Gen. 35:9–15). During the divided monarchy, Jeroboam I set up a temple in Bethel, and he placed a golden calf there as a rival to the temple in Jerusalem (1 Kings 12:26–30). Bethel was likely destroyed in 721 B.C. by the Assyrians when they conquered the northern kingdom.

There is much disagreement among scholars regarding the archaeological history of Beitin, and the archaeological reports have been criticized for reaching unwarranted chronological conclusions. In general, it looks like the site was first settled during the EB Age, since numerous sherds were found on the mound from this time. Beitin was not, however, fortified until the MB II period, when an 11-foot-thick city wall surrounded the site. This city was destroyed in the sixteenth century B.C. and not reoccupied until the second half of the LB Age. This site appears to have been a prosperous Canaanite city, as Kelso remarks: "This represents the finest architectural phase in the city's history" (Kelso 1975, 192). It included large houses with flagstone pavements and drainage/sewer systems. The excavators were convinced that the LB level was destroyed by the invading Israelites in the thirteenth century B.C., and other archaeologists concur with that assessment (Mazar 1990, 333).

The ancient Israelite leaders assigned Bethel to the inheritance of the tribe of Benjamin (Josh. 18:22). The initial Israelite occupation during the Iron I period was sparse, and meager remains have been uncovered at Beitin from this time. The city became important at the close of the tenth century B.C. during the reign of Jeroboam I, and it flourished until the end of the eighth century B.C. The prophet Amos in about 750 B.C. mentions Bethel as still serving as a place of worship (Amos 5:5).

FOR FURTHER READING

Kelso, James L. "Bethel." *EAEHL*, 1:190–93 (1975).

Kelso, James L. *The Excavation of Bethel*. AASOR 39. Cambridge, MA: American Schools of Oriental Research, 1968.

Mazar, Amihai. *Archaeology of the Land of the Bible: 10,000–586 B.C.E.* New York: Doubleday, 1990.

GIBEON

The biblical site of Gibeon is located on a mound near the village of el-Jib, about 6 miles north-northwest of Jerusalem. That identification appears to be solid, as James Pritchard states, "The discovery at el-Jib (during the excavation of 1956, 1957, and 1959) of thirty-one jar handles inscribed with the name *gb'n* has now confirmed the identification of Gibeon with el-Jib" (Pritchard 1976, 446). The city was first settled in the EB I period, and its final habitation during the Old Testament period ended near the close of the sixth century B.C.

Gibeon's role in the Old Testament is extensive; it is mentioned over forty times. Its first appearance is in Joshua 9–10, where the Gibeonites deceived the invading Israelites in order to secure a covenant of protection. When Gibeon came under attack from five kings of the land, the Israelite army came to the rescue. After the conquest, Gibeon was allotted to the tribe of Benjamin (Josh. 18:25), and it was designated a Levitical city (Josh. 21:17). Another significant event occurred during the kingship of David, in which the warriors of David, under Joab's leadership, defeated Abner and the men of Israel at the pool of Gibeon (1 Sam. 2:12–17).

James Pritchard led the excavations at Gibeon on behalf of the University Museum of the University of Pennsylvania, the Church Divinity School of the Pacific, and ASOR. Five seasons of digging were undertaken between 1956 and 1962.

Among the most impressive finds at the site were two systems to supply water to the city dating to the Iron Age. The construction and form of the two systems are discussed in chapter 14, to which the reader may refer. One of those systems may, in fact, include the pool of Gibeon mentioned above. Another important discovery came from the Israelite occupation of the eighth through seventh centuries B.C.: 63 rock-cut wine cellars that were bottle-shaped and averaged 6 feet in depth and 6 feet in diameter. The jars in which the wine was stored each had a capacity over 9 gallons, and it is thus estimated that the cellars would have held up to 25,000 gallons of wine.

FOR FURTHER READING

Pritchard, James B. "Gibeon." *EAEHL*, 2:446–50 (1976).

Pritchard, James B. *Gibeon, Where the Sun Stood Still: The Discovery of the Biblical City*. Princeton: Princeton University Press, 1962.

Pritchard, James B. *The Water System at Gibeon*. Philadelphia: University of Pennsylvania, 1961.

JERUSALEM

Jerusalem was the most important city in ancient Israel. It was "the city of the great King" (in reference to Yahweh, Ps. 48:2) and "the city of David"

(45 times in the Old Testament, including 2 Sam. 5:7). Jerusalem served as the capital of the united Israel and then as the capital of Judah after the division. The Lord was the one who chose Jerusalem as the worship center for his people, and the temple was located there on Mount Zion (Deut. 12:5, 21; 2 Chron. 7:12). Jerusalem sits in the central highlands, about 2,400 feet above sea level. Of course, many prominent and defining biblical events took place in this city. Abraham took his son Isaac to be sacrificed on Mount Moriah, which was later identified with Jerusalem (Gen. 22:2; 2 Chron. 3:1). David captured the city from the Jebusites, purchased the threshing floor of Ornan the Jebusite there (1 Chron. 21:18–27), and planned the building of God's temple on the site. Of course, Jesus's work and ministry climaxed in Jerusalem, where he was tried, crucified, buried, and resurrected.

Large-scale excavations have taken place in Jerusalem since 1865, beginning with the investigations of the Palestine Exploration Fund under the direction of Charles Warren. This work concentrated on the area of the Old City and the Temple Mount. From that time to today, many other excavation projects have been undertaken; here we will discuss only a few that provide important information for the Old Testament period. In this regard, the excavations carried out between 1961 and 1967 by the British School of Archaeology in Jerusalem, under the direction of Kathleen Kenyon and Roland de Vaux, ought to be highlighted. Their work focused on the Ophel (hill) and other areas south of the Temple Mount. Further work was accomplished by the City of David Project from 1978 to 1985, supervised by Yigal Shiloh of the Institute of Archaeology at Hebrew University. Shiloh's work concentrated on the eastern slope of the spur known as the Ophel / City of David, and on the area of the Gihon Spring. Excavations in this area have continued, beginning in 1995, with the labors of Ronny Reich and Eli Shukron. Much of their study has been a reassessment of the form, function, and date of the Siloam Tunnel.

Since so much material has been uncovered in Jerusalem, I will take time only to highlight some of the more important remains. The earliest settlement of Jerusalem was on the ridge of the Ophel, and the earliest city wall found here came from the MB II period. Other remains of the Canaanite/Jebusite occupation have been unearthed, such as a large structure that they called the "stepped structure." It appears to have been of Jebusite origin and later reused in David and Solomon's building activity. "The purpose of the structure is uncertain, although it has been suggested that it served as a retaining wall, about 50 feet (15 m) high, for an earthen platform on which stood a royal building from the time of the united monarchy" (Currid and Barrett 2010, 129). In the Iron II period, the stepped structure was plastered and made into a glacis as part of the city's fortifications. In front of the structure, during the Iron II period, archaeologists discovered several typical Israelite four-room houses. Because of the steep slope of the area, the houses were built on terraces.

Another major discovery was the complex water system built around the Gihon Spring, the most dependable water source for Jerusalem in antiquity. Because I deal with this site in chapter 14, I will not repeat myself here. I would add, however, that recent work in the area has led some scholars to argue that the Iron II tunnel of this system, normally attributed to Hezekiah, actually pre-dated Hezekiah's kingship (Reich and Shukron 2011, 147–57). This reconstruction has met with a mixed reception from the archaeological community.

The settlement of Jerusalem began to expand northward during the united monarchy. Solomon built the temple north of the Ophel on Mount Zion. Excavations immediately west of the Temple Mount by Benjamin Mazar found no architectural elements from the tenth through ninth centuries B.C., except for some Iron II burials. Since Israelite burials were invariably placed outside city walls, this area would not have been occupied at that time. Expansion did take place to the west in the eighth century B.C. Nahman Avigad conducted excavations in the Jewish Quarter of Jerusalem west of the Temple Mount from 1969 to 1982. He discovered a 20-foot-thick wall from the eighth century B.C., and houses from that time to the east of the wall. Hezekiah likely built the wall in response to Assyrian military threats (2 Chron. 32:5).

FOR FURTHER READING

Currid, John D., and David P. Barrett. *Crossway ESV Bible Atlas*. Wheaton, IL: Crossway Books, 2010.

Geva, Hillel. *Jewish Quarter Excavations in the Old City of Jerusalem*, vol. VII, *Conducted by Nahman Avigad, 1969–1982*. Jerusalem: Israel Exploration Society, 2017.

Kenyon, Kathleen. *Digging Up Jerusalem*. London: Praeger, 1974.

Mazar, Benjamin. *Excavations in the Old City Near the Temple Mount*. Jerusalem: Institute of Archaeology, Hebrew University, 1971.

Reich, Ronny, and Eli Shukron. "The Date of the Siloam Tunnel Reconsidered." *Tel Aviv* 38 (2011): 147–57.

Shiloh, Yigal. *Excavations at the City of David*. 6 vols. Jerusalem: Institute of Archaeology, Hebrew University, 1984–.

Yadin, Yigael. *Jerusalem Revealed*. Jerusalem: Israel Exploration Society, 1975.

KHIRBET RADDANA

The mound of Khirbet Raddana is located in the central highlands about 9 miles north of Jerusalem near the modern city of Ramallah. Although some EB I sherds were found scattered on the tell, there was no evidence of any structures from that period. The primary settlement at the site was during the Iron I period. The excavators suggest that the mound ought to be identified with biblical Beeroth, a city of the Hivites during the Israelite conquest (Josh. 9:17); however, that site is probably located at Khirbet el-Burj. Khirbet Raddana was excavated by Joseph A. Callaway from 1969 to 1974 on behalf of the Israel Department of Antiquities and Museums.

Khirbet Raddana appears to have been a typical Iron I (probably Israelite) settlement in the hill country. It was a small village that was extensively excavated. Building at the site began in the late thirteenth century B.C., and it was finally destroyed in the middle of the eleventh century B.C. Excavations uncovered seven houses in Areas R, S, and T; all of them were three-room, pillared houses. The rear walls of the houses served as part of an outer defensive wall for the town. The inhabitants of the settlement were agriculturalists, as is clear from the many tools of food production found in the town. Both cereals and fruits were probably cultivated on the steep hillsides around the site by means of agricultural terracing.

An inscribed jar handle in a stratified deposit of the early Iron I period was found. It is dated no later than the twelfth century B.C. (Cross and Freedman 1971, 19). It contains three letters that perhaps are a personal name of the owner of the jar.

FOR FURTHER READING

Aharoni, Yohanan. "Khirbet Raddana and Its Inscription." *IEJ* 21 (1971): 130–35.

Callaway, Joseph A., and Robert E. Cooley. "A Salvage Excavation at Raddana in Bireh." *BASOR* 201 (1971): 9–19.

Cross, Frank M., and David N. Freedman. "An Inscribed Jar Handle from Raddana." *BASOR* 201 (1971): 19–22.

Lederman, Zvi. "An Early Iron Age Village at Khirbet Raddana: The Excavations of Joseph A. Callaway." PhD diss., Harvard University, 1999.

RAMAT RAHEL

The mound of Ramat Rahel lies about 2 miles south of Jerusalem, midway between Jerusalem and Bethlehem, on the spine of the Judean highlands.

Its settlement began at the close of the eighth century B.C., and it was destroyed at the hands of the Babylonians around 600 B.C. Identification of the site is uncertain, although many scholars agree with Aharoni that it was biblical Beth-hakkerem, which is mentioned in Jeremiah 6:1 and Nehemiah 3:14. Ramat Rahel has been excavated several times. In 1930–31, Benjamin Mazar and Moshe Stekelis, under the auspices of the Israel Exploration Society, excavated a burial cave from the Second Temple period. Exploration of the mound itself began in 1954 under the direction of Yohanan Aharoni, and it continued for five seasons until 1962 (for the Department of Antiquities). Brief excavations took place in 1984 (led by Gaby Barkay) and in 1999 (conducted by Gideon Suleimany). Finally, major excavations began in 2004, and continue today, on behalf of Tel Aviv University and Heidelberg University, with Oded Lipschitz and Manfred Oeming directing them.

The first settlers of the site arrived at the end of the eighth century B.C. The first stratum, which Aharoni designated VB, contained few remains because the builders of the next period (stratum VA) destroyed much of the architecture of the earlier period. However, the excavators did uncover a casemate wall system that was perhaps part of a small citadel (Aharoni 1978, 1001). In addition, much pottery was found from the late eighth and early seventh centuries B.C., along with over 100 *lmlk* ("to the king") seal impressions.

The settlement of stratum VA lasted until it was destroyed by the Babylonians about 600 B.C. This settlement was large, covering about 5 acres on top of the mound, and it contained an external fortification system with a large citadel. The outer town wall was about 10–12 feet thick and it surrounded the entire site. At the northeastern corner of the settlement, the excavators uncovered a citadel, which measured about 245 by 160 feet; it was surrounded by a 15-foot-wide casemate wall system. The citadel was entered through a gateway at the eastern side of the building. The structure is a good example of Israelite building technique of the period. The builders used dressed stones of fine workmanship, and some Proto-Aeolic capitals were found in the ruins of the building.

FOR FURTHER READING

Aharoni, Yohanan. *Excavations at Ramat Rahel 1: Seasons 1959 and 1960.* Roma: Universita di Roma, 1962.

Aharoni, Yohanan. *Excavations at Ramat Rahel 2: Seasons 1961 and 1962.* Roma: Universita di Roma, 1964.

Aharoni, Yohanan. "Ramat Rahel." *EAEHL*, 4:1000–1009 (1978).

Na'aman, Nadav. "An Assyrian Residence at Ramat Rachel?" *Tel Aviv* 28 (2001): 260–80.

SAMARIA

The tell of Samaria lies on a main highway from Shechem, about 8 miles to the northwest. The settlement was on a high hill that overlooked its surroundings. The area was one of good agricultural potential. The city of Samaria was founded by the Israelite monarch Omri (884–874 B.C.). First Kings 16:23–24 says, "In the thirty-first year of Asa king of Judah, Omri began to reign over Israel, and he reigned for twelve years; six years he reigned in Tirzah. He bought the hill of Samaria from Shemer for two talents of silver, and he fortified the hill and called the name of the city that he built Samaria, after the name of Shemer, the owner of the hill." Samaria became the capital city of the northern kingdom, and Omri was buried there (1 Kings 16:28). Ahab (874–853 B.C.) succeeded his father as king of Israel, and he was well known for his building activities at Samaria (1 Kings 16:32; 22:39) and elsewhere. After Ahab, there was an economic decline in the north until the reign of Jeroboam II (782–753 B.C.); under his rule, Samaria reached its zenith in power and economic prosperity. In 721 B.C., however, the city was conquered by Sargon II of Assyria and its population was deported.

Two major excavations have taken place at Samaria. The first was under the codirectorship of Clarence Fisher and George Reisner, under the auspices of Harvard University, from 1908 to 1910. The second was led by John Crowfoot from 1931 to 1935, under the sponsorship of the British Academy, the British School of Archaeology in Jerusalem, Harvard University, Hebrew University, and the Palestine Exploration Fund. Smaller-scale excavations took place in the 1960s for the Jordanian Department of Antiquities, super-

Fig. 12.1. Samaria Ivory

vised by F. Zayadine (1966, 77–80), and another by J. B. Hennessy in 1968 (Hennessy 1970, 1–21).

The summit of the mound has been the most extensively excavated part of the site. A palace or royal citadel was found there, and its foundations derived from the time of Omri (designated Building Level I). Two fortification walls enclosed the palace: an inner wall built by Omri, and an outer wall erected by his son Ahab. The palace was built on top of a 13-foot-high, rock-cut platform. Omri's wall was constructed of ashlar masonry, and the stones were set in a header-stretcher fashion. Building Level II, attributed to Ahab, was an expansion of the area of the acropolis by means of a massive fill. North of the palace, excavators found a large depository of Phoenician ivories, and they assumed that the "ivory house" constructed by Ahab (1 Kings 22:39) was in the vicinity.

In the 1910 excavations, archaeologists discovered over sixty potsherds with Hebrew writing on them (called ostraca) in the storerooms of a building they called the Ostraca House. Many of them are tax records dealing with shipments of oil and wine to the royal household in Samaria. The dating of the ostraca is uncertain, although many scholars hold to the time of Jeroboam II, when Samaria appears to have been flourishing economically (Building Level IV).

FOR FURTHER READING

Avigad, Nahman. "Samaria." *EAEHL*, 4:1032–50 (1978).

Crowfoot, John W., Kathleen M. Kenyon, and E. L. Sukenik. *The Buildings at Samaria*. London: Palestine Exploration Fund, 1942.

Hennessy, J. B. "Excavations at Samaria-Sebaste, 1968." *Levant* 2 (1970): 1–21.

Reisner, G. A., C. S. Fisher, and D. G. Lyon. *Harvard Excavations at Samaria I–II*. Cambridge, MA: Harvard University Press, 1924.

Zayadine, F. "Samaria-Sebaste: Clearance and Excavations (October 1965– June 1967)." *Annual of the Department of Antiquities of Jordan* 12 (1966): 77–80.

SHECHEM

Tell Balatah (Shechem) lies in the north-central hill country about 40 miles north of Jerusalem and 7 miles southeast of Samaria. Located between the two mountains of Ebal and Gerizim, the mound is strategically situated. The main roads of the region pass by it. It was a pivotal site in antiquity, as it was positioned on the "spine" route, which traversed the highlands from Hebron in the south to Samaria in the north. In the Old Testament, Shechem was an important city. It was the first town in Canaan visited by Abraham (Gen. 12:6). During the period of the conquest, Shechem was on the northern border of the tribal allotment of Ephraim (Josh. 17:7). Although the city came into the possession of the Israelites, there is no recording of its capture in the Old Testament. It was designated a Levitical city out of Ephraim (Josh. 21:20–21), and appointed as a city of refuge (Josh. 20:7). At Shechem, Joshua addressed the people of Israel for the last time (Josh. 24:1–28). During the time of the judges, Abimelech was crowned king there (Judg. 9:6). After the death of Solomon, all Israel came to Shechem to make Rehoboam king (1 Kings 12:1); after the division, King Jeroboam of the north resided in Shechem (1 Kings 12:25). The name Shechem appears often in extrabiblical literature, such as in the Egyptian Execration Texts (nineteenth century B.C.). It is also mentioned in an inscription of Khu-Sebek, which tells of Pharaoh Senwosret III (1878–1841 B.C.) campaigning in Canaan and reaching the area of *skmm* (= Shechem).

The first excavations of the site began in 1913 under the direction of Ernst Sellin, and they continued sporadically into the 1930s. Unfortunately, "most of Sellin's records, his completed excavation report, and many small objects . . . were destroyed during the bombing of Berlin in the Fall of 1943" (Wright 1978, 1086). American excavators, under the direction of G. E. Wright, began major excavations at the site in 1956; the final campaign occurred in 1973, led by W. G. Dever. Finally, in the years 2010–12, the Palestinian Department of Antiquities did some archaeological work at the site as part of a project to make it into an archaeological park.

The earliest urbanization at Shechem began in the MB I period, about 1900 B.C. However, it was not until the MB II period that Shechem began to flourish. The crowning structure of the site appeared at this time, and was unearthed in the northwest quadrant of the mound in an area designated Field V by the American excavators. Field V contains the largest extant pre-Roman temple remains in Palestine. This temple complex was used continuously through the LB Age, and some scholars argue that it was not destroyed until the end of the twelfth century B.C. in the Iron I period. This so-called Fortress Temple "was the largest known from ancient Canaan—70 feet wide and 86 feet long, with stone wall foundations 17 feet thick. The thick foundations supported a multistory temple made of mudbricks and timber. Two large towers flanked the entrance on the east side of the temple and projected 16 feet in front of it" (Stager 2003, 29–31). Although there is disagreement, this temple may be the Temple of Baal-Berith mentioned in Judges 8:33; 9:4, 46. After the destruction of the temple during the Iron I period, a large granary was built in Field V on top of the temple area during the eighth century B.C. (Currid 1989, 42–46).

FOR FURTHER READING

Campbell, Edward F., and James F. Ross. "The Excavation of Shechem and the Biblical Tradition." *BA* 26 (1963): 2–27.

Currid, John D. "A Note on the Function of Building 5900 at Shechem—Again." *ZDPV* 105 (1989): 42–46.

Stager, Lawrence E. "The Shechem Temple: Where Abimelech Massacred a Thousand." *BAR* 29 (2003): 26–35, 66–69.

Wright, George E. "Shechem." *EAEHL*, 4:1083–94 (1978).

Wright, George E. *Shechem: The Biography of a Biblical City.* London: McGraw-Hill, 1965.

SHILOH

The site of Khirbet Seilun lies about 20 miles north of Jerusalem and about 10 miles south of Shechem in the highlands of Ephraim. It was first settled during the MB II period, and its final phase of occupation during Old Testament times was in the eighth century B.C. Shiloh was an important Israelite city during the periods of the conquest and the judges. The Israelite leaders assigned the bulk of the tribal land allotments at Shiloh (Josh. 18:1–19:51), and they erected the tabernacle there at that time (Josh. 18:1). Shiloh remained the religious center of Israel throughout most of the Iron I period (1 Sam. 1:3).

Shiloh was first excavated by the Danish in 1922 with initial soundings under the supervision of Aege Schmidt; these were followed by three major seasons of digging in 1926–32 under the direction of Hans Kjaer. The Danish returned to the site in 1963 and Svend Holm-Nielsen carried out further soundings. From 1981 to 1984, Israel Finkelstein, under the auspices of Bar-Ilan University, excavated the site and published a final report in 1993. Hananya Hizmi conducted further excavation work on the summit of the site in 2012–13. Finally, beginning in 2017, ABR (Associates for Biblical Research) began a planned multiyear excavation led by Scott Stripling.

Excavations at Shiloh have uncovered a large MB II city. It had an outer wall, at places about 15 feet wide, and retaining walls supported by a huge earth and lime glacis. Some unique finds came from this level, such as a bronze axe shaped like the palm of a human hand and a silver pendant decorated with a symbol of the weather deity. This city was destroyed at the end of the MB

Age, and it was the resettled in the LB Age. The LB settlers continued to use much of the MB infrastructure, but the settlement was smaller and poorer.

An Iron I settlement, which served as the main cultic center of Israel, was established in the twelfth century B.C. and flourished in the eleventh century B.C. It was an intensive settlement. The site had no outer fortification wall, although the back walls of houses formed the city's defense. Pillared, elongated storehouses were also discovered. One of the major indicators of time and culture was the appearance of many collared-rim storage jars. This type of jar was a hallmark of the Iron I highland culture, and it is often used as an identifying trait of an Israelite presence. The site was deserted in about 1000 B.C., and not resettled until the eighth century B.C. The Iron II site was sparsely populated and small in size. It was destroyed, perhaps by the Assyrians in 721 B.C.

FOR FURTHER READING

Finkelstein, Israel, et al., eds. *Shiloh: The Archaeology of a Biblical Site.* Tel Aviv: Institute of Archaeology of Tel Aviv University, 1993.

Hizmi, Hananya, and Reut Livyatan-ben-Arie. "The Excavations at the Northern Platform of Tel Shiloh, the 2012–2013 Seasons." *Near East Archaeological Society Bulletin* 62 (2017): 35–52.

Kaufman, Asher S. "Fixing the Site of the Tabernacle at Shiloh." *BAR* 14 (1988): 42–49.

PART 3

ASPECTS OF SOCIETY

CHAPTER 13

Agriculture and Herding

"For the Lord your God is bringing you into a good land, a land of brooks of water, of fountains and springs, flowing out in the valleys and hills, a land of wheat and barley, of vines and fig trees and pomegranates, a land of olive trees and honey." (Deut. 8:7–8)

SINCE MANKIND'S FIRST appearance on earth, a principal concern of his has been to control his food supply. Despite considerable natural opposition, such as climatic unpredictability, humanity has continued to pursue this domination in order to achieve economic stability. Without proper regulation of the subsistence base, a fixed economy (and a settled society based upon it) is impossible to establish or maintain. Because man seems to have an inherent desire to congregate in settled communities founded upon a strong subsistence base, he has been compelled throughout history to search for ways and means to secure a stable food supply.

During antiquity, people in Palestine developed an increasing ability to maintain their food supply.[1] Prior to the Neolithic period (beginning about 8000 B.C.), humankind relied solely on hunting and gathering to supply food.[2] Even though man remained a hunter and gatherer for many centuries in the pre-Neolithic period, he was able to ameliorate his management of the food base. During the earliest times, humanity seems to have had a severely limited capacity to control food income. For example, the earliest tool kits, by which they hunted animals, gathered cereals, and prepared them for consumption, were very small, consisting primarily of core tools (the Acheulean tradition). Consequently, few settled communities were established in these early ages. Closer to the Neolithic period, on the other hand, mankind greatly increased his capacity to regulate his hunting and

---

1. For concise and good summaries of this history, see Lawrence E. Stager, "Agriculture," *Interpreter's Dictionary of the Bible Supplementary Volume* (Nashville: Abingdon, 1976), 11–13; Rivka Gonen, *Grain* (Jerusalem: Shikmona, 1979).

2. See, in particular, the classic works of Peter J. Ucko and Geoffrey W. Dimbleby, eds., *The Domestication and Exploitation of Plants and Animals* (London: Duckworth, 1969), and Dan Brothwell and Patricia Brothwell, *Food in Antiquity: A Survey of the Diets of Early Peoples* (New York: Praeger, 1969).

gathering activities. First of all, his tool kit, which enabled him to collect cereals and hunt game, expanded to a large degree, now including a flake industry, flint tools, and microliths. Knives, scrapers, chisels, and a variety of points began to appear (e.g., at El Wad and Emirah).[3] Second, humanity's ability to capture, kill, and butcher animals was improved by the development of an intricate base-camp hunting system, such as that found by Anthony Marks at Har Harif.[4] These innovative techniques resulted in mankind securing a broad spectrum economy, in which a variegated food supply was available. It is consequential and not coincidental that perhaps the oldest site in Palestine with permanent architecture has been unearthed from this period at the site of Ein Gev.[5]

The Pre-Pottery Neolithic is the period of initiatory agriculture and herding in Palestine. A few Pre-Pottery Neolithic A (beginning about 8000 B.C.) sites show evidence of domestication, such as Beidha, where ibex were probably herded and grain (barley and wheat) was cultivated.[6] Many sites during this period were year-round settlements with permanent domestic architecture. In the ensuing Pre-Pottery Neolithic B period, many more settled communities relying greatly on domestication were established (e.g., Tell Ramad, Tell Munhata).[7] The diet of mankind in the PPNB was more diversified than what it was in the PPNA. In the later period, cereals such as einkorn appeared, along with legumes and lentils. There seems to be a strong correlation between mankind's increasing control of his subsistence base through domestication and the greater stability and duration of his living situation.

In the Pottery Neolithic and Chalcolithic periods, a few innovations were introduced in mankind's attempt to regulate his food supply. A major development was the appearance of new domesticated animals: cattle (Beersheba) and swine (Munhata) were now included in the herds of the settlers. Oxen were commonly used at many sites, which may indicate, as Lawrence Stager suggests, the introduction of the plow into the agricultural system.[8] Moreover, it is likely that slash/burn agriculture was first used during these periods. It is an agricultural technique that improves the quality of soil by

3. For recent work at the El Wad terrace, see Mina Weinstein-Evron, *Archaeology in the Archives: Unveiling the Natufian Culture of Mount Carmel* (Leiden: Brill, 2009).

4. Anthony E. Marks et al., "Prehistoric Sites near Har Harif," *IEJ* 22 (1972): 73–85.

5. Moshe Stekelis and Ofer Bar-Yosef, "Un habitat du Paléolithique supérieur à Ein Gev (Israel), note préliminaire," *L'Anthropologie* 69 (1965): 176–83.

6. See Diana Kirkbride, "Beidha: Early Neolithic Life South of the Dead Sea," *Antiquity* 42 (1968): 263–74; Kirkbride, "Five Seasons at the Pre-Pottery Neolithic Village of Beidha in Jordan," *PEQ* 98 (1966): 8–72.

7. See Sandor Bokonyi, "Development of Early Stock Rearing in the Near East," *Nature* 264 (1976): 19–23; Henri de Contenson, "Tell Ramad, a Village of Syria of the 7th and 6th millennia B.C.," *Archaeology* 24 (1971): 278–85.

8. Stager, "Agriculture," 12.

destroying weeds with the burning of branches and then letting the ashes sink into the soil. In addition, horticulture, although not widespread, is in clear evidence from this time. Significant olive processing appears to have begun during the Chalcolithic age.[9] Once again, the interrelation between the improvements in mankind's control of his subsistence base and his ability to lead a stable, settled communal life was apparent, and it resulted in the villages of the time being larger than ever. Many of them even had site specialization.

An example of site specialization is found in what is called the Beer-sheba group, in which three sites are clustered and each site had a different economic base. The site of Tell Abu Matar, for instance, focused its labors on smelting and processing, whereas Safadi had a strong ivory craft. Specific sites appear to have specialized in manufacturing specific types of pottery in the central highlands of Palestine during the Chalcolithic period.[10]

At the outset of the Bronze Age in Palestine (ca. 3000 B.C.), there was a striking expansion of the population and the number of settlements. In order to support this considerable increase with an adequate food supply, Bronze Age man had to find new ways in which to expand the areas under cultivation and to regulate better those regions already being farmed. One of the primary developments was that the incipient horticulture of the Chalcolithic period became full-fledged, widespread cropping in the Bronze Age. In fact, Palestine became a major fruit and wine center of the ancient Near East during this time. The Egyptian "Story of Sinuhe," which dates to the time of the Middle Kingdom, describes the horticultural wealth of Palestine as follows: "Figs were in it and grapes. It had more wine than water. Plentiful was its honey, abundant its olives. Every (kind of) fruits was on its tree."[11] Another improvement in the Palestinian regulation of the subsistence base was the development of a brisk international trade, especially with Egypt, which provided a more secure and stable food supply. Lastly, zone specialization of agricultural products best adapted to each region began.[12] Zone specialization indicates the beginnings of an intricate agricultural system, in which one region is dependent on another for particular agricultural products.

Probably the primary technical advance contributing to the development of Bronze Age agriculture was the invention of the bronze plowshare. This invention allowed farmers to cultivate new areas more freely and more

9. J. L. Lovell, "Shifting Subsistence Patterns: Some Ideas about the End of the Chalcolithic in the Southern Levant," *Paleorient* 28 (2002): 89–102.

10. Shimon Gibson and Yorke M. Rowan, "The Chalcolithic in the Central Highlands of Palestine: A Reassessment Based on a New Examination of Khirbet es-Sauma'a," *Levant* 38 (2006): 85–108.

11. John A. Wilson, "Egyptian Myths, Tales and Mortuary Texts," in *Ancient Near Eastern Texts*, ed. James B. Pritchard (Princeton: Princeton University Press, 1955), 19.

12. Stager, "Agriculture," 13.

quickly and thus to expand their food supply more easily. An example of a bronze plowshare comes from the Bronze Age levels at Beth-Shemesh.[13]

During the Bronze Age, the systematic clearance of forests began on a massive scale.[14] The primary purpose of the deforestation was to clear land for cultivation and population settlement. During the Bronze Age, and continuing into the Iron Age, there was a need for a larger food supply because of population pressure. Population growth induced people to enlarge their areas of cultivation through the process of artificial deforestation. Pastoral overgrazing was also a major contributor in deforestation; transhumant moving of flocks of sheep and goats between pasture lands helped in this process because these animals eat regrowth and seedlings of trees and young palatable plants. In addition, they can destroy tracts of vegetation by appropriating vast areas for grazing. "Once grazing pastures have completely deteriorated, the flocks are impelled to search for more grazing lands and thereby widen the areas of destruction."[15] Augustin Bernard goes so far as to suggest that pastoralism was the main cause of deforestation and even calls pastoralists "haters of trees."[16]

At the beginning of the Iron Age, when Israel was settling the land of Canaan, the population pressure seems to have increased dramatically, and many settlements appeared in areas that previously had been sparsely settled. The book of Joshua comments on this settlement activity:

> Then the people of Joseph spoke to Joshua, saying, "Why have you given me but one lot and one portion as an inheritance, although I am a numerous people, since all along the LORD has blessed me?" And Joshua said to them, "If you are a numerous people, go up by yourselves to the forest, and there clear ground for yourselves in the land of the Perizzites and the Rephaim, since the hill country of Ephraim is too narrow for you." The people of Joseph said, "The hill country is not enough for us. Yet all the Canaanites who dwell in the plain have chariots of iron, both those in Beth-shean and its villages and those in the Valley of Jezreel." Then Joshua said to the house of Joseph, to Ephraim and Manasseh, "You are a numerous people and have great power. You shall not have one allotment only, but the hill country shall be yours, for though it is a forest, you shall clear it and possess it to its farthest borders." (Josh. 17:14–18a)

The major new areas of settlement were the highlands and the deserts.

---

13. Avraham Negev, ed., *Archaeological Encyclopedia of the Holy Land* (Englewood, NJ: SBS, 1980), 13–18.

14. So Michael B. Rowton, "The Woodlands of Ancient Western Asia," *JNES* 26 (1967): 261–77; John D. Currid, "The Deforestation of the Foothills of Palestine," *PEQ* 116 (1984): 1–11.

15. Currid, "Deforestation," 6–7. See also E. P. Eckholm, *Losing Ground* (New York: W. W. Norton, 1976), 31.

16. Augustin Bernard, *Afrique septentrionale et occidentale*, vol. 1 (Paris: Colin, 1937), 721–36.

In order for the land to support human settlement in areas that were not so easy to cultivate, people were forced to diversify and to develop or learn fresh agricultural techniques. One principal result of the expansion of settlers into the mountainous areas of Palestine was the incipient use of agricultural terracing.[17] The object of terracing was to transform continuous slopes into series of level surfaces. This prevented erosion, enhanced accumulation of water, and provided an area of cultivable soil. Small-scale, limited terracing activity occurred during the Bronze Age, but in the Iron I period it was apparently more common, especially among the highland villages such as Khirbet Raddana.[18] These small sites were likely Israelite settlements, and the terracing helped them to survive by providing areas of cultivation for cereals, olives, and grapes. In the Iron II period, terracing became much more widespread throughout the hill country of Palestine.

In the desert areas, farmers created terrace dams for cultivation in order to have greater control over their limited water supply.[19] Floodwater farming appears to have begun during the tenth century B.C. and continued to the end of the Iron II period. According to Lawrence Stager, who excavated a few of these farms in the Buqe'ah basin of the Judean desert, the farmers "were able to grow modest stands of wheat and barley as well as legumes by harnessing floodwaters and raising the water yield well beyond that supplied by direct rainfall."[20]

Another important advancement in the agricultural activity of the Iron Age was the introduction of the beam press for use in the production of olive oil. Archaeological discoveries of oil installations at Beth-Shemesh, Dan, Gezer, and Tell Beit Mirsim from the Iron Age demonstrate that the beam press was probably in use no later than the eighth or seventh centuries B.C.[21]

THE PROCESS OF CEREAL CULTIVATION

Since the time of the Neolithic period, when agriculture began in earnest, grain has been the staple food of Palestine. The land of Israel is described

17. See C. H. J. de Geus, "The Importance of Archaeological Research into the Palestinian Agricultural Terraces with an Excursus on the Hebrew Word *gbi*," *PEQ* 107 (1975): 65–74; Zev Ron, "Agricultural Terraces in the Judean Mountains," *IEJ* 16 (1966): 33–49, 111–22; Lawrence E. Stager, "Archaeology of the Family in Ancient Israel," *BASOR* 260 (1985): 1–35.

18. Joseph A. Callaway and Robert E. Cooley, "A Salvage Excavation at Raddana, in Bireh," *BASOR* 201 (1971): 9–19.

19. Lawrence E. Stager, "Farming in the Judean Desert during the Iron Age," *BASOR* 221 (1976): 145–58.

20. Stager, "Farming in the Judean Desert during the Iron Age," 157.

21. For further discussion, see David Eitam, "Olive Presses of the Israelite Period," *TA* 6 (1979), 146–55; David Eitam and Michael Hetzer, *Olive Oil in Antiquity: Israel and Neighboring Countries from Neolithic to Early Arab Period* (Padova: Sargon, 1996); Lawrence E. Stager and Samuel R. Wolff, "Production and Commerce in Temple Courtyards: An Olive Press in the Sacred Precinct at Tel Dan," *BASOR* 243 (1981): 95–102.

in the Bible as a "land of wheat and barley" (Deut. 8:8). For centuries, the common folk worked in the fields to produce crops, and then they either ground the grain into foodstuffs or stored what they produced for later use. This was the common lot of the Israelite farmer. At this point, it may be instructive to view this process from beginning to end, and to consider the various steps of Iron Age husbandry.[22]

1. Plowing. The purpose of plowing is to break up the soil and remove weeds, so that seed may be sowed. The Israelites employed the ox-pulled plow. We read, for example, of the first meeting of the prophets Elisha and Elijah, in which Elijah "found Elisha the son of Shaphat, who was plowing with twelve yoke of oxen in front of him" (1 Kings 19:19). In the early centuries of Israel's settlement, the Hebrews were at a great disadvantage economically and militarily because:

> There was no blacksmith to be found throughout the land of Israel, for the Philistines said, "Lest the Hebrews make themselves swords or spears." But every one of the Israelites went down to the Philistines to sharpen his plowshare, his mattock, his axe, or his sickle, and the charge was two-thirds of a shekel for the plowshares and for the mattocks, and a third of a shekel for sharpening the axes and for setting the goads. (1 Sam. 13:19–21)

Iron plow points have been found in Israelite contexts from as early as the eleventh century B.C. at the sites of Gibeah and Beth-Shemesh.[23]

2. Sowing. The most basic way to scatter seed into the furrowed ground is by hand (see, e.g., Matt. 13:1–9), and this is still practiced today. After the sower scattered the seed, it was common to drive the yoked oxen back over the field to trample the seed deeply into the earth. It was also a common practice to sow the seed as the first step in cultivation, and then plow the seed into the ground afterward.

In ancient Mesopotamia, around 1500 B.C., the seed drill for plowing was invented. It combined the two tasks of plowing and sowing into one step: the plow was worked by an animal pulling, and the plow made furrows in the ground, then seeds in a seed box were poured through a funnel into the furrows. The apparatus was attached to the plow itself. This invention made farming more efficient and faster.

3. Reaping and Gleaning. Grain was harvested in the late spring. The reapers would hold several stalks of grain at a time and then cut off the heads of the grain with a short-handled sickle. "The sickle, which is a much more sophisticated tool than either the hoe or the axe, is composed of a row of

---

22. The evidence for this process derives from three primary sources: written evidence, archaeological evidence, and the present-day farming practices of villages in Israel.

23. Lawrence A. Sinclair, "Gibeah," *EAEHL*, 2:445 (1976).

small, serrated flint blades, inserted into a handle made of wood or bone."[24] The flint sickle was used for thousands of years, and is found in the very earliest stages of human plant gathering.[25] Sometime during the Iron I period in Palestine, the iron sickle began to replace the flint sickle. However, in Israel during this period, due to poverty and the scarcity of metal, the Israelites continued to use flint scythes (cf. 1 Sam. 13:20). By the Iron II period, iron sickles were more common in Israel.

The reapers would then lay the cut grain on the ground, and the gleaners would follow by tying the stalks into bundles. These bundles would then be taken to the threshing floor. For a biblical picture of this process, see Ruth 2.

4. Threshing and Winnowing. After harvesting, crops were brought to a threshing floor, laid down flat on the surface, and then crushed in the process of threshing in order to separate the grain from the stalks.[26] To thresh the grain, the ancient farmer employed heavy sledges. Because the two parts of the cereals were still mixed together, the cultivator then winnowed the grain by tossing the stalks in the air, and the chaff would be blown away while the grain would drop into a pile on the ground. Often the farmer used a winnowing fork in this process (see Isa. 30:24).

Fig. 13.1. Winnowing

24. Gonen, *Grain*, 29.

25. Robert J. Braidwood, *Prehistoric Men*, 8th ed. (Glenview, IL: Scott, Foresman and Company, 1975). On page 110, Braidwood comments, "We know a sickle blade of flint when we see one, because of a strange polish or sheen which seems to develop on the cutting edge when the blade has been used to cut grasses or grain, or perhaps reeds."

26. See the recent study by Jaime L. Waters, *Threshing Floors in Ancient Israel: Their Ritual and Symbolic Significance* (Minneapolis: Fortress Press, 2015).

Threshing floors are difficult to identify archaeologically.[27] One appears to be in evidence at the site of Gezer from the early twelfth century B.C. A large public granary was discovered in strata XIII–XI that had a large plastered surface next to it that perhaps was a threshing floor. Others have purportedly been found at Kh. Abu Masarrah, Kh. 'Almit, and Qibbutz Sasa.[28]

5. Grinding. Grinding of grain for the purpose of making flour or other products was a common activity of everyday life (Isa. 47:1–2; Jer. 25:10). The oldest implement for grinding grain was the quern, which consisted of a large, flat stone on the bottom and a smaller grinding stone for the worker's hand (called a rider). It was a simple process in which the worker would grind the cereals in a forward and backward movement. Querns have been discovered in the earliest tool assemblages in the ancient Near East.[29] They are commonly found throughout the archaeological record of ancient Palestine. The story of the woman killing Abimelech when she "threw an upper millstone on Abimelech's head and crushed his skull" is probably a reference to this agricultural tool. Another variation of the quern was the saddle quern, which was also used for millennia in Palestine. It was composed of a large, concave lower stone (thus the name "saddle") and a cylindrical hand stone.

There was not much development in the nature of grinding stones in antiquity, at least until the Israelite Iron II period. According to Rivka Gonen, an important innovation occurred at that time:

> In the First Temple period (first half of the first millennium B.C.E.), a new kind of quern was invented, in which two sticks were inserted into holes in the upper stone, one in front and one in the back. This allowed two people to operate the mill by pushing the stone to and fro. Now the mill could be enlarged and the output increased. In addition, the grinding surfaces were grooved to facilitate the grinding action and allow the flour to flow freely.[30]

6. Storage. Grain that was not immediately used for everyday foodstuffs was placed in storage.[31] Grain storage was critical to a settled community. First of all, it allowed for short-term preservation of grain from one harvest to the next. Second, it provided for long-term preservation in case of drought, famine, or war. The first form of food storage in ancient Palestine was the

27. Ruth Shahack-Gross, Mor Gafri, and Israel Finkelstein, "Identifying Threshing Floors in the Archaeological Record," *Journal of Field Archaeology* 34 (2009): 171–84.

28. Waters, *Threshing Floors*, 9.

29. Braidwood, *Prehistoric Men*, 128, 131.

30. Gonen, *Grain*, 36.

31. For an extended analysis of grain storage practices during the Iron Age in Israel, see John D. Currid, "Archaeological Investigations into the Grain Storage Practices of Iron Age Palestine" (PhD diss., University of Chicago, 1986).

practice of storing grain and other perishables in subterranean pits. They have been discovered in pre-Neolithic contexts at the site of 'Ain Mallaha. They were found in the floors of houses. They are bell-shaped and are either plastered or stone-lined. During the subsequent Neolithic and Chalcolithic periods, subterranean pits were commonly used to preserve grain. Also, pottery made its appearance in the Neolithic period, and the jar became a common means of grain storage. It was an improvement over pit storage because it allowed for easier handling of the foodstuff, it could be opened and closed with little difficulty, and it was immune to the hazards of pests and moisture.

During the Bronze Age, a crucial development occurred, and that was the appearance of storehouses and large-scale granaries. The earliest such structure is the Beth Yerah granary that dates to about 2500 B.C.[32]

During the Iron Age, there was great advancement in the technique of grain storage. The number of storehouses increased greatly, and the forms and construction of the buildings were much more diversified. New storehouse designs, such as the tripartite pillared, corridor, and four-room styles, were introduced. In addition, large communal silos appeared widely for the first time.

From the time of the united monarchy in Israel, a state storage economy was in existence. The writer of 1 Chronicles reports that King David had warehouses in various towns and villages throughout his empire, and a complicated bureaucracy was organized around the storage system (27:25–30). Solomon erected centralized store cities, in which large granaries collected monthly supplies for the upkeep of the state and the court (1 Kings 4:7–19; 9:19). The kings of the divided monarchy all constructed store cities and storage complexes (e.g., 2 Chron. 17:12–13; 32:27–29). In addition, private and individual storage facilities have been found in many Iron Age sites excavated in Palestine.

AN AGRICULTURAL CALENDAR

In 1908, the excavator at the site of Gezer, R. A. S. Macalister, discovered what has come to be known as the Gezer Calendar. It was written in paleo-Hebrew script and dates to the last half of the tenth century B.C. The inscription records the main agricultural activities according to months in a one-year cycle. It was not an official calendar, but perhaps a schoolboy's text that copied a popular ditty of the time. However, it is helpful in setting down the pattern of everyday agricultural life in Israel. It reads as follows:

---

32. See John D. Currid, "The Beehive Buildings of Ancient Palestine," *BA* 49 (1986): 20–24.

Two months of gathering (harvesting)
Two months of winnowing (scattering)
Two months of spring planting
A month of hoeing flax
A month of reaping barley
A month of reaping and (feasting?)
Two months of pruning
A month of summer fruit
Abijah (the scribe's name = "Yahweh is my father")

Fig. 13.2. Gezer Calendar

KEY TERMS

broad spectrum economy
seed drill
slash/burn agriculture
terracing
tripartite-pillared building

DISCUSSION QUESTIONS

1. Explain why the domestication of plants and animals would have been necessary for the founding of permanent settlements in ancient Palestine.
2. The main settlement of the Israelites in the Land of Promise was in the hill country of Canaan. What agricultural practices did the Israelites employ in order to cultivate this hilly land? What were the primary types of fruits and vegetables that they grew?
3. In the second half of this chapter, we presented the process of grain production in antiquity. How does this differ from the methods and practices of farmers today in the West? How do you think the labor intensity of agriculture in antiquity affected the way people lived?

FOR FURTHER READING

Borowski, Oded. *Agriculture in Iron Age Israel*. Winona Lake, IN: Eisenbrauns, 2009.
Gonen, Rivka. *Grain*. Jerusalem: Shikmona, 1979.
Hopkins, David. *The Highlands of Canaan: Agricultural Life in the Early Iron Age*. Sheffield: Sheffield Academic Press, 1987.
Stager, Lawrence E. "Agriculture." In *Interpreter's Dictionary of the Bible Supplementary Volume*, 11–13. Nashville: Abingdon, 1976.

CHAPTER 14

Water

"The distribution of water, then, unequal as it is, is another factor in heightening the complexity of this land of contrasts."—George Adam Smith[1]

I N ANTIQUITY, WHEN people searched for a place to settle, there were a variety of factors that played into their decision. Perhaps the most important feature of human settlement is access to a permanent water supply. Prior to the invention of huge water systems, cisterns, aqueducts, and other forms of water management, settlements were established in limited regions where perennial water sources existed. The two great civilizations of the ancient Near East, Egypt and Mesopotamia, began with human settlement alongside the rivers of the Nile basin and the Tigris and Euphrates valleys. In Palestine, the site of 'Ubeidiya is perhaps the oldest known human habitation discovered in the area, and it is located less than 2 miles south of the Sea of Galilee on the western side of the Jordan River. It is not in Palestine, but the site of Latamne is older than 'Ubeidiya, and it lies on the banks of the Orontes River in Syria. Such is commonly the case. The point is simply that from the beginning of human settlement, water played an essential and critical role in where people lived.

EARLY FORMS OF WATER MANAGEMENT

The precise date that man began to practice agriculture is uncertain. Some investigators place it very early, sometime before 10,000 B.C.[2] Others, such as Andre Parrot, date the domestication of plants as late as 5500 B.C. during the Neolithic period. The best option is likely between the two, when cultivation appears to be in evidence at the site of Jericho as early as the Pre-

1. George Adam Smith, *The Historical Geography of the Holy Land*, 16th ed. (London: Hodder and Stoughton, 1910), 78.
2. See, e.g., Eric S. Higgs, ed., *Papers in Economic Prehistory: Studies by Members and Associates of the British Academy Major Project in the Early History of Agriculture* (Cambridge: Cambridge University Press, 1972).

Pottery Neolithic period (ca. 8000 B.C.). In the PPNA period, according to the excavator, Kathleen Kenyon, the site covered 10 acres, contained large town defenses, and experienced a large population increase over the previous period. The settlers practiced agriculture, and there is evidence that they grew barley and emmer. The area in which Jericho is located, however, is limited in rainfall and, therefore, other means are necessary to provide water for the crops. Kenyon argues that the settlers developed a system of irrigation, so that much more land could be cultivated. She discovered during this period curved linear structures that were three meters deep, and she argues that they served as water tanks that were used for irrigation. It was irrigation, in her opinion, that enabled Jericho to expand and its population to increase at that time. Kenyon concludes, "It is also possible to assume that the developing agriculture was accompanied by developing irrigation, for the spring in its natural state could not have watered an area large enough for the fully grown town. The organization required to create a system of irrigation could produce the community organization of which the imposing defenses provide evidence."[3]

The next great innovation in water management occurred in the following period, called the Pottery Neolithic. It was at this time that pottery made its first appearance in Palestine. Whether the knowledge of pottery and pottery making came from elsewhere or developed independently in Palestine is a matter of debate.[4] In any event, archaeologists have unearthed specimens of large vessels from this time period, called *pithoi* (sing. *pithos*), which would have been used for storage of liquids and grains. At the site of Wadi Rabah, for example, Jacob Kaplan discovered this type of storage jar along with hole-mouthed jars that were smaller, but also would have been used to store liquids, mostly water and wine, and grain.[5] This was an important development because it allowed for greater accessibility to water, its long-term availability, and an ease of transporting water from one place to another.

In the ensuing Chalcolithic period (4000–3200 B.C.), probably due to some major climatic change, the population of Palestine was centered in more arid areas. Many of the settlements were situated on the banks of wadis (seasonal streams) or brooks. For example, the sites in the Beersheba group, including Abu Mater, Khirbet Beitar, and Safadi, are all located on the banks of the Nahal Beersheba. There is no evidence that these sites employed irrigation, but they depended on underground water supplies. New types and forms of pottery to hold liquids appeared during this period. For instance, the so-called Beersheba churn looked like an imitation of a goat skin, and its purpose was to hold water products.

3. Kathleen Kenyon, "Jericho," *EAEHL*, 2:554 (1976).

4. See the discussion in Ruth Amiran, *Ancient Pottery of the Holy Land* (New Brunswick, NJ: Rutgers University Press, 1970), 17–21.

5. Jacob Kaplan, "Excavations at Wadi Rabah," *IEJ* 8 (1958): 149–60.

The digging of wells was certainly an ancient practice, although we are uncertain when it began. They were particularly important for semino-madic peoples and shepherds who moved their flocks through desert areas. Abraham and Isaac, living during the Middle Bronze II period (2000–1550 B.C.), dug wells wherever they were sojourning (Gen. 21:30; 26:18–22; 26:25).

Cisterns probably first began to be used at the beginning of the Early Bronze Age (3200 B.C.) and became widely utilized during the Middle Bronze Age. A cistern is a reservoir dug in the ground to collect and store rainwater. Two prominent types of cisterns are known from the archaeological record. First, the individual or private cistern was bulb-shaped with a neck wide enough for the man digging it to climb through (see many examples at Tell Ta'anek). Water was often channeled into the cistern by drains from streets and roofs when the cistern was located in a town or village. Joseph was likely imprisoned by his brothers in this type of cistern (Gen. 37:24).

During the Iron I period, in which the Israelites were in the process of settling the highlands of the land of Canaan, cisterns were a common feature of their towns and villages. For example, at the twelfth through eleventh century B.C. site of Khirbet Raddana, located in the hill country 10 miles north of Jerusalem, the excavator, Joseph A. Callaway, discovered a series of Israelite pillared houses.[6] Under the floors of the houses, cisterns were found that had been cut into the bedrock, and they were bell-shaped and lined with plaster. These cisterns provided a ready source of water for the inhabitants, and this technology perhaps helped to facilitate the settling of the highland areas of Canaan.

The second type of cistern is large and communal. An early example comes from the site of Arad, occupied during the Early Bronze period (ca. twenty-ninth through twenty-seventh centuries B.C.). The site is shaped like a saddle, and, as the excavator, Yohanan Aharoni, explains, there is in the lowest place in the site "an artificial depression, the remnant of a big water cistern in which water could be collected from the entire town area." Also, "a large public pool was discovered recently in the excavations at Ai. Additional cisterns for catching rainwater were surely hewn out of the limestone rock within the town and outside of it."[7] A late example from the Roman period comes from the site of Masada, next to the Dead Sea. Fresh water was criti-cal to the survival of a settlement in this arid area. The builders constructed a dam across a wadi that runs north of the site to trap the seasonal flow of water, and they also built an aqueduct to bring it to Masada. Twelve large cisterns were uncovered at the site that were cut from bedrock and lined

6. For a discussion of these discoveries, see Lawrence E. Stager, "The Archaeology of the Family in Ancient Israel," *BASOR* 260 (1985): 1–36.

7. Yohanan Aharoni, *The Archaeology of the Land of Israel* (Philadelphia: Westminster Press, 1978), 61.

with plaster to prevent seepage. A typical cistern at Masada could hold up to 40,000 cubic yards of water.

MAJOR WATER SYSTEMS OF THE ISRAELITES

Many Israelite settlements were constructed near natural water sources, but often these sources were outside of the city walls. In order to have access to good supplies of fresh water, the Israelites performed some remarkable engineering feats at a number of sites. These building projects were particularly important in times of war, when an enemy would lay siege to a city and attempt to subdue it through want of food and water. Such water systems, however, often proved to be a weakness in the defense of a city and, therefore, the engineers had to take that deficiency into account when building them.

The Iron Age biblical site of Gibeon (el-Jib) is located in the highlands of Judea, about 5.5 miles north of Jerusalem. In 1838, Edward Robinson correctly identified the site, and in the late 1800s the Iron Age water system was initially investigated. James Pritchard explains:

> In 1889 the rock-cut tunnel at the back of the cave was entered and its lower course was measured by a Russian who is known only by the name "Mr. Risky." A plan and a section of as much of the installation as the Russian could actually explore were published the following year by Barauth C. Schick, a well-known German resident of Jerusalem, in the *Quarterly Statement of the Palestine Exploration Fund*.[8]

Major excavations took place at Gibeon between 1956 and 1962 under the direction of Pritchard. He found that there were two water systems constructed during the Iron Age, which provided water to settlers within the walled city. The first was a cylindrical cutting into bedrock within the confines of the city that measured about 37 feet in diameter and about 35 feet deep. A spiral staircase goes further down into a tunnel that provides access to a kidney-shaped water chamber fed by the natural water table. Consequently, the shaft burrows about 80 feet below the level of the city. Pritchard estimates that about 3,000 tons of limestone was quarried and removed during the original construction. The exact date of the system's construction is uncertain, but it was likely in the ninth century B.C. Pritchard suggests that this "may have been the 'pool of Gibeon' mentioned in II Samuel 2:13," where Abner and his men fought with Joab and his forces.[9]

---

8. James B. Pritchard, *Gibeon: Where the Sun Stood Still* (Princeton, NJ: Princeton University Press, 1962), 54.

9. James B. Pritchard, "Gibeon," in *Encyclopedia of Archaeological Excavations in the Holy Land*, ed. Michael Avi-Yonah (Englewood Cliffs, NJ: Prentice-Hall, 1976), 2:447.

The second water system was built later in the Iron Age. It consists of a stepped tunnel, beginning inside the city walls and sloping to a spring outside the walls. The stepped tunnel, about 130 feet in length, leads into a water chamber or cistern room that is fed from a spring through a feeder tunnel. There is an entrance to the chamber from the outside, but it could have been easily camouflaged in time of siege warfare.

During the period of the divided monarchy in Israel, Megiddo served as a royal center under the kingship of Ahab. A major level of occupation has been revealed through excavation of this time (stratum IVA). It contained a massive 10-foot-wide city wall with a large outer and inner gate system. Elaborate palaces and other public buildings, such as the tripartite pillared structures identified by the original excavators as stables, dominate the interior of the city.[10] The major water supply for the city was a tunnel system built by Ahab that brought access to a spring outside the city walls. First, a shaft, about 115 feet long, was cut into bedrock within the city. A stairway was then cut along the sides of the shaft for people to ascend and descend. At the bottom of the shaft, the engineers cut a horizontal tunnel, about 200 feet long, that reached the spring outside the city. Apparently two teams cut this tunnel, one crew proceeding from each end, as engineers plotted a straight line between them from above.

Another ninth-century B.C. Israelite water system was discovered at Hazor under the direction of Yigael Yadin in 1968.[11] It was built during the occupation of stratum VIII of the site, probably by King Ahab of the northern kingdom. The complex had three parts to it: an entrance building at ground level led to a vertical shaft and then to a sloping tunnel. According to the excavators, the shaft was cut through the strata of the mound to a depth of 98.5 feet. The sloping tunnel continues another 82 feet or so, and its slope descends about 33 feet. At the bottom of the tunnel is a pool that would have been fed by the water below the water table in the area.

Charles Warren discovered the most famous and elaborate water system of the Israelites in Jerusalem in 1867. The only major source of water for Jerusalem in antiquity was the Gihon Spring, which is located in the Kidron Valley to the east of the City of David on the Ophel. It lay outside the walls of the ancient city. In antiquity, three water systems, fed by the Gihon Spring, were constructed to bring the water inside the city walls for the purposes of efficient water management and as a deterrent against siege warfare. The three systems were planned and built at different times, but were used in conjunction with one another during the Israelite period to serve as the city's main water supply.

10. See Robert S. Lamon and Geoffrey M. Shipton, *Megiddo I*, OIP 42 (Chicago: University of Chicago Press, 1939).

11. Yigael Yadin, *Hazor: Schweich Lectures* (Oxford: Oxford University Press, 1972).

Fig. 14.1. Water System, Iron II, Hazor

Warren's initial discovery was a system located on the eastern slope of the Ophel, and it consists of an underground, rock-hewn tunnel that begins within the city walls. The tunnel slopes down steeply and proceeds under the city walls. It has a stairway cut into the rock. The length of the tunnel is about 135 feet, and it descends about 43 feet. At its end is a vertical shaft that is about 7 feet wide, which plunges to a depth of about 41 feet. At the bottom of the shaft are the waters of Gihon. To get water, someone would perhaps descend to the end of the tunnel and then drop a bucket by rope to retrieve water from the spring.

The date when "Warren's shaft" was built has been a matter of debate. A dominant opinion until recently has been that the entire system "should probably be dated to the period of the Divided Monarchy—sometime before the time of Hezekiah, who made use of the lower horizontal gallery to begin his own tunnel."[12] This position argues against some of the earlier interpreters, who claimed this was the "water shaft" that David's men went up and surprised the defenders of the city of Jebus/Jerusalem (2 Sam. 5:8). Yohanan Aharoni concludes that this "conjecture . . . has no factual basis."[13] Amihai Mazar goes so far as to say that this identification was one of the "major

12. Amihai Mazar, *Archaeology of the Land of the Bible* (New York: Doubleday, 1990), 480–81.
13. Aharoni, *Archaeology of the Land of Israel*, 234.

mistakes . . . made in the interpretation of archaeological discoveries in Palestine."[14]

However, recent excavations near the Gihon Spring have uncovered remains of a water system from a much earlier time than the kings of Israel.[15] The archaeologists uncovered two large towers bracketing a deep, rock-hewn pool. They believe that part of Warren's shaft may have fed that pool. This system, according to the investigators, dates to the early second millennium B.C., and thus would have been part of the Jebusite/Canaanite city of Jerusalem prior to Israel's capture of it in the early tenth century B.C. Consequently, the interpretation that the breach of the water system by David's men took place in the area of the Gihon Spring comes back into play as a possible historical reality.

A second water project related to the Gihon Spring is the Siloam channel. It is an aqueduct-canal that emerges from the Gihon Spring and travels south along the eastern slope of the City of David for about 1300 feet, where it empties into a large reservoir at the bottom of the Tyropoeon Valley. Openings regularly appear in the canal, and these allowed water to flow out and irrigate fields along the Kidron Valley. This canal has been identified with the "waters of Shiloah that flow gently" (Isa. 8:6) during the reign of King Ahaz of Judah (732–716 B.C.).

The next Judean king was Hezekiah (716–687 B.C.), and he stopped up the Siloam canal from providing water for Jerusalem. Second Chronicles 32:2–3 says, "And when Hezekiah saw that Sennacherib had come and intended to fight against Jerusalem, he planned with his officers and his mighty men to stop the water of the springs that were outside the city; and they helped him." In its place, he built what has come to be known as Hezekiah's Tunnel,

Fig. 14.2. Siloam Inscription

14. Mazar, *Archaeology of the Land of the Bible*, 31.

15. Ronny Reich, *Excavating the City of David* (Jerusalem: Israel Exploration Society and Biblical Archaeology Society, 2011).

which was hewn out of the rock beneath the City of David. The tunnel is about 1,750 feet long and it gently slopes from the Gihon Spring into the Pool of Siloam inside the city walls. Two teams digging toward each other, one from the spring and the other from the pool, cut Hezekiah's Tunnel. "It was not chiseled in a straight line but was serpentine, due to the frequent shift in terrain. The two teams also made adjustments as they drew near to each other and heard the picks of the other team. Approximately 20 feet from the Siloam pool, an inscription was discovered that describes the last moments of the meeting of the two cutting teams."[16] It says:

> [. . . when] (the tunnel) was driven through. And this was the way in which it was cut through: While [. . .] (were) still [. . .] axe(s), each man toward his fellow, and while there were still three cubits to be cut through, [there was heard] the voice of a man calling to his fellow, for there was *an overlap* in the rock on the right [and on the left]. And when the tunnel was driven through, the quarrymen hewed (the rock), each man toward his fellow, axe against axe; and the water flowed from the spring toward the reservoir for 1,200 cubits, and the height of the rock above the head(s) of the quarrymen was 100 cubits.[17]

The Bible mentions this project as one of the great achievements of Hezekiah: "The rest of the deeds of Hezekiah and all his might and how he made the pool and the conduit and brought water into the city, are they not written in the Book of the Chronicles of the Kings of Judah?" (2 Kings 20:20).

Other water systems have been discovered at tells, but the dating of their construction is uncertain. For example, excavators at Gezer found waterworks at the site that may have been built during the divided monarchy (although some suggest a date during the Late Bronze Age, which would make it a Canaanite structure). It consists of a round shaft with a flight of steps, about 23 feet deep, which leads to a sloping tunnel that descends another 148 feet or so. The tunnel ends in a large cavern, where the water table has been reached. Another one was unearthed at the site of Ibleam (Kh. Belameh), which may date to the Iron Age, although clear-cut dating evidence is lacking. Although the waterworks have not been completely excavated, its general design is clear: a sloping tunnel that begins inside the city walls on top of the tell descends at least 380 feet to a spring outside the city.[18]

A unique water system has been discovered at the site of Tel Beersheba that dates to the Israelite Iron II period. In the northeast quadrant of the site,

16. John D. Currid, "Ten Most Significant Discoveries in the Field of Archaeology," in *Crossway ESV Archaeology Bible*, eds. John D. Currid and David Chapman (Wheaton, IL: Crossway, 2017), xxi–xxii.

17. William F. Albright, "The Siloam Inscription," *ANET*, 321.

18. Gerrit van der Kooij and Hamdan Taha, *The Water Tunnel System at Khirbet Bal'ama* (Ramallah: Khirbet Bal'ama Archaeological Project, 2008).

the excavators unearthed a broad stairway descending to a pool or chamber cut deeply into the natural rock. It is not, however, a shaft designed to tap into the groundwater. Rather, "it would seem that this installation served to gather rainwater that had been channeled to subterranean cisterns—a project involving considerable moving of earth and stone."[19] This large water receptacle would have assured a regular water supply for the city during times of protracted siege. The archaeologists also discovered that below the pavement of the city streets there were channels by which water was conveyed from the roofs and walls of houses to central cisterns in the city.

KEY TERMS

cistern
Hezekiah's Tunnel
wadi
Warren's Shaft

DISCUSSION QUESTIONS

1. Why was access to a permanent water supply perhaps the most fundamental reason that people settled where they did in ancient Palestine?
2. Why was the development of pottery so important for water management in an ancient society?
3. According to 2 Samuel 5:8, David commanded his soldiers to "get up the water shaft to attack" the Jebusites in Jerusalem. What is it about water systems that make them vulnerable to enemy attack? If you were an ancient engineer, how would you conceal an exposed water system?

FOR FURTHER READING

Lamon, R. S. *The Megiddo Water System*. Chicago: OIP, 1935.
Macalister, R. A. S. *The Excavations of Gezer 1902–1905 and 1907–1909*. London: John Murray, 1912.
Pritchard, James B. *Gibeon: Where the Sun Stood Still*. Princeton: Princeton University Press, 1962.
Reich, Ronny. *Excavating the City of David*. Jerusalem: IES and BAS, 2011.

---

19. Yohanan Aharoni, "Tel Beersheba," *EAEHL*, 1:165 (1975).

CHAPTER 15

Architecture

"Architecture starts when you carefully put two bricks together.
There it begins."—Ludwig Mies van der Rohe

W HAT ARE THE factors relevant in a society's construction of its buildings? What affects the design and form of a culture's architecture? There are indeed many variables. For example, medieval churches commonly contain an apse with an altar that is pointed east. The reason for this orientation is certainly religious; the people are thus worshiping and praying toward Jerusalem, and it may reflect the belief that in his second coming Christ will come from the east (Matt. 24:27). Perhaps the dominant factor in building construction is the availability of building materials. For instance, in the southwestern United States, the principal construction material has always been adobe (unburnt, sun-dried brick) because of its abundance and the lack of other building materials, such as wood. While other factors, such as climate, geography, religion, and tradition play a significant role, access to building materials stands at the top of the list.

CONSTRUCTION MATERIALS

Mud-brick. One of the most common materials used in building in ancient Palestine was mud-brick, and it is often used in the present day. Normally, it consisted of natural clay that was mixed with straw for holding power (called *temper*). The builder would place the tempered mud into a mold or frame, and then let it harden in the sun. Some of the bricks appeared to have been fired in some type of oven in order to make them fireproof.

Mud-brick structures have been discovered as early as the Pre-Pottery Neolithic A period at the site of Jericho (eighth millennium B.C.). Circular houses/huts were found there that were made of "hog-backed" bricks: they are called that because they had a flat base and a curved upper surface. In the following period, Pre-Pottery Neolithic B (ca. 7000 B.C.), mud-bricks were still in use, but their shape had changed. They were now cigar-shaped,

with thumb indentations that perhaps served to hold mortar more firmly.
For example, at the site of Munhata, about 15 km south of the Sea of Galilee,
archaeologists discovered a rectangular-shaped house with mud-brick walls
and plastered floors that measured about 15 square meters.

Fig. 15.1. Mud-Brick Construction, Iron II, Beersheba

In the Early Bronze Age (ca. 3200–2200 B.C.), mud-bricks took on rectangular and square forms that became standardized for the remaining history
of Palestine. These brick shapes dominated the architecture of the Middle
and Late Bronze Ages in Palestine. In fact, both forms of bricks, rectangular
and square, appear in the same wall, even in the same course, at Tell Beit
Mirsim during the Middle Bronze Age.

Stone. Many structures were built with stone from the earliest times.
Good building stone was freely available in most parts of Palestine, particularly in the form of limestone and basalt.[1] In fact, Palestine could be described
as a land flowing with rocks and stones! By far, the greatest amount of stone
construction in ancient Palestine was *rubble masonry*. This standard wall
construction, especially during the Middle Bronze Age, consisted of two faces
of sizeable field stones with the interior made up of smaller stones and earth.

During the Late Bronze Age, stone construction became more monu-

1. Yigal Shiloh and Aharon Horowitz, "Ashlar Quarries of the Iron Age in the Hill Country of Israel,"
BASOR 217 (1975): 46.

mental. Some large and imposing public buildings are known from this period: the Migdol Temple and East Gate at Shechem, the Orthostat Temple and K Gate at Hazor, and the Migdol Temple and VIII (South) Gate at Megiddo. The building technique was also better than the mere coursed random rubble of the Middle Bronze Age—some of these buildings were constructed with squared blocks that were set into an orderly bond. In addition, it is likely that the technique of using solid piers in a wall in order to bear some of the load of the structures first appeared at this time. That method became standard in Iron Age (Israelite) construction.

Fig. 15.2. Field Stone Construction, Iron II, Arad

One of the characteristic building methods of the Iron Age (Israelite) was ashlar masonry. This heavily dressed stone was often arranged in header-stretcher fashion. That is, courses of stones whose shorter ends were exposed (headers) alternated with courses whose longer ends were exposed (stretchers).

Combination. In Bronze Age construction, the lower part of the wall was often stronger or more solid than the upper part of the wall. Lower areas were subject to more wear and tear because of weight, activity, and thoroughfare. To offset these problems, builders sometimes constructed walls with a stone base and mud-brick layers on top of it. Good examples of this combination were the Middle Bronze II East Gate at Shechem and the Middle-Late Bronze Age Orthostat Temple at Hazor.

Finish. Invariably, mud-brick walls of the Bronze and Iron Ages were plastered. Often mud plaster was used with a good amount of sand mixed in. Lime plaster was also used. Plastering of walls certainly had an aesthetic appeal, but that was not its main purpose. Its primary purpose was to guard the walls from damage, especially that caused by inclement weather.

Wood. Wood remains from the Bronze and Iron Ages are not rare. According to Nili Liphschitz and Gideon Biger, between the years 1975 and 1995, "more than 9,000 wood remains have been collected from archaeological excavations at some 150 sites throughout Palestine, from Mt. Hermon in the north to the Arava and Sinai desert, from strata dating to various periods."[2] Wood was used in construction from the Early Bronze Age down through the Iron Age, especially for monumental buildings, such as temples, gates, palaces, and storehouses. "Such buildings demanded long logs for roofs, as well as timber for inside the buildings: doors, wall-posts, wall-cupboards, shelves, etc."[3] Examples are abundant: At Byblos during the Early Bronze Age, massive timber-structured houses and temples have been discovered. At Middle Bronze Gibeon, carbonized remains of a roof support have been found.[4]

There were other types of building construction. I have simply reviewed the more important and common ones in ancient Palestine. It should be noted that building materials are not a good indicator of chronology. Many of the materials employed by ancient builders were used over a long span of time and over a large geographical area. One therefore needs to be wary of assigning a particular material or construction technique to a specific time period. It is much more dependable to use pottery to resolve chronological issues.

As already indicated, numerous factors influenced how the ancients designed and constructed their buildings, including space, functionality, climate, geography, and customs. We will not take time to consider each one of these, but the reader ought to examine the relevant literature.[5]

CONSTRUCTION FORM AND DESIGN

The Greek philosopher Heraclitus famously commented that "everything changes and nothing stands still." That is a useful adage to describe the history of architecture in ancient Palestine. Our aim in this section is to examine the evolving variations in building form from the very earliest times down to the Israelite Iron Age. Ancient architecture that has been

2. Nili Liphschitz and Gideon Biger, "The Timber Trade in Ancient Palestine," *TA* 22 (1995): 121.

3. Liphschitz and Biger, "The Timber Trade in Ancient Palestine," 121.

4. James B. Pritchard, *Gibeon: Where the Sun Stood Still* (Princeton, NJ: Princeton University Press, 1962), 154.

5. A most helpful book on this topic is Amos Rapoport, *House Form and Culture* (Englewood Cliffs, NJ: Prentice-Hall, 1969).

revealed through excavation is generally divided into two major categories: buildings and fortifications. The first category includes many different types of man-made structures, which fall into three groups: domestic, public, and sacred buildings. The second major category, fortifications, includes defensive structures such as a gate, an outer wall system, a revetment wall, a moat, and a glacis.[6]

Neolithic Period (8000–4000 B.C.)

Architecture appeared in ancient Palestine prior to the Neolithic period, but it was quite primitive. For example, at the Natufian site of Ain Mallaha, located on the edge of Lake Huleh, about 16 miles north of the Sea of Galilee, the archaeologist Jean Perrot discovered a large domestic quarter (ca. 10,000 B.C.). The houses were circular structures with subterranean floors and stone walls. Wooden posts would have held up roofs that probably consisted of light timber or animal hides. The walls of the houses were decorated; for instance, the first house had stone walls that were decorated with lime coating beneath red paint. These houses were hut-like, but they reflect an early stage of house building. Substantial architecture does not begin to appear in the archaeological record in Palestine until the PPNA period.

Domestic architecture. Houses from the earliest phase of the Neolithic Period (PPNA) did not differ all that much from the previous Natufian age. At the site of Jericho, for example, the houses were huts made of hog-backed bricks with subterranean floors of camp mud. Some of them had postholes to support roofs made of wood. In the subsequent PPNB period, the design and form of housing changed. At Jericho, houses were now rectangular, and they were built with cigar-shaped bricks with thumb indentations (for securing mortar). The walls were plastered, and they were highly burnished and painted with red ochre. Floors were made with hard limestone plaster. The houses were built around courtyards, and many of the courtyards contained hearths for cooking. Similar structures have been found at the site of Abu Gosh from the same period. The following PN period was a dark age, in which architectural remains are scarce and dating sequences are difficult to define. A number of sites that had been occupied in the PPN period were now unoccupied or sparsely populated, such as Jericho and Abu Gosh. In fact, people at Jericho and Hazorea during this time lived in sunken, shallow pit dwellings. It is likely that a shift took place from sedentarism back to pastoralism.

Sacred architecture. It is almost an adage to say that the minute an

6. A glacis may be defined as a long fortification slope running from the bottom of a mound to the defensive wall on the top. It was usually made of layers of rubble, sometimes plastered, that encircled the entire mound. It acted much like a girdle, and it served to prevent erosion and thus helped to hold the mound together.

archaeologist puts a shovel in the ground, he or she finds a temple. That of course is an overstatement, but it does reflect the history of excavation, in which building after building has been identified as a religious structure by mere speculation. For the Neolithic period, that is not a problem, because religious structures were few and far between, if any existed at all. In the broader region of the Levant, there may have been some shrine architecture. For example, James Mellaart believed that some of the Neolithic houses at Catal Huyuk in modern-day Turkey were "so decorated as shrines and the area so far exposed as a priestly quarter."[7] But, truthfully, that reconstruction is uncertain and speculative.

Public Architecture. Some buildings appeared in the PPN period that perhaps served a communal, public purpose. For instance, at the site of Beidha in Transjordan, a few large, centrally located structures were discovered that appear to be specialized workshops for particular crafts at the site. These public buildings date to the PPNB period, about 7000 B.C. A sacred precinct with a temple was excavated from the same time period just east of the main settlement.[8] Another large structure, filled with stone tools for some type of public craft, was also found at Nahal Oren. The date of this building was somewhat earlier than the Beidha buildings, probably originating in the very late PPNA period. This initial appearance of public, communal architecture in the archaeological record coincides with the domestication of plants and animals that occurred during the Neolithic period. Food control and production were major reasons that people began to live in year-round settlements, and that led to the building of civic structures.

Fortifications. Archaeologists discovered a thriving settlement at the site of Jericho during the earliest times of the Neolithic (PPNA). It was the largest site known from the time, covering 10 acres of ground. On the west side of the mound, the diggers uncovered a series of protective walls that stood at a height of almost 15 feet and were 5 feet wide; they were constructed partially of large field stones. On the outside of the walls was a fosse or moat that had been dug into the rock, and it measured 10 feet wide. Inside the walls was a massive, round tower that was 32 feet high and had a base diameter of 42 feet. A passage with 22 steps led up to the top of the tower from the inside. The tower was constructed prior to the city walls and, therefore, was perhaps a freestanding watchtower. The archaeologist of Jericho, Kathleen Kenyon, concluded that this was a fortification system, and so declared Jericho to be the earliest known urban community.[9] Amihai Mazar correctly concludes,

7. Cited by Robert J. Braidwood, *Prehistoric Men*, 8th ed. (Glenview, IL: Scott, Foresman and Company, 1975), 137.

8. Brian F. Byrd, *Early Village Life at Beidha, Jordan: Neolithic Spatial Organization and Vernacular Architecture* (Oxford: Oxford University Press, 2005).

9. Not all agree. Ofer Bar-Yosef argues that the massive walls at the site were to protect the site from

"The massive structures at Jericho reflect the existence of social organization and central authority which could recruit, for the first time in human history, the necessary means and manpower for such building operations."[10]

Chalcolithic Period (4000–3200 B.C.)

The primary areas of settlement during the Chalcolithic period were in the Negev, the Jordan Valley, and the Transjordanian Plateau. The occupation was more intense in the semiarid regions of the land rather than the more fertile areas of central and northern Palestine. The reason for this shift is uncertain, although a likely culprit was some type of major climate change in the area. The population, however, continued to live in villages, and these settlements were much larger than those at the end of the Neolithic period.

Domestic architecture. In the region of Beersheba in the northern Negev, Chalcolithic settlers constructed underground villages (e.g., Tell Abu Matar). They carved out clusters of subterranean dwellings, including anywhere from five to seven rooms, which were connected by underground galleries. The houses were oval in design, and some of them had paved floors. The nature of these dwellings reflected how the settlers adapted to the semiarid Negev. In the last phase of the Chalcolithic period at Tell Abu Matar, the inhabitants constructed rectangular stone houses that were built entirely on the surface of the site. These so-called broad-room houses have been found at many other Chalcolithic sites, such as at Shiqmim and Teleilat Ghassul. The broad-room house was the common form and design employed by the Chalcolithic settlers, and the subterranean complexes were unique.

Sacred architecture. Archaeologists have found what they consider to be temple structures at the Chalcolithic site of Teleilat Ghassul.[11] One temple in Area E consisted of two broad-rooms with a circular installation (an altar?), and it was surrounded by a *temenos* (sacred precinct) wall. These buildings contained famous wall paintings, such as the eight-pointed Star of Ghassul, which combined geometric forms with imaginary creatures. The design of this temple and the pottery found within it are similar to a temple found at the site of Ein Gedi near the Dead Sea.

A sacred area was discovered at Ein Gedi on a terrace overlooking Nahal David, which flows into the Dead Sea. It contained a long-roomed shrine surrounded by a *temenos* wall. Entrance to the complex was accessed through a double-doored gateway that led to a courtyard in front of the temple.

---

the natural elements, such as silt coming from a nearby wadi. It thus was more or less like a modern levee. See Ofer Bar-Yosef, Avner Goren, and A. Nigel Goring-Morris, "Netiv-Hagdud: A 'Sultanian' Mound in the Lower Jordan Valley," *Paleorient* 6 (1980): 201–6.

10. Amihai Mazar, *Archaeology of the Land of the Bible* (New York: Doubleday, 1990), 42.

11. Milena Gosic, "Temples in the Ghassulian Culture: Terminology and Social Implications," *Issues in Ethnology and Anthropology* 11 (2016): 869–93.

The temple itself was broad-room, and it was nearly empty of finds. David Ussishkin has argued that another find in the area, called "The Cave of the Treasure," may, in fact, be the missing artifacts of the Ein Gedi temple.[12] It may be that priests hid this hoard of cultic objects in a remote cave when the temple was no longer in use.

Recent work at the site of Gilat has uncovered another Chalcolithic sanctuary.[13] Few other public buildings are known from the Chalcolithic period. Thus, Mazar rightly concludes that "it would appear that the religious institutions played a leading role in the social and economic life of the time."[14]

Public architecture and fortifications. Very few, if any, public buildings have been found from the Chalcolithic period. The so-called "corporate" buildings at Shiqmim may prove to be an exception to this statement. No fortifications have been uncovered, either.

Early Bronze Age (3200–2200 B.C.)[15]

Domestic architecture. The Early Bronze Age was the first real period of urbanization in Palestine, and it was then that tells began to appear on a wide scale. In the early stage of this period, round-shaped houses were common. However, for most of the remainder of the time, the principal form was the broad-room house that continued the tradition of the Chalcolithic house design. It had an entrance in one of the long walls, benches along the inside walls, and a central post to hold up a roof (probably made of sticks). Many of these had courtyards at the front of the property. Fine examples of this style can be seen at the Early Bronze site of Arad in the Negev.

Sacred architecture. There was a wide diversity of temple architecture during this period. At the site of Megiddo, for instance, two broad-room sanctuaries were discovered from the Early Bronze II period: they were attached to and flanked an altar, and the whole complex was surrounded by a wall. In the following EB III period, a series of sacred shrines called megaron temples were found, each with an antechamber. In Area T at Arad, two structures bound by a common wall have been named the Twin Temples. One of the rooms contained a raised platform (*bamah*) and a stone-lined basin, both of which were probably used for cultic purposes. A monumental temple with a surrounding *temenos* wall has been found on the acropolis of Ai.

Public architecture. Several palaces have been uncovered from this period,

---

12. David Ussishkin, "The 'Ghassulian' Temple in Ein Gedi and the Origin of the Hoard from Nahal Mishmor," *BA* 34 (1971): 23–39.

13. See Thomas E. Levy, ed., *Archaeology, Anthropology and Cult: The Sanctuary at Gilat, Israel* (New York: Routledge, 2016).

14. Mazar, *Archaeology of the Land of the Bible*, 68.

15. From this point on, the material is deeply dependent on my work *Doing Archaeology in the Land of the Bible* (Grand Rapids: Baker, 1999), 90–98.

and the most notable was the elaborate Palace 3177 at Megiddo. An unusual building design for this time was the charnel house, examples of which have been found at Bab edh Dhra and Megiddo. They served as repositories for the bones of secondary burials. Their form was similar to the broad-room domestic residence that was so common. There were, however, a few that had a circular configuration.

Another unusual structure was the circular, aboveground granary. Found in clusters at Arad and Khirbet Kerak, they were shaped like beehives and measured anywhere from 12 to 24 feet in diameter. Presumably workers poured grain in at the top of the beehive through a trap door, and the grain was extracted at the bottom through a similar trap door. Examples of this type of building are known from ancient Egypt.[16]

Fortifications. Early Bronze Age defensive systems were larger and stronger than any previous fortifications. A prime example can be seen at the site of Arad in the northern Negev. The outer wall of the settlement, which enclosed the entire site of 22 acres, was about 8 feet thick and extended for two-thirds of a mile. Every 60 to 80 feet, depending on the contours of the site, a semicircular bastion/tower was built into the outer wall. These towers measured 10 to 12 feet in diameter, and they extended away from the city wall. One entered the tower through an entrance in the city wall. Entrance into the city was gained through postern gates that measured no more than 3 to 4 feet wide.

There was a continuity of design and form of buildings throughout Palestine during the Early Bronze Age. The glacis, a man-made sloping revetment used to protect the base of a tell's outer fortification wall, probably made its first appearance in Palestine at this time.

Middle Bronze Age (2200–1550 B.C.)

The transition from the Early Bronze Age to the Middle Bronze Age was quite pronounced. The main regions of settlement now shifted to the more arid confines, in particular the central Negev and the Sinai. In the early parts of the Middle Bronze Age, buildings were smaller and more meager than in the Early Bronze Age, and that demonstrates the stark transition of the time. Not until the second half of the Middle Bronze Age did a highly developed architectural tradition emerge.[17]

Domestic architecture. Instead of the common broad-room house of the Early Bronze Age, the domiciles of the early centuries of the Middle Bronze

16. See the discussion in John D. Currid, "The Beehive Granaries of Ancient Palestine," *ZDPV* 101 (1985): 151–64; Currid, "The Beehive Buildings of Ancient Palestine," *BA* 49 (1986): 20–24.

17. Michelle Daviau, *Houses and Their Furnishings in Bronze Age Palestine: Domestic Activity Areas and Artifact Distribution in the Middle and Late Bronze Ages* (Sheffield: JSOT, 1993).

Age were comparatively slight. They consisted of a single rounded chamber, very small, with a stone pillar at the center to hold up a roof. Partway through the period, house form changed, and the dwellings now became multiroom complexes built around a central hall or courtyard. Many of these structures also had a second story.

Sacred architecture. Temples built in the broad-room style of the Early Bronze Age continued into the Middle Bronze Age. Examples of this design can be seen at the sites of Hazor (Area A) and Ebla (in Syria).[18] A new temple architectural form appeared during this period, as well. The so-called Migdol temple design consisted of monumental square or rectangular structures with two massive towers at the entrance. Eminent examples of this temple form and design have been unearthed at the sites of Megiddo and Shechem.

Public architecture. Town planning became more defined and precise in the Middle Bronze Age. George R. H. Wright comments, "It may be hazarded that as a minimum there was a continuous way around the periphery of the tell and that each sector, quarter or division was served by at least one street offering direct access to the peripheral way. . . . Within the terms of its layout the significant difference from the EB period in the over-all aspect of the city was that in this later period the towns were much more densely occupied and thus building development was more closely packed together."[19] Within this more defined town plan, several palatial structures have been uncovered through excavation. In the context of Palestine, these buildings were large architectural complexes. For example, one of the palaces at Megiddo contained two courts and at least ten subsidiary rooms.

Fortifications. The defensive systems of tells became quite elaborate and large during the Middle Bronze II period. Many of the cities now had large, solid outer walls with monumental, multichambered gateways. At Gezer during the seventeenth century B.C., for instance, a 12-foot-wide city wall surrounded the city. The main entrance into the settlement was through two huge mud-brick towers that flanked the roadway. At the base of the outside city wall was a glacis, which was plastered and sloped to the foot of the tell. At Tel Dan, a fully preserved vaulted, mud-brick gate was discovered from the nineteenth through eighteenth centuries B.C. This arched gate was an improvement over previous forms, which were flat and made largely of timbers, and thus could be more easily destroyed. The gateway was the most vulnerable spot in a city's fortifications and had to be protected. The Tel Dan gate was also secured by a pavement of stones that led up to it. That design hindered access to the gate by chariots, battering rams, and other vehicles

18. Mazar, *Archaeology of the Land of the Bible*, 212.
19. G. R. H. Wright, *Ancient Building in South Syria and Palestine*, 2 vols. (Leiden: Brill, 1985), 1:55.

of war. At the base of the outer wall at Tel Dan was a glacis, and the arched gateway was joined to it.

The glacis was widely used during the Middle Bronze Age. Hazor, for instance, was the largest mound in Palestine at this time (180–200 acres), and it had one glacis (sloping revetment) surrounding the lower city and another one around the upper city (acropolis). Moats were also employed for the first time. At both Acco and Achzib, a moat and a glacis were used together.

Late Bronze Age (1550–1200 B.C.)

There does not appear to have been a break in population between the Middle Bronze and Late Bronze Ages. There was, however, a decline in the number of sites that were occupied. Many of them seem to have simply been abandoned, and Egyptian raids into Palestine perhaps destroyed some. By the second half of the Late Bronze period, some of these sites, like Jericho and Tell Beit Mirsim, were resettled. Because of the population continuity between the two periods, the architectural forms and designs remained the same or were similar.

Domestic architecture. House form in the Late Bronze Age reflected the continuity with the Middle Bronze Age. The most common style consisted of a central courtyard surrounded on several sides by rooms of varying sizes. This house design was first seen during the Middle Bronze period, and now it dominated the Late Bronze Age. Large patrician homes have been unearthed at Megiddo, Taanach, and Aphek, and they also consisted of a central court-yard encircled by good-sized rooms and hallways.[20]

Sacred architecture. Not surprisingly, there appears to have been a fundamental uniformity between the temple architecture of the Late Bronze Age and the preceding period. Some of the major temple structures of the later period were first built during the Middle Bronze period and then rebuilt or renovated in the Late Bronze period. Important temples at Megiddo (Tower Temple) and Hazor (Temple H) underwent this process. The Tower Temple at Megiddo was first constructed during the Middle Bronze II period, and then had a continuous use through renovation until the beginning of the Iron Age (ca. 1200 B.C.). The basic design of this type of temple was a monumental broad-room that was entered from a porch into a main hallway. The inner holy place was located in the main hallway opposite the entrance.

Other temple plans were also used from this period. For example, at the city of Lachish, the so-called Fosse Temple was built inside the moat fortification of the earlier Middle Bronze city. They had a bent entrance that

---

20. Mazar, *Archaeology of the Land of the Bible*, 246.

was located near one of the long walls, and this gave access to the main hall that contained an altar and benches. The ceiling was held up by a series of wooden supports on which wooden beams would have been diagonally laid.

Fig. 15.3. Four-Room House, Iron II, Beersheba

Public architecture. Perhaps the most notable structure during this period was a palace discovered at Megiddo. Its design was similar to another palace at the site from the Middle Bronze period. It was first built in the sixteenth century B.C. in a square configuration of a series of rooms surrounding a central courtyard. By the fourteenth century, it had evolved into a rectangular-shaped building that had massive walls. The latter building was destroyed during the thirteenth century.

Fortifications. Defensive systems at Late Bronze Age sites in Palestine were, for the most part, lacking. Major city walls have not been found at important sites like Megiddo and Lachish. Towns that did have fortification systems, such as Hazor, simply copied the previous plans of the Middle Bronze period.

Iron Age I (1200–1000 B.C.)

This period reflects the time when both the Israelites and the Philistines were settling into the land: the Philistines had established themselves in the coastal plain along the Mediterranean Sea, and the Israelites had conquered and inhabited, primarily, the highland areas of Palestine. The Israelites at this time were a loose tribal confederation, and the archaeology of the Iron I period reflects that sociopolitical reality.

Domestic architecture. The common house form and design for the people of Israel at this time was the four-room house. It had a rectangular design with an entrance on one of the short sides. Inside were four rooms: three parallel long rooms and a broad room at the rear.[21] Rows of pillars separated the parallel rooms and perhaps also served to support a roof. While these domiciles are often referred to as "Israelite" four-room houses, one needs to be careful in assigning an ethnic origin to them. A four-room house has been found at Tel Batash from the Late Bronze period, prior to the Israelite settlement in the land. Such houses have also been discovered in Philistine contexts during the Iron Age. One has even been uncovered in Egypt, in western Thebes, and it dates to the time of Ramses IV (1153–1147 B.C.).

Sacred architecture. No temples have been uncovered within Israelite contexts from this period. Some archaeologists have proposed, however, that they have uncovered some religious shrines from this period, although they would not be considered full-fledged temple complexes. Adam Zertal has discovered a good example of a shrine from the Early Iron Age on the slopes of Mount Ebal.[22] It should be noted that not all scholars agree that this complex was for religious purposes. Aharon Kempinski argues that, in fact, this site was of a secular nature, and that it was simply an Israelite farm with a watchtower at its center.[23]

The situation in Philistia, along the Mediterranean coast, is much different. At the site of Tell Qasile, next to the Yarkon River on the coast, archaeologists unearthed three major, successive temple complexes that were built between 1150 and 1000 B.C. A similarly designed temple has been found at Tell es-Safi (Gath), but its dating is a little bit later (ca. tenth century B.C.). Another shrine was excavated at Sarepta, which was a port belonging to the Phoenicians.

Public architecture and fortifications. Many of the Israelite settlements of this time were isolated, individual villages that consisted of clusters of four-room houses and little else architecturally. Most of these towns were unfortified and had no city walls. William Dever concludes, "The picture we get in these early Israelite hill-country villages is of a very simple, rather impoverished, somewhat isolated culture with no great artistic or architectural tradition behind it."[24] There are exceptions to this state of affairs,

21. Yigal Shiloh, "The Four-Room House: Its Situation and Function in the Israelite City," *IEJ* 20 (1970): 180–90.

22. Adam Zertal, "Has Joshua's Altar Been Found on Mt. Ebal?," *BAR* 11 (1985): 26–43.

23. Aharon Kempinsky, "Joshua's Altar—An Iron Age I Watchtower," *BAR* 12 (1986): 42–49.

24. William G. Dever, "How to Tell a Canaanite from an Israelite," in *The Rise of Ancient Israel*, ed.

however, as excavations at Har Adir and Giloh have revealed, respectively, a square fortress and a tall, fortified tower. In addition, it may be that the clustering of four-room houses at some sites, such as Khirbet Raddanah and 'Izbet Sartah, were, in a sense, a domestic fortification.[25]

Again, we see that the Philistine architectural culture was more advanced than its Israelite counterpart. Many Philistine cities were strongly fortified. Huge city walls have been discovered at Ashdod and Ekron from this time period. Large palace complexes appeared at Tel Miqne and Tell Qasile. Overall, town planning and architectural development far exceeded what was displayed in Israelite culture.

Iron Age II (1000–586 B.C.)

This period coincides with the monarchic times in Israel, including most of the united monarchy under David and Solomon and the divided monarchy that concluded with the destruction of Judah at the hands of the Babylonians in 586 B.C. Whereas public buildings and fortifications played a small role in the Iron I period, they were central to the monarchic culture of the Iron II period: there was a movement from a mere village-centered existence to a more urban existence.

Domestic architecture. The four-room house design, which first widely appeared during the Iron I period, also dominated the Israelite settlement of the Iron II period. Reconstruction of such domiciles can be seen at Beersheba today. Some of the homes, however, contained only three rooms, although they were clearly a variation on the four-room plan. Many of the houses at this time had two stories.[26]

Sacred architecture. According to the Old Testament, the main temple of the Hebrews was the Solomonic temple built in the tenth century B.C. by King Solomon (1 Kings 6; 2 Chron. 3–4). There are no archaeological remains of that structure. Many scholars believe that it was located on top of the platform in Jerusalem where the second temple, built by Herod the Great, was later erected. The design of the Solomonic temple looks similar to a later temple, from the eighth century B.C., uncovered at Tell Tainat in northern Syria.

A small Israelite temple was discovered in the excavations at Arad from the Iron II period. Its design was generally similar to the Solomonic temple. It had three sections: a courtyard containing an altar for burnt offerings, an entrance hall (holy place), and an inner holy place (holy of holies) with two incense altars and two standing stones. The latter objects

Hershel Shanks et al. (Washington: Biblical Archaeological Society, 1992), 42.

25. Israel Finkelstein, *The Archaeology of the Israelite Settlement* (Jerusalem: Israel Exploration Society, 1988), 76.

26. Stager, "The Archaeology of the Family," 1–36.

would suggest that some type of deviant Hebrew religion was being practiced at this site.

On the northern border of the northern kingdom of Israel, excavators uncovered a ritual center at Tel Dan from the ninth century B.C. Dan was one of the two worship centers that Jeroboam I set up for the northern kingdom, and the other was at Bethel on the southern border of his kingdom (1 Kings 12:28–31). The shrine that excavators found consisted of a square enclosure with a podium inside (possibly for a temple on top) and a sacrificial altar. These remains are likely those from the heretical temple complex established by Jeroboam I. Another altar was discovered from the late eighth or early seventh century B.C. in southern Judah at the site of Beersheba. The specific context of this hewn ashlar altar is uncertain.

Public architecture. Monumental architecture appeared at this time in the kingdoms of Israel and Judah. In the northern kingdom, for example, two palaces have been identified at Megiddo (1723 and 6000). The design of the structures was similar to the Syro-Hittite *bit hilani* buildings that consist of a pillared entrance, central courtyard, and surrounding rectangular rooms. A palace from the early part of the Iron II period has been found at the site of Bethsaida. The capital of the northern kingdom was at Samaria, and archaeologists excavated a palace there that may have been Ahab's "ivory house" (1 Kings 22:39). Within the debris of the building, many lavish, costly ivory items were unearthed.

In the southern kingdom of Judah, the city of Lachish was elaborately constructed during the Iron II period. It had a massive podium that supported two massive palaces. Nothing remains of the palaces, but their design was reflected in the foundations on the podium. They were similar to the Megiddo palaces; that is, they were formed around a central courtyard with surrounding storerooms. A smaller palace was excavated at Ramat Rahel, outside of Jerusalem, and it consisted of two buildings surrounded by storerooms.

One major type of building that has been found in both the northern and the southern kingdom has generated quite a debate regarding its purpose. At numerous sites, such as Megiddo, Hazor, and Beersheba, there were buildings that had three long rooms divided by two rows of pillars. Various scholars have claimed that these "tripartite pillared" buildings served as stables, storehouses, barracks, or markets.[27]

Fortifications. Defensive systems during the Iron Age II period displayed a variety of forms. For example, there were various types of outer walls in city fortifications. In the tenth century B.C., casemate walls surrounded the towns of Gezer and Hazor, but Chinnereth had a solid wall. In the ninth through eighth centuries B.C., Lachish had a solid wall for protection, Beth Shemesh

---

27. See John D. Currid, "Puzzling Public Buildings," *BAR* 18 (1992): 52–61.

had a casemate system, Rabud had a zig-zag wall, and Tell en-Nasbeh had an offset-inset wall. This diversity in form and design lasted well into the sixth century B.C.[28]

Fig. 15.4. Iron Age Gate Complex, Megiddo

Diversity of construction was evident in the outer gates of the Iron II cities. In the early part of that time period, gates had six chambers. In the middle part of the period, many were built with only four chambers and were smaller in construction. But that was not a significant trend, because during much of the period the gates at Gezer had two chambers, Beersheba had four chambers, and 'Ira had six chambers.

Some of the settlements were strictly fortresses, built for the primary purpose of defense.[29] The best example of such a construction can be seen at the site of Arad.

KEY TERMS

ashlar masonry

bamah

28. Larry Herr, "The Iron II Period: Emerging Nations," *BA* 60 (1997): 126, 144, 157–58.
29. Rudolph Cohen, "The Iron Age Fortresses in the Central Negev," *BASOR* 236 (1979): 61–79.

fosse
header-stretcher
offset/inset
rubble masonry
temper

DISCUSSION QUESTIONS

1. Imagine you were a settler in ancient Canaan, and you decided to build a house for your family. What factors would play into the type and form of the building you would construct? What would be the most important factor or condition in your building a house?
2. A common activity of ancient builders was to "rob" materials from previous occupations of a site. Why is this a problem for an archaeologist, especially in regard to dating different occupational levels?
3. Buildings uncovered through excavation are in ruins. How does an archaeologist know the purpose or function of a building from such limited remains?
4. What do you think would be solid archaeological indicators that a building under excavation served as a temple or other sacred structure?

FOR FURTHER READING

Rapoport, Amos. *House Form and Culture*. Englewood Cliffs, NJ: Prentice-Hall, 1969.

Wright, G. R. H. *Ancient Building in South Syria and Palestine*. 2 vols. Leiden: Brill, 1985.

Wright, G. R. H. *Ancient Building Technology*. 3 vols. Leiden: Brill, 1999–2009.

CHAPTER 16

Ceramics

"I do pottery."—Marcia Gay Harden

P EOPLE FIRST MADE pottery in Palestine during the Pottery Neolithic period, although at a later date than elsewhere in the ancient
Near East. Prior to this time, clay had been used for a variety of purposes, such as house construction, ovens, storage chambers, and some figurine art. The remains indicate that these clay objects had been purposefully
fired. For example, at the Mesopotamian site of Susa, fired balls of clay used
as receipts in commerce have been found from the ninth millennium B.C.
They had been fired to a temperature of about 500 degrees. The reason for
the invention of pottery in the ancient Near East is unknown, although at
some sites it appears to have been connected to sedentarization and the
domestication of plants and animals.[1] It is commonly suggested that pottery
"may have evolved out of basketry . . . from the custom of covering a basket
with clay in order to make it waterproof. . . . Another way in which pottery
originated may have been with the clay-lined pits which were used for cooking. Examples have been found at Jericho."[2]

The pottery during this early period exhibited "primeval simplicity in
its forms,"[3] with plain, unsophisticated decorative techniques. The basic
forms included bowls, kraters, and jars. Some of the wares were plain with
no decoration, while others had various degrees of ornamentation. We will
deal with variations in form characterizing Palestinian pottery later in this
chapter.

From the Pottery Neolithic period onward, pottery, by far, has been
the most common object found in the excavation of ancient sites. It is found
everywhere. Part of its value for the archaeologist is its *ubiquity*.

---

1. Some authors dismiss this connection; see, e.g., Charlotte F. Speight and John Toki, *Hands in Clay*, 5th ed. (New York: McGraw-Hill, 2004), 17.

2. Edward Lucie-Smith, *The Story of Craft: The Craftsman's Role in Society* (Ithaca, NY: Cornell University Press, 1981), 25. I want to thank my TA at RTS-Charlotte, Katy McIlvaine, for this reference.

3. Ruth Amiran, *Ancient Pottery of the Holy Land: From Its Beginnings in the Neolithic Period to the End of the Iron Age* (New Brunswick, NJ: Rutgers University Press, 1970), 18.

Pottery's second great virtue for archaeology is its *durability*. Although vessels easily break, and only a few of them are found intact in excavation, potsherds are virtually indestructible. They do not rot, rust, melt, evaporate, crumble, or corrode. Pottery is extant in every layer of a site because it lasts.[4]

The importance of pottery also derives from its *changeability*. For the most part, the features of pottery vessels, including form and design, were remarkably standardized during any particular period within a geographical region. However, these characteristics changed at frequent intervals. Consequently, each period within a region had its own distinctive and typical ceramic. Archaeologists have been able to construct a chronological scheme for the history of ancient Palestine based, for the most part, on the type of pottery that appears in various levels of a site. Some of the more important features of pottery that help to distinguish one period from another are decoration, form, ware, ornamentation, and method of manufacture.[5]

Pottery, then, is the most fundamental tool for developing the dating sequence of a site. George Ernest Wright correctly says, "Given a sufficient quantity of broken or whole pieces from a given stratum, the date of that stratum can be established."[6] Once the ceramic is established at several sites in a region, the archaeologist can compare the pottery corpus and arrive at a relative dating sequence for the area. As Amihai Mazar aptly comments,

> Relative chronology is ascertained by typological sequences of objects, particularly of pottery, established by comparative studies of stratified assemblages from various sites in a certain region. Comparison of the assemblages within the regions enables us to define a relative sequence in each area, and to establish a chronological order for the entire country.[7]

All of this is to say that pottery "is incomparably the most useful class of object for dating."[8] William M. Flinders Petrie, in 1891, was the first to recognize the immense value of pottery for archaeology in Palestine. He commented, "Once settle the pottery of a country, and the key is in our hands for all future explorations. A single glance at a mound of ruins, even without dismounting, will show as much to anyone who knows the styles of pottery, as weeks of work may reveal to a beginner."[9] Since Petrie's time, the study of pottery has become a fundamental aspect of excavation in ancient Palestine.

---

4. Oded Borowski, "Ceramic Dating," in *Benchmarks in Time and Culture*, ed. Joel Drinkard, Gerald Mattingly, and J. Maxwell Miller (Atlanta: Scholars Press, 1988), 223.

5. Givka Ronen, *Ancient Pottery* (London: Cassell, 1973).

6. George Ernest Wright, *Biblical Archaeology* (Philadelphia: Westminster, 1962), 24.

7. Amihai Mazar, *Archaeology of the Land of the Bible* (New York: Doubleday, 1990), 28.

8. William F. Albright, *From the Stone Age to Christianity*, 2nd ed. (Garden City, NY: Doubleday, 1957), 49.

9. William M. Flinders Petrie, *Tell el Hesy (Lachish)* (London: Watt, 1891), 40.

THE VARIABLE FEATURES OF POTTERY

It is rare for excavators to uncover pottery vessels that are whole. Almost all pottery has been found broken, and most of these potsherds cannot be related to other sherds of the same vessel. Every sherd, however, bears characteristics of the whole vessel from which it derived. There are two types of potsherds. The first is what archaeologists call a diagnostic or indicator sherd; included in this category are handles, bases, and rims of a vessel. These pieces help to indicate, or identify, the original shape, size, and use of a vessel. The second category of pottery sherds is the simple body sherd; it is ubiquitous in an excavation, but limited in its help to identify shape, size, and purpose of an original vessel.

Different periods of the history of Palestine are represented in the archaeological record by variations in the shape of handles, bases, and rims of pottery. So, for example, a common vessel found during the Iron I period (1200–1000 B.C.) was the collared-rim storage jar, in which the rim of the vessel looks like a priest's collar. This large vessel rarely appeared in the previous Late Bronze Age. "The earliest example of such a pithos is known from Aphek in a context dating to the thirteenth century B.C.E.; the widespread use of these pithoi in Iron Age I settlement sites led scholars to identify them as distinctive of the material culture of the Israelites."[10] Also during that time period, kraters had multiple handles, from four to eight, whereas the previous Late Bronze kraters had only two handles. Bowls from some periods have flat bases, and from other periods curved bases. So, *form* is a fundamental and critical indicator of chronological sequencing of a site, region, and land.

Another feature of pottery that is used as a chronological indicator is *decoration*. The outward appearance of pottery changed from one period to the next in antiquity. So, for example, the ceramic of the Iron I period was generally of coarse workmanship, and it had little ornamentation. The preceding Late Bronze II period, in contrast, employed painted decoration frequently. Even during the same time period there were distinctions in decorative style of pottery between regions. Whereas the pottery of much of inland Palestine during the Iron I period was drab and coarse, along the coastal plain, where the Philistines had settled, the ceramic was highly decorated with paint. Amiran observes:

> The salient characteristics of the painted decoration may be defined as follows: the decoration covers the upper and middle parts of the body . . . and contain a geometric pattern, like spirals, concentric circles enclosing a cross, checkerboards, lozenges, or, most characteristically, a bird-motif.

10. Mazar, *Archaeology of the Land of the Bible*, 347.

. . . Generally, this decoration is black and red on a white slip, but it occurs also in one color, with or without the slip.[11]

Fig. 16.1. Philistine Beer Jug

This ware is called "Philistine" pottery. Its ethnic association appears to be justified because of its predominant appearance at Philistine sites and its clear relationship with pottery from the Aegean (where the Philistines perhaps originated).

Various decorative techniques were used in ancient pottery making. A vessel might be polished or burnished; it might be painted or glazed; it might be surfaced with wash or slip; or it might be perforated with holes, or shaved, or incised. It might have an external decoration, such as the cooking pots of the Middle Bronze IIA period, which had outside ornamentation that looked like rope. The following definitions of some of the techniques of pottery making should be helpful for our later discussion of specific ceramic distinctions between various periods of settlement in Palestine.

1. *Burnishing.* This is a technique in which a potter polished a vessel to seal pores and to create a lustrous finish.

2. *Slip.* A potter may have added a thin surface coat of untempered clay on a vessel. This slip process made the outside of the vessel harder, and thus easier to polish or paint. A slip also made a vessel less permeable, and it often changed the color of the piece.

3. *Wash.* Some potters covered vessels with wash, which is a thin, watery coating of paint usually applied to the outside of the jar.

Another important characteristic of ceramic that can be used as a chronological indicator is *ware*. Ware may be simply defined as the composition of pottery according to its raw materials. The essence of pottery is the combination of clay with nonplastics, which are minerals and fossils. Ware varied by region because raw materials varied by region.

Ancient pottery makers added other materials to the clay mixture in order to bind it more strongly, to help minimize shrinkage, and to prevent cracking. "This process is called tempering. Straw, dung, sand, salt, and grog are a few of the substances employed in antiquity. Specific periods and locations normally adopted one technique over others. For example, dark-faced

11. Amiran, *Ancient Pottery of the Holy Land*, 266–67.

burnished ware of the Neolithic period almost always contains straw temper, whereas other periods did not use it at all."[12]

Pottery can also be distinguished by the manufacturing process used to make it. During the Pottery Neolithic and Chalcolithic ages, pottery was produced by hand. The slow wheel did not make its appearance in Palestine until about 3000 B.C. At Megiddo during the EB I period, for example, much of the pottery corpus was handmade, but some of it was manufactured on the slow wheel. This perhaps represented the transition from the one process to the next. The fast wheel did not arrive in Palestine until the MB II period. The appearance and "widespread use of the potter's wheel is mainly responsible for the technical advances in pottery making and for the greater refinement of forms."[13]

POTTERY EXCAVATION

As we have shown, archaeologists use pottery as the primary indicator of date for the different settlement levels of a site and the artifacts found in them. Close attention must be given to the pottery at a site, and if it is not, then the value of an excavation is called into question. For example, Gottlieb

Fig. 16.2. Excavating Pottery

12. John D. Currid, *Doing Archaeology in the Land of the Bible* (Grand Rapids: Baker, 1999), 82. Grog is ground up pottery vessels used for temper.

13. Amiran, *Ancient Pottery of the Holy Land*, 90.

Schumacher excavated at Megiddo during the years 1903–5, but he did little work with stratigraphy and pottery analysis. As a result, much of his work is useless to later archaeologists.[14] For instance, the important fragment of the so-called Shishak stele was later found in one of Schumacher's dumps that were made for a huge trench he dug through the site. It was found outside the stratigraphic context and, therefore, was without value for dating.

Retrieval and recording of pottery must be done in a controlled and systematic way. The first step when digging up pottery is for the diggers to put the sherds into a bucket. Each bucket has a tag that identifies the locus from which the pottery was taken. The area supervisor, at the end of each day, draws a top plan of the area of discovery, thus correlating the pottery, the locus, and the stratum/level of the site. The many top plans for each area are finally correlated by the field archaeologist.

Fig. 16.3. Pottery Washing, Bethsaida

After excavation, pottery is immediately washed and then examined for any inscriptions, painting, ornamentation, and so forth. At the end of each day, the archaeologist "reads" the pottery, especially the indicator sherds, in order to date each locus. The indicator sherds are then marked with a locus number.

Important diagnostic sherds and whole vessels are drawn in the laboratory of the excavation. They are drawn in profile: whole vessels are depicted with the left side of the illustration representing the exterior of the vessel, and the right side representing the vessel in section. These pieces are also photographed. Great care given to all aspects of pottery excavation—digging, recording, and illustrating—is of immense value in site reconstruction and the dating of settlements.

IRON AGE POTTERY IN PALESTINE

So much material has been excavated and published on the history of pottery in ancient Palestine, from the Neolithic to the Hellenistic periods,

14. William Foxwell Albright, *The Archaeology of Palestine*, rev. ed. (Gloucester, MA: Peter Smith, 1971), 33.

that we must limit our study to the Iron Age (the main period of Israel's presence in the land).[15] Our intention, however, is not to be exhaustive even in that limited study. There is simply too much material.[16] Our design is to present a brief overview of the ceramic history of the Iron Age in order to give the reader an introduction to the material finds.

Iron Age I (ca. 1200–1000 b.c.). During these centuries, the Israelites entered the Promised Land. They settled primarily in the highland and foothill regions of Palestine. The Philistines controlled much of the coastal plain, and the indigenous Canaanites held on to many of the valley areas. In the hill country and Shephelah of central Palestine, the number of settlements greatly increased at this time. For example, in the Shephelah the density of settlement became much higher than it was in the previous Late Bronze Age. The Iron I site distribution was nearly 50 percent greater than that of the earlier period.[17] Throughout the highland and foothill region, roughly 300 villages were settled during this period and, in my view, it is appropriate to call them Israelite.[18]

The pottery at these Iron I sites was of poor, crude, and limited quality. The corpus included only some of the most basic forms, and decoration was mostly lacking: there was no painted ware, and some of the vessels contained only fairly primitive ornamentation, such as incisions impressed on the outside of the ware. Common forms were large *pithoi*, called collared-rim storage jars (which were probably used to store water), cooking pots, and small jars to hold wine or oil.

The collared-rim storage jars were a prominent artifact found in these villages, and that fact led some archaeologists to suggest that its appearance was to be tied specifically to the Israelite settlement. This ethnic identification is perhaps too simplistic, because this type of storage container appeared occasionally in earlier periods. In addition, "similar pithoi were found also at Megiddo and Tell Keisan, where Canaanite culture survived until the eleventh century b.c.e., and at Sahab in Transjordan, probably an Ammonite site."[19]

15. See, e.g., Amiran, *Ancient Pottery of the Holy Land*; Rivka Gonen, *Ancient Pottery* (London: Cassell, 1973); Hendricus J. Franken, *A History of Pottery and Potters in Ancient Jerusalem: Excavations by K. M. Kenyon in Jerusalem, 1961–1967* (London: Equinox, 2005); Bryant G. Wood, *The Sociology of Pottery in Ancient Palestine: The Ceramic Industry and the Diffusion of Ceramic Style in the Bronze and Iron Age* (Sheffield: Sheffield Academic Press, 1990).

16. See Seymour Gitin, *The Ancient Pottery of Israel and Its Neighbors from the Iron Age through the Hellenistic Period* (Jerusalem: Israel Exploration Society, 2015); Orna Zimhoni, *Studies in the Iron Age Pottery of Israel: Typological, Archaeological, and Chronological* (Tel Aviv: Institute of Archaeology, 1997).

17. See John D. Currid, "The Deforestation of the Foothills of Palestine," *PEQ* 116 (1984): 1–11.

18. Some scholars refer to them as "proto-Israelite" settlements; see, for example, William G. Dever, "How to Tell a Canaanite from an Israelite," in *The Rise of Ancient Israel*, by Hershel Shanks et al. (Washington: BAS, 1992), 43.

19. Mazar, *Archaeology of the Land of the Bible*, 347.

The corpus of Israelite pottery in central Palestine differed greatly from the Philistine pottery found along the Mediterranean coastline. Philistine pottery included as its main forms kraters, bowls, jugs with strainer spouts, and stirrup vases. In regard to decoration, there were several prominent and distinctive features; many of the vessels had a thick white slip with a bichrome (red and black) painted decoration. This decoration was often a geometric pattern like spirals, concentric circles, or checkerboards. Perhaps the most characteristic motif was a bird drawn in several different postures. This highly decorated ware derived from the Aegean, and probably came with the Sea Peoples when they migrated to the eastern coastlands of the Mediterranean at the beginning of the Iron I period. Typical Canaanite pottery, stemming from the Late Bronze Age, was also found within the ceramic corpus of the Philistine culture in Palestine.

Iron Age II (ca. 1000–586 B.C.). The united monarchy in Israel coincided with the end of the eleventh century and most of the tenth century B.C. This period was characterized by the introduction of a variety of new shapes and forms in the ceramic corpus. The most important innovations were the applying of a red slip to bowls and the burnishing of them by hand. These techniques were found at several sites, as Walter Rast reports:

> The Taanach evidence suggests a date for the introduction of red-slip burnishing at approximately 1000 which is supported by comparative evidence. At Tell Beit Mirsim the practice was noted as the chief feature distinguishing Stratum B3. It made its main appearance at Megiddo VA-IVB. At 'Ain Shems it was discovered to be the most characteristic treatment of the pottery of Stratum IIb. The same may be noted of Deir 'Alla where red-slip burnishing began in Phase E and then became ubiquitous, especially on bowls, by the time of Phase G.[20]

To be more specific regarding the ceramic chronology of the united monarchy is a difficult task. Thus, for instance, the difference between Davidic pottery and Solomonic ware remains a mystery.[21]

Once the Israelite nation divided into two kingdoms in the second half of the tenth century B.C., two ceramic traditions developed, one in the north (Israel) and one in the south (Judah). Thus, in the northern kingdom of the ninth through eighth centuries B.C., the so-called Samaria Ware made its appearance; it was so-named because of its discovery at Samaria, the capital of the northern kingdom. Amiran describes the workmanship of this ware—in particular, of its bowls—as follows:

20. Walter E. Rast, *Taanach I: Studies in the Iron Age Pottery* (Cambridge, MA: ASOR, 1978), 21.

21. John D. Currid, "The Re-Stratification of Megiddo During the United Monarchy," *ZDPV* 107 (1991): 28–38.

Eggshell-thin, fine, throughly [*sic*] baked ware; thick slip, continuously burnished on the wheel, or, rarely, by hand. The color or colors of the slip are very striking: red slip inside and outside, or red and yellow slip alternating in bands, or sometimes, red inside and yellow outside, or vice versa.[22]

Some scholars want to abandon the name "Samaria Ware" because the style did not originate in Samaria, but perhaps was imported from Phoenicia.[23]

The Judean (southern) tradition during the ninth through eighth centuries B.C. consisted of vessels that "are for the most part undecorated, wheel-burnishing is an innovation in and characteristic of this period . . . painted decoration is very rare, mainly on amphoriskoi."[24]

During the final stage of the Iron II period (ca. 700–586 B.C.), the distinct ceramic traditions remained in the north and the south. In the northern cities of Samaria, Shechem, and Tell el-Farah (North), most of the pottery forms demonstrated a continuation of the eighth-century forms. What was new at this time was the appearance of great numbers of Assyrian ware, whether imported or imitated, at the sites. This makes sense in light of the Assyrian conquest of the north in 722–721 B.C. and the resettlement of the region under the tutelage of Assyria.

The pottery of Judah in this final stage also reflected the earlier repertoire of the ninth through eighth centuries B.C.; many of the forms were simply a continuation of previous ceramic types. For example, the types of bowls found in the seventh century, including "rice" bowls and shallow bowls with cut rims, first appeared in Judah in the ninth century. More foreign forms were represented in the seventh-century repertoire, including Assyrian, Philistine, and Cypriote traditions.

KEY TERMS

burnishing

collared-rim storage jar

diagnostic sherd

grog

locus

slip

ware

wash

22. Amiran, *Ancient Pottery of the Holy Land*, 207.

23. Mazar, *Archaeology of the Land of the Bible*, 508.

24. Ze'ev Herzog and Lily Singer-Avitz, "Iron Age II A-B: Judah and the Negev," in *The Ancient Pottery of Israel and Its Neighbors from the Iron Age through the Hellenistic Period*, ed. Seymour Gitin (Jerusalem: Israel Exploration Society, 2015), 218.

DISCUSSION QUESTIONS

1. Why are the remains of pottery so important for the reconstruction of the history of an ancient site?
2. Why do you think Israelite pottery of the Early Iron Age was so drab and crude in comparison to Philistine and Aegean pottery of the same time period?
3. Remains of whole clay pots are rare finds in an excavation. How does an archaeologist reconstruct the type and form of a vessel from broken sherds? How does the investigator determine the date of the vessel?

FOR FURTHER READING

Amiran, Ruth. *Ancient Pottery of the Holy Land*. New Brunswick, NJ: Rutgers University Press, 1970.

Gitin, Seymour, ed. *The Ancient Pottery of Israel and Its Neighbors from the Iron Age through the Hellenistic Period*. 2 vols. Jerusalem: IES, 2015.

Gonen, Rivka. *Ancient Pottery*. London: Cassell, 1973.

CHAPTER 17

The Hebrew Language in Archaeology

"Just as the Torah was given in the Holy Tongue, so was the world created with the Holy Tongue."—Genesis Rabba 18:4

THE SCIENCE OF LINGUISTICS

One of the principal tasks of the science of linguistics is to investigate and trace the history of language families. Such studies are obviously plagued by the unknown. There is much speculation. However, there generally seems to be a basic assumption that the various languages that constitute a "family" ultimately developed or evolved from a single language of the past. There are over 5,000 languages in history, but there are only about twenty families from which they all descend.

The general family to which ancient Hebrew belongs is a broad one. It is often called by one of two names: either Hamito-Semitic or Afro-Asiatic. This large family includes the following:

1. Semitic languages of the Middle East
2. Cushitic languages of Ethiopia, Somalia, and Sudan
3. Egyptian languages
4. Languages of North Africa, such as Berber

The most common feature of the languages of this family is the similarity in the conjugation of the verb.

Ancient Hebrew belongs to the first branch of that large family: it is a Semitic language. The mother language of the Semitic branch is called Proto-Semitic. It was used prior to 3000 B.C., but we know almost nothing about the people who spoke it, whether it be their ethnicity, their precise areas of settlement, or whatever. It is customary to divide the Semitic languages into five smaller branches:

1. The oldest branch is Northeast Semitic from the early third millennium B.C., which includes Babylonian and Assyrian (Akkadian).
2. The Northwest Semitic branch appeared as early as the middle of the third millennium B.C. with Eblaite and later with Ugaritic, Phoenician, and Hebrew during the second millennium B.C.
3. Aramaic was spoken by Aramaean tribes for centuries prior to the oldest extant inscriptions in Aramaic, which come from the beginning of the first millennium B.C. "As the Aramaeans moved into Assyria and Babylonia, their language gradually superseded Accadian as the lingua franca of the region, eventually becoming the official language of the Persian Empire."[1]
4. The Southwest Semitic branch includes the languages of Hejaz, Nejd, Qays, and Yemen. The earliest inscriptions appeared in the mid-first millennium B.C. The Hejaz dialect dominated and developed into the classical Arabic language spoken (in many dialects) between 300 and 600 A.D.
5. Languages included in the Southeast Semitic branch are South Arabic (including the Sabaic dialect) and Ethiopic.

THE ORIGIN OF HEBREW

It is difficult to determine when Hebrew was first spoken and written because of the complexities involved in language development and by our lack of understanding the processes by which a language is formed. Key to our knowledge was the discovery of the palace archives of the city of Ebla during the 1970s. Archaeologists unearthed thousands of tablets that dated to about 2300 B.C. The language of the writings demonstrates close ties to the vocabulary, grammar, and syntax of the later Northwest Semitic languages of Canaanite, Phoenician (Ugaritic), and Hebrew. Eblaite is the oldest language of this branch, and it precedes the dating of the Ugaritic texts by about 1000 years. Giovanni Pettinato, the paleographer for the Ebla investigations, concluded that Eblaite should be classified as "Early Canaanite" or "Palaeo-Canaanite."[2]

---

1. Alger F. Johns, *A Short Grammar of Biblical Aramaic*, rev. ed. (Berrien Springs, MI: Andrews University Press, 1972), 1.
2. See Giovanni Pettinato, "The Royal Archives of Tell Mardikh-Ebla," *BA* 39 (1976): 44–52; Kenneth A. Kitchen, *The Bible in Its World: The Bible and Archaeology Today* (Downers Grove, IL: InterVarsity Press, 1977), 38–39.

The Ugaritic texts from Ras Shamra all date to the fourteenth through thirteenth centuries B.C., although some of the compositions reflect an earlier origination. This Northwest Semitic language is quite close to Hebrew in many grammatical and lexical aspects.

At the site of el-Amarna in ancient Egypt, archaeologists found about 350 clay tablets that were written in Akkadian. Akkadian had a cuneiform script, and it was the diplomatic language of the time. The texts date to the fourteenth century B.C. These tablets were letters that constituted part of the diplomatic correspondence between the Egyptian suzerains Amenophis III (ca. 1391–1353 B.C.) and Amenophis IV (Akhenaton; ca. 1353–1335 B.C.) and their vassals concentrated primarily in Syria and Palestine.[3] The letters from the vassals, though written in Akkadian, possess many characteristics of the Northwest Semitic native language of the writers.

There is no reason to believe that Hebrew, as a Northwest Semitic language, was not in development during the second millennium B.C. Although one cannot be more precise than that general chronology, the appearance of Eblaite appears to push the date of the origination of Hebrew back to the early second millennium B.C.

THE LANGUAGE OF THE PATRIARCHS

The Hebrew patriarch Abraham left his native land of Mesopotamia and migrated to Canaan (Gen. 11:31). It is safe to assume that he and his clan spoke Akkadian (Assyrian/Babylonian) and perhaps an early form of Aramaic. When they arrived in Canaan, they would have had to learn the language(s) of the land.

A clue to that linguistic transition may be seen in Genesis 31:44–47, which begins with Laban, the Aramaean, saying to the Hebrew patriarch Jacob,

> "Come now, let us make a covenant, you and I. And let it be a witness between you and me." So Jacob took a stone and set it up as a pillar. And Jacob said to his kinsmen, "Gather stones." And they took stones and made a heap, and they ate there by the heap. Laban called it Jegar-sahadutha, but Jacob called it Galeed.

Laban, the Aramaean, called the pile of rocks Jegar-sahadutha, which in his native, early Aramaic means "a heap of stones."[4] Jacob, on the other hand, called it Galeed, which is Hebrew that means "a heap of stones of the

---

3. See William L. Moran, ed. and trans., *The Amarna Letters* (Baltimore: Johns Hopkins University Press, 1992).

4. *HALOT*, 1080.

witness."[5] Language helps to define and give an identity to a people, and in this episode we see that the family of Abraham, two generations after leaving Mesopotamia, have adopted a new language. Obviously the patriarchs were multilingual, but we see in this text that there is a transition to employing Hebrew as their common language.

THE ARCHAEOLOGICAL REMAINS OF ANCIENT HEBREW

In this section, we will discuss item by item the most important archaeological finds that contain the Hebrew language written on them. We limit ourselves to the period of the Old Testament that concludes with the destruction of the first temple by the Babylonians in 586 B.C.

1. At 'Izbet Sartah, excavators discovered a poorly constructed settlement that originated in the twelfth century B.C., but had become more established in the eleventh century B.C. The town lay in the foothills of the tribal land of Ephraim to the east of the town of Aphek. It is probably to be identified as the biblical Ebenezer, where the Israelites mustered their army to battle the Philistines (1 Sam. 4:1). During the course of the excavations, an ostracon was found at the bottom of a storage pit from the Iron I period.[6] On the ostracon was written a text four lines long, and another line that was an alphabet. William Shea translates it as follows:

> Line 1. "Unto the field we came/, (unto) Aphek from Shiloh."

> Line 2. "The Kittim took (it and) came to Azor/ (to) Dagon lord of Ashdod (and to) Gath."

> Line 3. "(It returned to) Kiriath-Jearim."

> Line 4. The companion of the foot soldiers, Hophni, came to tell the elders, "a horse has come (and) upon (it was my) brother for us to bury."

> Line 5. Alphabet.[7]

The precise context of the composition of this piece is uncertain, although it appears to have been a copyist's exercise. As expected, there is some scholarly debate regarding whether or not this is truly a Hebrew document. In my opinion, the archaeological context, script, and language all argue in favor of it being the oldest Hebrew inscription that we have in our possession.

---

5. *HALOT*, 186.
6. Moshe Kochavi, "An Ostracon of the Period of the Judges from 'Izbet Sartah," *TA* 4 (1977): 1–13.
7. William H. Shea, "The 'Izbet Sartah Ostracon," *AUSS* 28 (1990): 59–86.

2. Beginning in 2007, archaeologists excavated the site of Khirbet Qeiyafa, which lies next to the Valley of Elah about 20 miles southwest of Jerusalem. The investigators uncovered a fortress city that dates to the end of the Iron I period and the beginning of the Iron II period (ca. 1050–970 B.C.).[8] An inscription was discovered there that some argue is the oldest Hebrew writing that is extant.

The find is an ostracon that contains five lines of text. The writing is poorly preserved and hard to decipher. Gershon Galil translates the text as follows:

Do not do (it), but worship [. . .].

Judge the slave and the widow, judge the orph[an]

and the stranger. Plead for the infant, plead for the poor and

the widow. Avenge (the pauper's vengeance) at the king's hands.

Protect the poor [and] the slave, su[pport] the stranger.[9]

Not all scholars agree that this was a Hebrew inscription. Some argue that it was Canaanite or proto-Canaanite. On the other hand, much of the vocabulary in the text appears to be common Hebrew, and the site was clearly located in territory belonging to the tribe of Judah.

3. In the excavations of Tel Zayit, a site located in the Judaean foothills, investigators uncovered an inscription dating to the middle of the tenth century B.C.[10] It was an abecedary carved into a stone. Richard Hess argues, "The announcement of a tenth century B.C.E. abecedary . . . provides further opportunity for reflecting on the development of literacy in ancient Israel" and "served the purpose of learning how to read and write in Hebrew."[11] He further concludes, on the basis of this inscription and other evidence, that literacy in Israel was widespread in many levels of Israelite society. For an opposing view, see the work of Christopher Rollston.[12]

8. Finkelstein extends the lower date to ca. 915 B.C. See Israel Finkelstein and Eli Piasetzky, "Khirbet Qeiyafa: Absolute Chronology," *TA* 37 (2010): 84–88.

9. Cited in Christopher Rollston, "The Khirbet Qeiyafa Ostracon: Methodological Musings and Caveats," *TA* 38 (2011): 67–82.

10. Ron E. Tappy et al., "An Abecedary of the Mid-Tenth Century B.C.E. from the Judaean Shephelah," *BASOR* 344 (2006): 5–46.

11. Richard S. Hess, "Writing about Writing: Abecedaries and Evidence of Literacy in Ancient Israel," *VT* 56 (2006): 342–46.

12. Christopher A. Rollston, "The Phoenician Script of the Tel Zayit Abecedary and Putative Evidence for Israelite Literacy," in *Literate Culture and Tenth-Century Canaan: The Tel Zayit Abecedary in Context*, ed. Ron E. Tappy and P. Kyle McCarter (Winona Lake, IN: Eisenbrauns, 2008), 61–96.

4. The Gezer Calendar is a limestone tablet containing a student's text of an agricultural calendar written in Hebrew. It dates to the second half of the tenth century B.C. Discovered by R. A. S. Macalister in 1908 at Gezer, about 20 miles west of Jerusalem, the tablet was not found in a secure archaeological context. The precise dating of the object is, therefore, uncertain. For a translation of the calendar, see page 166 above.

5. An inscription that is known as the Widow's Petition Ostracon was written in Hebrew on a potsherd. Scholars date its composition anywhere between the ninth and the seventh century B.C. It was eight lines long, and was a legal document from a woman petitioning an official regarding the property of her deceased husband. I translate it as follows:

May Yahweh bless you in peace.

And may my lord, the ruler, hear your maidservant.

My husband is dead. No sons.

And may your hand be with me.

And may you give in the hand of your maidservant the property which you pledged to 'Amasyahu.

But the field of wheat which is in Na'amah you gave it to his brother.

Fig. 17.1. Widow's Plea Ostracon

The problem with this text is that its provenance is unknown; neither its place nor date of discovery is known. The ostracon is held in a private collection.

6. The Harvard excavations at Samaria (1908–10), the capital city of the northern kingdom of Israel, unearthed numerous ostraca that were written in Hebrew. They were found in a room appropriately named the Ostraca House, and they numbered over a hundred ostraca (although only sixty-three are legible). "These sherds were records of shipments of oil and wine sent by various settlements in the district of Samaria to the royal household as taxes in kind. These very short inscriptions are of considerable value for the light they shed on the language, script, personal names, taxation system, and organization of the kingdom of Israel and of the topography of the territory of the tribe of Manasseh."[13] The precise date of the ostraca is under debate, although 850–750 B.C. would cover most of the scholarly suggestions.

13. Nahman Avigad, "Samaria," *EAEHL*, 4:1043 (1978).

7. The Siloam Inscription was composed during the rule of the Judaean king Hezekiah (ca. 716–687 B.C.) inside a tunnel that he was having built in Jerusalem. The tunnel was constructed to connect the Gihon Spring (outside the city) to the Pool of Siloam (inside the city). Approximately 20 feet from the pool inside the tunnel, this Hebrew inscription was found that describes the meeting of the two digging teams. It says,

> [. . . when] (the tunnel) was driven through. And this was the way in which it was cut through: While [. . .] (were) still [. . .] axe(s), each man toward his fellow, and while there were still three cubits to be cut through, [there was heard] the voice of a man calling to this fellow, for there was an *overlap* in the rock on the right [and on the left]. And when the tunnel was driven through, the quarrymen hewed (the rock), each man toward his fellow, axe against axe; and the water flowed from the spring toward the reservoir for 1,200 cubits, and the height of the rock above the head(s) of the quarrymen was 100 cubits.[14]

The digging of the tunnel during Hezekiah's kingship is confirmed by 2 Kings 20:20 and 2 Chronicles 32:30.

8. In numerous excavations of Judaean sites during the eighth through seventh centuries B.C., storage jar handles have been found that were stamped with Hebrew lettering and some symbols. Many of them contain the words "belonging to the king," and beneath the writing are often found a winged disc and the name of a town, such as Hebron, Ziph, or Socoh. Some researchers believe these cities were royal centers for taxation, and the commodities in the stamped jars were the taxes paid by the people. Others say the jars were for the distribution of the commodities to the people from the royal cities. And yet

Fig. 17.2. La Melech Jar Handle

other scholars argue that the jars were produced by royal potters, and the stamps represent official measures of quantity (see 1 Chron. 4:23).

9. Archaeologist Joseph Naveh excavated the site of Mesad Hashavyahu in 1960. It was an ancient fortress located next to the Mediterranean Sea that was occupied from about 639 to 609 B.C. The site may have been an Egyptian fort that included both Judahite and Greek mercenaries.

---

14. William F. Albright, "The Siloam Inscription," in *ANET*, 321.

Naveh discovered there an ostracon written in good, common Hebrew.[15] It contains fourteen lines of writing, and conveys a complaint made by a worker to an official at the fortress that his cloak has been unjustly confiscated. I translate it as follows:

My lord, the leader, hear

a word of his servant. Your servant

is a harvester. Your servant was in

Hatsar-ʿAsam, and your servant harvested.

And he finished, and he stored (it) in the days before

Sabbath. When your servant finished (the) harvest

and (the) storage in (those) days that Hoshabyahu
    the son of Shobi came.

And he seized the garment of your servant when I completed

my harvest. This has been days (since) he seized the
    garment of your servant.

And all my brothers can answer for me, the ones harvesting
    with me in the heat.

Yes [. . .] my brothers can answer for me. Truly, I
    am innocent from guilt.

(Too few letters are preserved to reconstruct lines 11–14 accurately).

This inscription bears the oldest extrabiblical reference to the Hebrew Sabbath.

    10. In 1979, archaeologist Gabriel Barkay excavated an Iron Age tomb in Ketef Hinnom just southwest of the city of Jerusalem. He found two small silver scrolls in a repository beneath one of the burial benches. The larger of the two scrolls was analyzed first, and it contained finely and delicately etched characters in Hebrew. The text was the priestly benediction from Numbers 6. Analysis of the smaller scroll revealed that it also contained that

---

15. Joseph Naveh, "A Hebrew Letter from the Seventh Century B.C.," *IEJ* 10 (1960): 129–39.

same text. The tomb in which the scrolls were discovered was a typical Judaean rock-cut cave from the late seventh century B.C. This find is the earliest direct citation of a biblical text in our possession.

　11. At the Judaean site of Lachish, the archaeologist J. L. Starkey discovered a destruction layer that corresponded to the defeat of the city by the Babylonians in 589/588 B.C. In the burnt debris, Starkey found eighteen ostraca in a guardroom located between the inner and outer gates of the city. These were letters written in Hebrew by a man named Hoshaiah to a military leader named Yaosh. A common interpretation is that Hoshaiah commanded a small fortress outside Lachish, and he was writing to Yaosh, who was the military commander at Lachish. Others, like Yigael Yadin, believe that Hoshaiah, the military commander at Lachish, was writing to Yaosh, a leading official in Jerusalem. The letters appear to have been composed just before the destruction of Lachish. One letter reads,

> And let (my lord) know that we are watching for the signals of Lachish, according to all the indications which my lord hath given, for we cannot see Azekah.[16]

Hoshaiah seems to have been speaking of fire warning signals that would have been sent from one Judaean city to another. The lack of signal fires may have indicated that the Babylonian army was nearby.

Fig. 17.3.
Ketef Hinnom
Inscription

　12. Numerous official seals containing Hebrew inscriptions have been discovered through excavation. For example, a clay stamp, or bulla, was recently found in an ancient dump in Jerusalem, and it was inscribed, "Belonging to Hezekiah (son of) Ahaz, king of Judah." Although it was not found in a stratified context, the date of the relic is likely from the time of Hezekiah's kingship in the eighth century B.C. Another important seal discovery took place during the excavations at Megiddo in the early 20th century. The bulla was inscribed with the words, "Shema servant of Yarob'oam." It probably refers to King Jeroboam II, who ruled the northern kingdom of Israel from about 782 to 753 B.C. For other examples of bullae containing the names of the kings of Israel and Judah, see Appendix 3.

16. *ANET*, 322.

ARCHAEOLOGICAL REMAINS OF OTHER SEMITIC LANGUAGES

Numerous Northwest Semitic, but non-Hebrew, inscriptions have been unearthed in or near the land of Palestine. We will consider two texts here that I do not examine in Appendix 3.

1. At the site of Deir 'Alla in southern Transjordan, investigators discovered ink-on-plaster inscriptions that can be dated to about 700 B.C. The texts present the sayings of Balaam, the son of Beor, who is known from the book of Numbers (chs. 22–24). The opening line of the texts is, "Warnings from the book of Balaam the son of Beor. He was a seer of the gods." The texts were composed in an Aramaic dialect. Although they were composed at the end of the eighth century B.C., they probably reflect an origination at an earlier date.

2. A royal dedicatory inscription was found at the site of Tel Miqne in the southern coastal plain (Philistia).[17] The text was incised on a limestone block, and it contains five lines written in a dialect similar to Phoenician. My translation reads,

> Achish, the son of Padi, the son of Yasid, the son of Ada, the son of Ya'ir, ruler of Ekron, built a temple/sanctuary for Patgayah, his lady, (so that) she might bless him and keep him and lengthen his days and bless his land.

The find dates to the seventh century B.C. It is an important discovery for a number of reasons. First, it identifies the site of Tel Miqne as Philistine Ekron, which was one of the Philistine capital cities. Second, the text mentions that Achish built a temple for the goddess Patgayah, who was the Aegean mother of Delphi. This connects the site of Ekron to the area of Greece from where the Philistines had initially migrated, and it evidences the continued cultural and economic ties between the two areas.

KEY TERMS

abecedary

stele (*pl.* stelae)

DISCUSSION QUESTIONS

1. Why is it important for an archaeologist to be trained in the languages of the ancient Near East?

17. Seymour Gitin, Trude Dothan, and Joseph Naveh, "A Royal Dedicatory Inscription from Ekron," *IEJ* 47 (1997): 1–16.

2. Why are ancient inscriptions so vital to the reconstruction of ancient history?
3. In comparison to other cultures of the ancient Near East, archaeologists have uncovered few inscriptional remains from ancient Israel. Why could that be the case?

FOR FURTHER READING

Davis, Graham I., ed. *Ancient Hebrew Inscriptions*. 2 vols. Cambridge: Cambridge University Press, 1991, 2004.

Pritchard, James B., ed. *Ancient Near Eastern Texts Relating to the Old Testament*. Princeton: Princeton University Press, 1955.

Thomas, D. Winton, ed. *Documents from Old Testament Times*. New York: Harper & Row, 1958.

CHAPTER 18

Burial Practices

"It's not that I'm afraid to die, I just don't want to be there when it happens."
—Woody Allen

ONE OF THE great responsibilities of every culture is to bury its dead. This task took on a variety of forms in antiquity. For example, by the year 1200 B.C., everyone on the island of Britain was cremating their dead and burying the remains in urns. Prior to that time, Britain's population had interred their dead in very different ways. Around 2000 B.C., a group of people called the Beaker folk settled in the southern and eastern regions of the island. Robert Braidwood comments on their settlement: "A few simple habitation sites and many burials of the Beaker folk are known. They buried their dead singly, sometimes in conspicuous individual barrows with the dead warrior in his full trappings."[1] Another group in Britain at this time were the Food-vessel folk, and they buried their dead, ironically, in their "food-vessel" pots.

Some of the earliest known burials in ancient Palestine came from the Natufian period (ca. 10,000–8,500 B.C.). For example, the excavations in the Mount Carmel cave uncovered burials in the ground of the cave where the people lived and some other burials on the outside terrace of the cave. The skeletons inside the living quarters were laid out in an extended

Fig. 18.1. Carmel Burial

1. Robert J. Braidwood, *Prehistoric Men*, 8th ed. (Glenview, IL: Scott, Foresman and Company, 1975), 187–88.

position on their backs, and the terrace skeletons were interred in a fetal pose. Objects were found in many of the graves, including many beads. In fact, two skulls were discovered that wore shell-bead headdresses. At the site of Ain Mallahah, both primary and secondary burials were found: the dead, in theory, were first buried in individual graves that were associated with their home, and then moved to a communal, collective burial ground with shallow pit graves. Some scholars suggest that the two types may simply reflect two different periods in the history of burials.

In many cases of burial, even from these earliest times, there were signs of ritual treatment of the dead. In addition, grave gifts were often present in the graves. These practices indicate that people had some notion of an afterlife even in the most primitive times and cultures.

NEOLITHIC PERIOD (CA. 8000–4000 B.C.)

During the PPNA period, Jericho was a village with a population of less than a thousand people.[2] Circular houses built with solid walls of hog-backed bricks indicate the establishment of a fully settled and sedentary occupation. Burials were still associated with living quarters; in one house, for example, seven skeletons were arranged in a circle beneath the floor. Many of the dead were lying in a contracted position, and some of them were headless. Around another house there were buried three groups of three skulls each. This may in fact indicate some type of ancestor worship, and the skeletal finds of the next period at Jericho (PPNB) may confirm that reality.

At the site of Beidha, located just north of Petra in Transjordan, excavators unearthed an occupation layer from the end of the PPNA. Interments there were similar to those at Jericho: skeletons were in a crouched burial position, and many, mostly children, were buried under the floors of houses. Some of the skeletons were also headless. Ornaments were found alongside the dead, such as a bone bracelet of tibias next to a child's body.

Fig. 18.2. Jericho Neolithic Skull

In the subsequent PPNB period, the style and form of burial evolved and became more elaborate. At Jericho, Kenyon discovered ten human skulls that were plastered and modeled. Seven were found in the floor of one house, and three in another. The skulls had been painted with black bands, and the lower jaws of the craniums were usually missing. Found

2. The excavator, Kathleen Kenyon, placed the population number at about two thousand, but that appears to be too high.

in the debris of the first house were forty skeletons without heads, but with the lower jaws. Jean Perrot found a plastered skull from the same period at Beisamoun/Mallaha in the Jordan Valley. The cranium was packed with plaster and colored with ocher, and the nose was artificially extended. Shells were inserted in place of the eyes. Similarly reworked skulls were found at Tel Ramad in Syria from this time period.

After the PPNB period, this flourishing settlement was abandoned in favor of small agricultural sites. Some have called it a dark age, and numerous scholars refer to it as the PPNC period (ca. seventh millennium B.C.). There are some burial remains from this transitional phase, such as at Atlit-Yam.[3] Forty-six graves were recovered at the site, and most were located in specific building areas. Grave goods were found in fifteen of the burials.

Burial remains from the Pottery Neolithic period are few and far between. This is true for much of the material culture of this time. Ahimai Mazar puts it this way: "Our knowledge of both the cultural history and the climatic and environmental conditions in Palestine in the sixth and fifth millennia B.C.E. is rather sparse."[4] Although pottery appeared for the first time in the archaeological record, the remains of the PN period are shabby, and dating sequences are difficult to determine. It was a dark age. Jericho is a good example of the scanty nature of things. People lived there in subterranean pit dwellings, and above those were paltry remains of other types of buildings.

CHALCOLITHIC PERIOD (CA. 4000–3200 B.C.)

The Chalcolitic period was characterized by movement and transition. The settlement pattern emphasized the peripheral regions, including semi-arid zones such as the Transjordanian Plateau and the Negev area around Beersheba. The desert fringes appear to have been the choice of settlement for many groups that based their economy on herding. Burial practices reflected the mobility of the time; people, for the most part, were not buried at home. Secondary burials were common, in which the body's decomposition took place where a person died, and then the bones were transported to a communal burial site.

Much evidence for this practice was found during the excavations of the cave site of Azor located just south of modern-day Tel Aviv. Archaeologists uncovered a collective burial tomb that measured about 36 by 26 feet. It was entered through a circular shaft. Inside they discovered clay ossuaries that

---

3. Ehud Galili, Avi Gopher, V. Eshed, and I. Hershkovitz, "Burial Practices at the Submerged Pre-Pottery Neolithic C Site of Atlit-Yam, Northern Coast of Israel," *BASOR* 339 (2005): 1–19.

4. Amihai Mazar, *Archaeology of the Land of the Bible* (New York: Doubleday, 1990), 49.

contained desiccated bones of the dead. Many of the ossuaries were shaped like houses with gabled roofs, and some of the houses were on stilts. Only parts of skeletons were brought and interred in the ossuaries, and often the ossuaries contained the bones of more than one person.

Fig. 18.3. Nawamis Burial

In the regions of the eastern and southern Sinai, beehive-shaped structures, measuring anywhere from 10 to 20 feet in diameter and up to 8 feet in height, have been found in clusters. They were aboveground tombs, and are called *nawamis* by the locals. Some of them contained multiple burials, and both primary and secondary burials were included. Many scholars agree that they were built at the end of the Chalcolithic period by indigenous pastoralists.[5]

EARLY BRONZE AGE (CA. 3200–2200 B.C.)

At the outset of the Early Bronze Age, a population shift occurred in which groups began to settle more heavily in the Mediterranean wet zone of Palestine. Instead of living in the desert fringes, settlement expanded into the highlands and the coastal plain. One site survey in the hill country around Hebron, for example, demonstrates that there was a 400 percent increase

5. Ofer Bar-Yosef, Israel Hershkovitz, Gideon Arbel, and Avner Goren, "The Orientation of *Nawamis* Entrances in Southern Sinai: Expressions of Religious Belief and Seasonality?," *TA* 10 (1983): 52–60.

in settlements from the Chalcolithic to the EB period. Most of these were new settlements.

The settlers brought with them a tradition of familial burial in caves. These were multigenerational, and the multiple burials contained a variety of grave offerings. A large cemetery was discovered at Bab edh-Dhra' that was in use during every phase of the EB Age. It is estimated that several thousand tombs were in the cemetery. Shaft tombs—burial caves entered through a shaft—dominated in the early part of the EB. No more than seven skeletons have been found in each cave, and most of them had been disarticulated (i.e., skulls were separated from bodies). The cemetery also included several hundred so-called charnel houses. These were broad-roomed buildings with burials inside, and the insides were charred from fire. The purpose of the burning was probably not for cremation, but archaeologists are uncertain regarding its meaning. Yohanan Aharoni is perhaps correct when he says about this vast cemetery complex, "Although a settlement from that period has been discovered in the near vicinity, it would appear that this burial ground not only served the needs of that community but also may have been a traditional burial center for a much larger population."[6]

By the close of the Early Bronze Age, there occurred a decline in urban life in Palestine. Although there is a great debate about why this took place, it seems likely to me that the population shifted away from urbanism to pastoralism due to climate change and deforestation. Shaft tombs continued to be used in this period, and they are in evidence at such sites as Gibeon and Megiddo.

MIDDLE BRONZE AGE (CA. 2200–1550 B.C.)

The physical remains of the Middle Bronze I period (ca. 2200–2000 B.C.) were clearly distinct from the Early Bronze period: pottery, weaponry, burial customs, building form, and other things were different. Instead of the communal, familial tombs of the previous periods, in which generations were entombed, individual interment became normative. Many of these were secondary burials, and the skeletons were incomplete and some were disarticulated.

In the Galilee and Golan regions, megalithic dolmens served as graves in the MB I period. Ahimai Mazar explains that these "are tablelike structures composed of two or more vertical basalt blocks roofed by large rock slabs. A heap of stones usually covered the dolmens creating a tumulus. Such structures are known in Transjordan from the Chalcolithic period, but in

6. Yohanan Aharoni, *The Archaeology of the Land of Israel* (Philadelphia: Westminster Press, 1978), 54.

Fig. 18.4. Golan Dolmen

the Golan and Galilee they definitely date to EB IV/MB I. Dolmens generally
served for the secondary interment of one person."[7]

During the subsequent MB II period, after a long hiatus, there was a
return to the practice of multiple burials in caves. The tomb assemblage from
Jericho at this time was a good example of this cultural behavior. Kathleen
Kenyon describes the methodology of burial as follows:

> Almost without exception there was a long narrow table, usually found
> laden with food. The structure of the table, with two legs at one end and
> one at the other, presumably was designed to enable it to stand on an
> uneven floor. Stools and beds were also found, but these were rare and only
> occurred in tombs of apparently important persons. In other tombs, the
> dead person lay on rush mats, and it can be concluded that beds and stools
> were luxury articles. Most adults were provided with baskets containing
> toilet equipment, alabaster vessels, wooden combs and boxes with applied
> bone decoration.[8]

As new burials took place, the attendants would simply push aside the bones
of the previously deceased and its associated grave gifts into a heap at the
back of the cave. Dozens of skeletons were found in individual caves.

7. Mazar, *Archaeology of the Land of the Bible*, 161. Cf., Clair Epstein, "Dolmens Excavated in the
Golan," *'Atiqot* 17 (1985): 20–58.
    8. Kathleen Kenyon, "Jericho," *EAEHL*, 2:563 (1976).

The revival of familial cave tombs in the MB II period probably coincided with the patriarchal period of the Old Testament. This is how the patriarchs buried their people. So, for example, Jacob refers to the burial place of his family in Hebron, which is "in the cave that is in the field at Machpelah, to the east of Mamre, in the land of Canaan, which Abraham bought with the field from Ephron the Hittite to possess as a burying place. There they buried Abraham and Sarah his wife. There they buried Isaac and Rebekah his wife, and there I buried Leah" (Gen. 49:30–31).

Another burial practice of the MB II period was the interment of bodies beneath houses inside a city. This was common practice at the site of Megiddo.[9] Another type of burial was infant interment in jars placed under the floors of houses and courtyards. At Megiddo, three, possibly four, infants were buried that way.[10]

LATE BRONZE AGE (1550–1200 B.C.)

During the Late Bronze Age in Palestine, numerous people groups were present in one form or another in the land. This reality is reflected in the Old Testament when Canaan is described as the land of "the Canaanites, the Hittites, the Hivites, the Perizzites, the Girgashites, the Amorites, and the Jebusites" (e.g., Josh. 3:10). The burial customs reflect that diversity, as various practices were prevalent in Palestine at that time.

Caves containing multiple burials continue to appear in the archaeological record, and they presumably were generational. The tombs were either natural caves or man-made ones. Grave objects, such as jewelry, were commonly found in them. There were, however, also cemeteries that contained individual burials, but they were found particularly along the coastal region.

While burials were predominately situated outside the city walls, one marked exception was that some tombs were built into the stone under some houses inside the cities.[11] At Megiddo, for example, three of them have been discovered. Burial T1 was constructed in a residential quarter, and it consisted of a burial chamber with a corbeled roof. It looked like a small royal tomb of antiquity. In the chamber was found "a stone bench on which a skeleton was lying in a supine position. On the floor were at least five other full-length skeletons."[12] Similar burial structures have been discovered at Tel Dan and Tel Aphek from the LB period.

9. See Kathleen Kenyon, "Middle and Late Bronze Age Strata at Megiddo," *Levant* 1 (1969): 25–60.

10. P. L. O. Guy, *Megiddo Tombs* (Chicago: University of Chicago Press, 1938), 137.

11. Kathleen Kenyon, *The Bible and Recent Archaeology* (Atlanta: John Knox Press, 1978), 23.

12. Rivka Gonen, *Burial Patterns and Cultural Diversity in Late Bronze Age Canaan* (Winona Lake, IN: Eisenbrauns, 1991), 139.

Other burial customs from the LB period perhaps reflect specific population groups. At the site of Deir el-Balah, located in the southern coastal plain, archaeologists unearthed a large cemetery dating to the fourteenth to early twelfth centuries B.C. The settlement appears to have been an Egyptian outpost. Graves there were dug into the sand, and then the deceased, interred in anthropoid clay coffins, were buried in them. This practice was clearly Egyptian or Egyptian-influenced; they mimicked the style of sarcophagus production in ancient Egypt. During the Early Iron Age, the Philistines in the southern coastal plain adopted this burial custom.

IRON AGE (CA. 1200–586 B.C.)

The beginning of the Iron I period (ca. 1200–1000 B.C.) was one of disruption, migratory movements, and military engagements in the land of Palestine. Various people groups were attempting to establish themselves in the land. Burial customs of the time reflected that diversity, and they may, in fact, be used as ethnic indicators. The areas settled by the Sea Peoples, for example, contained cemeteries and burial remains that were perhaps peculiar to them at the time. The anthropoid clay coffins first seen in the LB II period in the southern coastal plain continued to be used, but now by the Sea Peoples. As mentioned above, this practice was certainly inspired by Egyptian burial custom and was adopted by the Sea Peoples. These later anthropoid coffins had two styles: some of the facial forms were grotesque, that is, with distorted and twisted features, and some were of a more natural appearance. At Tell el-Farah (South) (Tell Sharuhen), William F. Petrie discovered two anthropoid clay coffins with the grotesque form; the associated cemetery contained many graves that contained especially large quantities of Philistine pottery from the twelfth through eleventh centuries B.C. The site of Beth Shean, located between the Jezreel and Jordan Valleys, appears to have been in the hands of the Sea Peoples during the Iron I period (see, e.g., 1 Sam. 31:12). Clay anthropoid coffins were discovered there, as described by Frances James:

> The lightly fired clay coffins are of two types: grotesqueries, of which no more than half a dozen are recorded; and what might be called normal faces. The latter give a definite impression of being individual portraits. It has been suggested, but that does not seem likely, that all of the latter type were women.[13]

Other burial types of the Sea Peoples in Palestine included individual cist burials, found at Azor and Tel Zeror. There were also unique styles of

13. Frances James, "Beth-shean," *EAEHL*, 1:220 (1975).

coffin making, which involved "breaking necks of and joining two large storage jars."[14] Recently, excavators unearthed a Philistine cemetery at Ashkelon, and publication of that material certainly has the potential of reshaping our understanding of Philistine burial practices.

Scant archaeological evidence exists for Israelite burial customs during the Iron I period. It appears that the Hebrews simply adopted the methodology of the Canaanites, which was to inter their dead in family burial caves that had often been naturally formed. During the monarchic period (ca. 1000–586 B.C.), the Hebrews purposefully created communal family tombs hewn from rock.[15] A network of such rock-cut chambers was found at Samaria, for example. They included rock-cut benches in the interior on which to place the recently deceased, and niches for bones to be placed of the not-so-recently deceased. Most of the cemeteries were located outside the towns, except notably Jerusalem, where many of the kings were buried inside the city walls (e.g., 1 Kings 14:31).

Fig. 18.5.
Anthropoid
Clay Coffin

Some have rightly suggested that the Hebrew rock-cut communal burial caves were designed to look like the common Israelite four-room house. If this be the case, it would not be surprising because a connection between one's earthly living space and one's future abode was commonly made in antiquity; see, for example, the ossuaries at Azor from the Chalcolithic period that resembled houses. The grave offerings discovered in many of the Israelite and Judaean tombs also argue in favor of a view of a future afterlife. Scholars used to believe that there were few burial gifts in these graves, but that has been disproved.

Numerous tombs from this time have been found in Jerusalem. Typical ones were found, for example, just southwest of the city in an area called the "Shoulder of Hinnom" (Ketef Hinnom). Several belong to the late Iron Age (ca. eighth through seventh centuries B.C.). Steps that had been hewn out of bedrock gave entrance to a tomb, and they led to an antechamber. Doors in the antechamber gave access to several burial chambers. The design of the tomb could be quite elaborate, including hewn recessed framing around each chamber doorway and a double cornice to crown the ceiling architecture. The burial chamber itself commonly had three burial shelves, one on each wall. Hewn out of the bench was a horseshoe-shaped headrest for the deceased. Beneath the bench was a repository, in which decayed bones and grave objects, such as pottery, metal, and glass wares were deposited.

14. Mazar, *Archaeology of the Land of the Bible*, 327.

15. For Judahite practices, see Elizabeth Block-Smith, *Judahite Burial Practices and Beliefs about the Dead* (Sheffield: JSOT Press, 1992).

In 1979, Gabriel Barkay unearthed seven Late Iron Age rock-cut tombs at Ketef Hinnom. Cave 24 contained five burial chambers, and a repository in one of them yielded remains of almost one hundred bodies and over one thousand objects. The most remarkable finds were two silver amulets containing the priestly benediction of Numbers 6 in Hebrew (see page 214–15 above).[16]

KEY TERMS

anthropoid clay coffin
dolmen
nawami
shaft tomb

DISCUSSION QUESTIONS

1. What are the glaring differences between how the ancients buried their dead and the way we bury our dead in Western society today? What do the differences underscore regarding the worldviews of antiquity and today?
2. Why did many of the ancients include grave goods in the burials of their people? Did that practice have anything to do with a concept of the afterlife?
3. Why do you think that the coffins found at Deir el-Balah were made to look like humans? Does this remind you of ancient Egyptian burial practices?
4. The Israelites commonly buried their dead in family burial caves. Why was that practice important? Did it have to do with the Old Testament concept of a person "sleeping with his fathers"? And what does that mean?

FOR FURTHER READING

Block-Smith, Elizabeth. *Judahite Burial Practices and Beliefs about the Dead*. Sheffield: JSOT Press, 1992.

Gonen, Rivka. *Burial Practices and Cultural Diversity in Late Bronze Age Canaan*. Winona Lake, IN: Eisenbrauns, 1991.

Guy, P. L. O. *Megiddo Tombs*. Chicago: University of Chicago Press, 1938.

16. See, most recently, Gabriel Barkay, Marilyn J. Lundberg, Andrew G. Vaughn, and Bruce Zuckerman, "The Amulets from Ketef Hinnom: A New Edition and Evaluation," *BASOR* 334 (2004): 41–71; Nadav Na'aman, "A New Appraisal of the Silver Amulets from Ketef Hinnom," *IEJ* 61 (2011): 184–95.

CHAPTER 19

Small Finds

"It is interesting to see that people had so much clutter even thousands of years ago. The only way to get rid of it all was to bury it, and then some archaeologist went and dug it all up."—Karl Pilkington

T HE THREE MAJOR finds in excavation work, especially on a tell, are architecture, fortifications, and pottery. We have already discussed in detail those various finds in ancient Palestine. Much less prominent, although critical for settlement reconstruction, are small finds that are more intermittent in their appearance in archaeological contexts. A *small find* may be defined as any man-made object discovered through excavation work that is not architecture, fortifications, or pottery. That description is vague, and could properly be categorized as a miscellaneous class. What is included in the category are such things as coins, stone idols, metal tools, jewelry, and so forth. The type of small finds varies from site to site, and they are helpful in determining a site's subsistence base, its trade connections, the natural resources of the area, and so forth. For example, the excavations at the mound of et-Tel, located just north of the Sea of Galilee, uncovered many remains of fishing gear (hooks, sinkers, sewing needles) from the Hellenistic / Early Roman periods. These small finds give weight to the proposal that et-Tel is to be identified with the ancient fishing village of Bethsaida that appears prominently in the New Testament gospel accounts.

In this chapter, we will briefly discuss the topic of small finds, and we will do so according to the material from which the objects were produced. The material composition of these relics may be subdivided into five general categories: stone, bone, wood, metal, and glass.

ANCIENT STONEWORKING

The earliest small finds in human history were stone implements used to hunt and gather, and then to prepare food. In the first human settlements in ancient Palestine, such as Ubeideyah, located just south of the Sea of Galilee, people used mostly what are called core tools. Robert Braidwood explains what a core tool is like: "The modification of an original, unworked piece of stone that produces any kind of chipped stone tool is always done by striking off or otherwise removing smaller pieces from the original larger piece. The general term for the smaller fragments so removed is *flake*; the larger piece is usually called a *core*."[1] The large core was used for various types of tools like hammers, axes, and choppers. The flake would have been employed as a smaller tool, such as a knife or scraper. Many of the flakes knocked off of a core were discarded. The flakes that were kept often would be modified, or retouched, for particular purposes. A flake industry appeared at the earliest sites in ancient Palestine, such as at Jisr Banat Yaqub, but the core tradition for making tools dominated the earliest periods.

Stone was used for other activities as well, like hunting, cooking, jewelry making, and idolatry (stone figurines). Arrowheads were discovered at early sites, such as En Gev. At Beidha, a Neolithic factory was uncovered that produced stone, shell, and bone beads (ca. 7000 B.C.). Some of the earliest housing was constructed of stone.

The dominance of stone was eclipsed and went into decline with the discovery of metals during the Bronze Age. Although some stone implements have been found in every period of the archaeological record, they became less vital as time progressed. By the Iron Age, stone tools comprised only a small percentage of the tool industry.

Fig. 19.1.
Neolithic
Goddess
Figurine

ANCIENT BONEWORKING

Bone tools also appeared in the archaeological record of early settlements, although at a later stage than stone tools. At Jisr Banat Yaqub, one of the earliest habitations in Palestine, archaeologists found a thriving tool industry that was primarily one of stone, but some bone tools were also extant. "There are knives, pins, needles with eyes, and little double-pointed straight bars of bone, called *gorges*, that were probably used for catching fish."[2] Examples of bone beads and picks have been found at certain early settlements like El Wad. Excavations at Ashkelon on the Mediterranean coast have revealed an extensive bone industry.[3]

1. Robert J. Braidwood, *Prehistoric Men*, 8th ed. (Glenview, IL: Scott, Foresman and Company, 1975), 41.
2. Braidwood, *Prehistoric Men*, 76.
3. Paula Wapnish, "Beauty and Utility in Bone—New Light on Bone Crafting," *BAR* 17 (1991): 54–57. For a general study of the topic, see Brian Hesse and Paula Wapnish, *Animal Bone Archaeology* (Washington: Taraxacum, 1985).

Bones were also used for weaponry in the early settlements. At Ksar Akil (in Lebanon), a large collection of bone and antler points was found, and they were employed as projectile points for arrows, darts, and spears.[4] Figurines and idols made of bone are known from these early times. A good example are four heads of bone figures discovered in the Nahal Hemar Cave excavation, which date to the beginning of the Neolithic period (ca. 8000 B.C.).

ANCIENT WOODWORKING

The value of wood in the processes of cultural development in ancient Palestine was considerable. Tree cover was denser than it is in modern times, and thus the people groups had a local resource that was conveniently available.[5] Local populations often utilized locally available materials.[6] In ancient Palestine, wood was used in a variety of ways. In building construction, it was an integral part of roofing, pillar beams, gates, and doors. Carpentry, such as shipbuilding and furniture making, was a prominent trade. Many tools had wooden handles, like hammers and axes. Perhaps the most important use of wood was as a fuel. It was critical to the development of many trades, crafts, and arts: cooking, metallurgy, and ceramics required wood for fuel.

One problem for the archaeologist is that wood easily decays in archaeological contexts. Remains of it survived almost exclusively in the arid atmosphere of the Dead Sea region. So, for instance, the excavations of the fortress of Masada uncovered numerous wooden objects, like a wooden comb and the wooden shaft of a Zealot's arrow. In tombs excavated at Jericho, the archaeologists discovered instances

> where even desiccated joints of meat still lay in the original wooden dishes. These tombs were cut in limestone and then walled up after the burials had been made. Carbon monoxide and methane gas seeping into closed tombs through cracks in the rock replaced the normal air that would have allowed bacteria to live. Consequently organic materials have survived.[7]

Extreme wet conditions can also preserve ancient wooden objects. A fishing boat from the Roman period was preserved for over two thousand years as it lay submerged near the muddy shoreline of the Sea of Galilee.[8] When I served

---

4. Christopher A. Bergman, "Hafting and Use of Bone and Antler Points from Ksar Akil, Lebanon," in *La main et l'outil: Manches et emmanchements préhistoriques*, ed. Danielle Stordeur (Lyon: Maison de l'Orient, 1987), 117–26.

5. John D. Currid, "The Deforestation of the Foothills of Palestine," *PEQ* 116 (1984): 1–11.

6. Amos Rapoport, *House Form and Culture* (Englewood Cliffs, NJ: Prentice-Hall, 1969), 108.

7. Peter R. S. Moorey, *Excavations in Palestine* (Guildford, UK: Lutterworth, 1981), 98.

8. Shelley Wachsmann, "The Galilee Boat—2,000-Year-Old Hull Recovered Intact," *BAR* 14 (1988): 18–33.

on the staff of the excavation of the commercial harbor at ancient Carthage, we uncovered a fragment of a wooden beam that perhaps was used as part of the cofferdam employed in building the city's quay wall.

ANCIENT METALWORKING

The first evidence of metal being used was at the outset of the Neolithic period (ca. 8000 B.C.). The first metal employed was natural or native copper that did not undergo any type of smelting process. The copper was simply "fashioned into small decorative pins and pendants, a phase that has aptly been called trinket metallurgy."[9] This was the first, small step in the development of metalworking in the ancient Near East.

Fig. 19.2. Nahal Mishmor Hoard

Mining and smelting industries did not appear to any degree prior to the fifth and fourth millennia B.C.[10] A good example of a thriving and sophisticated copper industry from the Chalcolithic period was discovered in a cave in the Judean Desert. The "Cave of the Treasure," or the Nahal Mishmor horde, included 436 copper objects that were perhaps used for ceremonial purposes. The items were well made and products of sophisticated casting methods. The industry included a "lost wax" process, in which an alloy of copper was mixed with a small amount of arsenic or some other substance to strengthen the metal.[11] Copper installations were in operation during this period in the Beersheba region, in particular at the site of Tell Abu Matar. Gold and silver also began to be used at this time, but in the limited capacity of jewelry making.

Bronze, an alloy consisting primarily of copper with the addition of tin, began to be used in the fourth millennium B.C. The mixture of the two made the metal harder and less brittle. Copper by itself was too soft to make

9. Paul T. Craddock, "Metallurgy in the Old World," in *The Oxford Companion to Archaeology*, ed. Brian Fagan (New York: Oxford University Press, 1996), 461.

10. Thomas Levy, "Craft Specialization First Appears in the Chalcolithic Period," *BAR* 16 (1990): 27.

11. Amihai Mazar, *Archaeology of the Land of the Bible* (New York: Doubleday, 1990), 73–74.

tools and weapons from it. This was a great metallurgical advancement, and it was commonly used until late in the second millennium B.C.

Iron was discovered as early as the fourth millennium B.C.. Examples of meteoric iron beads have been found in Egypt from that time. Most scholars used to believe that the smelting process to get iron from rock probably began with the Hittites in the middle of the second millennium B.C. From them, the practice spread throughout the ancient Near East, and by the end of that millennium it was in common use. This view is no longer widely accepted. The first iron implements found in Palestine date to the Iron I period, and they were all discovered in Philistine contexts (e.g., Tell Qasile).[12] Although we are uncertain of the origins of iron production, it may have developed in the Aegean region and then was spread by the Sea Peoples throughout the Mediterranean area.

The advantage of iron over bronze has been hotly debated. Certainly iron was more locally available and more easily produced (not being an alloy). Not all agree, but iron is stronger than bronze, and an iron weapon holds a finer edge.

We will consider now four principal ways in which metalworking was used throughout antiquity.

1. *Weaponry.*[13] The primary metal used throughout the third millennium B.C. in the ancient Near East was copper. Weapons are rarely discovered from the EB period, perhaps due partly to cost factors. Those that have been found were all copper. For example, a hoard of weapons and tools was found at Kfar Monash, which dates to the middle of the third millennium B.C. Weapons included in the stash were axes, spearheads, and ribbed daggers—all made of copper.

By the beginning of the second millennium B.C., bronze weaponry began to appear, and by the MB II period it had replaced copper hardware for the most part. New types of weapons were found from this time, which include duckbill axe heads, shafted spearheads, and ridged daggers. Late Bronze Age weaponry was much like that of the earlier Middle Bronze II period, although there was a great increase in the number and style of bronze weapons. Workshops for bronze production were discovered at several sites, such as at Tel Zeror, where copper ingots were alloyed with tin to make bronze for weapons and tools. In the Timna' Valley, eleven copper mining camps have been found, containing several substantial slag heaps that witness to the mining activity.

---

12. According to 1 Samuel 13:19–22, the Israelites were late to the game. They were at a great military disadvantage to the Philistines because they had no workers of facilities to oversee the production of metalworking, including iron making.

13. For this topic in general, see Boyd Seevers, *Warfare in the Old Testament: The Organization, Weapons, and Tactics of Ancient Near Eastern Armies* (Grand Rapids: Kregel, 2013).

Although it was a gradual process, during the Iron I period the transition was made from bronze to iron as the principal metal used in weapons.[14]

2. *Tools.* The earliest tool industry in the ancient Near East was a stone tradition that included both core tools and flake tools.[15] Not until the Chalcolithic period did copper smelting appear in the semiarid regions around Beersheba, in particular at the site of Abu Matar. Copper adzes, used for scraping wood, were found there that were produced from a single mold. Of the 436 objects found in the Nahal Mishmar horde, twenty of them were copper chisels.

Copper and bronze tools have been discovered from the Early Bronze Age at many sites. There appears to have been some site specialization dedicated to metallurgy. For example, a copper-mining complex was found at Nebi Salah in the Sinai, which included mining, refining, and casting activities. Copper tools were found there, such as square-cut awls. Metal tools, however, were relatively rare at this time: perhaps the best tool assemblage was that of the Kfar Monash horde. It seems to have been a stash of tools for woodcutters, including copper adzes, pegs, chisels, and a saw for felling trees.

With the introduction of iron at the close of the second millennium in Palestine, previous types of tool production gradually disappeared. For instance, replacement of stone sickles by metal ones occurred late in the area. Even into the Iron Age, farmers continued to reap their harvest with flint sickles, just like their Neolithic ancestors.[16] Iron tools eventually dominated because the metal was stronger than copper and bronze. For example, bronze plow points broke easily in the ground, but iron ones did not.

3. *Jewelry.* One of the earliest purposes of metal in the ancient Near East was for human adornment. At the outset of the Neolithic period (ca. 8000 B.C.), beads hammered out of native copper have been found, such as at the site of Cayonu in modern-day Turkey.[17] By the Chalcolithic period in Palestine, metal jewelry appeared more frequently. At Tell Abu Matar, which contained smelting and processing facilities, copper beads have been unearthed. The Nahal Mishmar horde included copper adornments from this time, such as armlets and perhaps a crown. All these objects were probably ceremonial, which may be the first use of jewelry prior to a public application.

Gold jewelry was clearly in evidence in the Early Bronze Age, in which a gold plaque with decoration was discovered in a tomb in Galilee. There was a great increase in gold jewelry in the Middle Bronze period throughout the

14. James D. Muhly, "How Iron Age Technology Changed the Ancient World—and Gave the Philistines a Military Edge," *BAR* 8 (1982): 40–54.

15. Braidwood, *Prehistoric Men*, 41.

16. Rivka Gonen, *Grain* (Jerusalem: Shikmona, 1979), 30.

17. Braidwood, *Prehistoric Men*, 136.

ancient Near East. At Byblos, along the Mediterranean coast, a cache of gold and silver ceremonial weaponry was found. A collection of fine gold jewelry was discovered at Tell el-Ajjul from the close of the Middle Bronze Age; it included earrings, bracelets, and amulets.

Metal jewelry from the Iron Age in Palestine is a rare find, and it was simply and oftentimes crudely manufactured.

4. *Coinage.* Metal coins appeared late in the history of the Old Testament. The first coins in the ancient Near East were likely struck during the seventh through sixth centuries B.C. in western Asia Minor.[18] Few coins have been discovered in Iron Age Palestine. Coins were not minted and circulated there until after the fall of Jerusalem in 586 B.C. The medium of payment in transactions in the Iron Age was silver; amorphic sheets or slabs of silver have been discovered at Israelite settlements, such as a silver horde from Eshtemoa from the tenth century B.C. Scales in which stone weights were used on one side of the instrument measured the value of the silver ingots. Bronze scales have been found in late Judean contexts of the seventh century B.C.

ANCIENT IVORY WORKING

It is unclear when ivory, material of the tusks of elephants and hippopotamuses, was first employed in human culture. In ancient Palestine, it appeared in a flurry during the Chalcolithic period in the Beersheba region. The site of Safadi, in fact, had an ivory craft specialization. Excavations there uncovered numerous fertility figurines of ivory, the ivory representation of a hippopotamus head, and an ivory bell with perforations. These were all manufactured at the site, perhaps from local hippopotamus tusks or from elephant tusks imported from Africa or Syria.

Ivory carving was rare in the ensuing Early and Middle Bronze Ages. Ivory objects, such as a comb and a dagger, have been found at Ai, Jericho, and Beth Yerah. An ivory plaque from Megiddo pictures a lion attacking a mountain goat, and it dates to the Middle Bronze period (ca. 1800 B.C.).

Perhaps the height of ivory production in ancient Palestine occurred during the Late Bronze Age. Amihai Mazar comments,

> In summary, the Late Bronze ivory collections from Canaan demonstrate a vivid local art as well as international connections and influences. Toward the end of the Late Bronze Age and in the first half of the twelfth century

18. John Betlyon, "Coinage," *ABD*, 1:1076–89.

19. For a general survey, see Richard Barnett, *Ancient Ivories in the Middle East* (Jerusalem: Hebrew University, 1982).

B.C.E. the Canaanite rulers possessed a variety of art objects reflecting the cosmopolitan nature of the period.[20]

The most spectacular collection was found in stratum VIIA at Megiddo. Excavators discovered in the "ivory rooms," which some scholars identify as a treasure-house for a king, almost 300 ivory artifacts. Other collections from this time, although not as elaborate as the Megiddo finds, were uncovered at Lachish and Tell el-Farah (South).

The Iron I period in Palestine was one of political upheaval. The Hittite Empire had collapsed, Egyptian power was in decline, and both the Israelites and the Philistines were attempting to get a strong foothold in the land. In the midst of those changes, however, some of the practices of the native Canaanites were integrated into the cultures of the new peoples in the land. Ivory works found at Iron I Megiddo and the Philistine sites of Tel Miqne and Tell Qasile demonstrate that the art of ivory carving was a continuation of Late Bronze Age Canaanite artistry.

Fig. 19.3. Samaria Ivory

During the Iron II period, beginning in the ninth century B.C., the demand for and use of ivory in the ancient Near East was "almost insatiable."[21] The primary ivory find in Israel was the grouping of over two hundred pieces from Samaria published by the Palestine Exploration Fund.[22] Most of these

20. Mazar, *Archaeology of the Land of the Bible*, 271.

21. Hershel Shanks, "Ancient Ivory," *BAR* 11 (1985): 40–53.

22. John W. Crowfoot and Grace M. Crowfoot, *Samaria-Sebaste II: The Early Ivories from Samaria* (London: Palestine Exploration Fund, 1938).

were uncovered in a building that may be identified with the "ivory house" of Ahab (1 Kings 22:39). They perhaps belong to the ninth century B.C., although some scholars date them to the eighth century B.C. Many of the ivories were small plaques used to adorn furniture or as paneling for the walls of the building. The style of the ivories reflected Phoenician techniques, and, of course, there was a close connection between Samaria and Phoenicia at this time, particularly through Jezebel, the wife of Ahab.

Ivory objects in Judah at this time were sparse. A few items have been uncovered, such as a bottle stopper in the shape of a goat's head from the ninth century B.C. at Lachish. No major collection, however, has been uncovered.

ANCIENT GLASSMAKING

Glass first appeared in the ancient Near East as a natural black volcanic glass called obsidian. In Palestine, it was first commonly used in the PPN period, having been found at Jericho, Beidha, Nahal Oren, and elsewhere. But since obsidian is not native to Palestine, it was likely imported from Anatolia to the north. The Anatolian site of Catal Huyuk had a major obsidian industry at this time. At this early date, "a bulk carrying trade had been established, the forerunner of commerce, and the routes were set by which, at later times, the metal trade was to move."[23]

The earliest man-made glass appeared in both Egypt and Mesopotamia at the beginning of the Early Bronze Age (ca. 3000 B.C.). In both regions, it was manufactured into beads for jewelry. "Man-made glass was produced by fusion of various raw materials, normally including silicates, soda, and lime. Often it also contained potash and lead oxide."[24]

Glass vessels were not produced until the close of the Middle Bronze Age (ca. 1600 B.C.). They appear at this time in both Egypt and Mesopotamia. In Palestine, the first glass vessels have been found in the Late Bronze Age levels at several sites, including Lachish and Beth Shean.

The process of glassblowing did not begin until the Roman period. That invention made glassmaking simple, and it became a common trade. Glass objects were ubiquitous during the Roman period, and in some ways characterize and define the time for the archaeologist. Jerusalem had a major glass factory at this time.[25]

---

23. Braidwood, *Prehistoric Men*, 129.

24. John D. Currid, *Doing Archaeology in the Land of the Bible* (Grand Rapids: Baker, 1999), 108.

25. Nahman Avigad, "Jerusalem Flourishing—A Craft Center for Stone, Pottery and Glass," *BAR* 9 (1983): 48–65.

KEY TERMS

core
flake
small find

DISCUSSION QUESTIONS

1. How can small finds in an excavation help to identify the subsistence base of a settlement?
2. What were the many uses of wood in an ancient society?
3. Why was the discovery of metalworking so important in ancient Near Eastern history?

FOR FURTHER READING

See the basic archaeological introductions that have been cited in this book, such as those by Amihai Mazar, G. E. Wright, W. F. Albright, Paul W. Lapp, and Yohanan Aharoni.

Appendix I

Basic Timeline of the Ancient Near East

Palestine	Egypt	Mesopotamia
Neolithic 8000–4000		
PPN 8000–6000		
PN 6000–4000		
Chalcolithic 4000–3200		
Early Bronze Age	Early Dynastic Period 2920–2575	
EB I 3200–2800		Early Dynastic Period 2700–2400
EB II 2800–2600		
EB III 2600–2350	Old Kingdom 2575–2134	Akkad, Ur III 2400–2000
EB IV 2350–2200		
Middle Bronze Age		
MB I 2200–2000	First Intermediate Period 2134–2040	
MB II 2000–1550	Middle Kingdom 2040–1640	Old Babylonian/Old Assyrian 2000–1600
Late Bronze Age	Second Intermediate Period 1640–1550	
LB I 1550–1400	New Kingdom 1550–1070	Middle Babylonian/Middle Assyrian 1600–1000
LB II 1400–1200		

Palestine	Egypt	Mesopotamia
Iron Age		
Iron I 1200–1000	Third Intermediate Period 1070–712	Neo-Babylonian/Neo-Assyrian 1155–539
Iron II 1000–586	Late Period 712–343	
Persian 539–332		Persian 539–332
Hellenistic 332–37		Seleucid Era 312–141
Roman 37 B.C.–A.D. 324		Parthian 141 B.C.–A.D. 228

APPENDIX 2

The Kings of Israel and Judah

The list of kings on these pages contains the names and approximate dates of the Hebrew monarchs in the Old Testament. Overlapping dates indicate coregencies, and these are highlighted in the list. Athaliah, who ruled Judah from 841 to 835, is marked with a QR: she became queen regnant due to the assassination of Ahaziah her son at the hands of Jehu (2 Kings 9:27). Pronunciation of names is anglicized according to common usage, but it should be noted that the original pronunciation of names in Hebrew is often much different. For example, Solomon's name in Hebrew is שְׁלֹמֹה (shelomoh).

United Monarchy of Israel and Judah (ca. 1050–930)

Saul	1050–1010
Ishbosheth	1010–1008 (north only)
David	1010–1002 (Judah only)
David	1002–970
Solomon	970–930

Divided Kingdom: Israel (930–722)

Jeroboam I	930–910
Nadab	910–909
Baasha	909–886
Elah	886–885
Zimri	885
Tibni	885–884
Omri	884–874

Ahab	874–853
Ahaziah	853–852
Jehoram/Joram	852–841
Jehu	841–814
Jehoahaz	814–798
Joash/Jehoash	798–782
Jeroboam II	782–753 [coregent from 793]
Zechariah	753–752
Shallum	752
Menahem	752–742
Pekahiah	742–740
Pekah	740–732
Hoshea	732–722

Divided Kingdom: Judah (930–586)

Rehoboam	930–913
Abijam	913–910
Asa	910–870
Jehoshaphat	870–848 [coregent from 872]
Jehoram/Joram	848–841 [coregent from 853]
Ahaziah	841
Athaliah	841–835 [QR]
Joash/Jehoash	835–796
Amaziah	796–767
Azariah/Uzziah	767–740 [coregent from 792]
Jotham	740–732
Ahaz	732–716 [coregent from 735]
Hezekiah	716–687
Manasseh	687–643 [coregent from 696]
Amon	643–640
Josiah	640–609
Jehoahaz	609
Jehoiakim	609–597
Jehoiachin	597
Zedekiah	597–586

APPENDIX 3

Extrabiblical References to the Kings of Israel and Judah

UNITED MONARCHY

David (1010–970)

The Tel Dan Inscription. This Aramaic inscription from the ninth century B.C. was probably a victory stele set up by the king of Damascus celebrating his defeat of several Israelite cities. It contains a line that says he "killed [Ahazi]yahu, son of [Joram, kin]g of the house of David." While some scholars attempt to explain away the reference by claiming *bytdwd* ("house of David") as either a place name or the name for a temple of a deity, it likely simply refers to the lineage of David, the second king of the united monarchy and perhaps the most significant ruler in Israel's history.

The Moabite Stone. This inscription from the ninth century B.C. is on a victory stele of the Moabite king Mesha commemorating a victory over the Israelites. Andre Lemaire translates lines 31–32 as "[. . . . . . .] the sheep of the land. And *the house [of Da]vid* dwelt

Fig. App. 3.1.
House of David
Inscription

in Horonen. [. . . . .] and Kamosh said to me: 'Go down! Fight against Horonen. And I went down.'"[1]

ISRAEL (NORTHERN KINGDOM)

Omri (884–874)

The Moabite Stone. Mesha, king of Moab, describing his rebellion against Israel, writes the text in the first person. He narrates how "Omri, king of Israel" had oppressed the Moabites and that Omri's "son" had proclaimed, "I will oppress Moab" (lines 4–6). The term "son" does not necessarily signify an immediate descendant, but one in Omri's line: 2 Kings 3 indicates that Mesha's rebellion took place during the reign of Jehoram (ca. 850 B.C.), who was a grandson of Omri.

The Black Obelisk of Shalmaneser III. Shalmaneser III, king of Assyria, records a list of cities he conquered in a military campaign in 841 B.C. In the inscription, he refers to "the tribute of Jehu, son of Omri." Again, "son" here refers to a descendant and not to a next generational son.

Long after the death of Omri, Assyrian documents of the eighth century B.C. continued to call Israel "the land of Omri."[2]

Ahab (874–853)

The Tel Dan Inscription. King Ahab of Samaria is secondarily cited in this inscription when Hazael boasts, "[And I killed Jo]ram, son of A[hab], king of Israel."

Joram/Jehoram (852–841)

The Tel Dan Inscription. This stele from the late ninth century B.C. commemorates the defeat of Israel by Hazael (king of Aram-Syria). One line reads, "[And I killed Jo]ram, son of A[hab], king of Israel, and [I] killed [Ahazi]yahu, son of [Joram, kin]g of the house of David." According to 2 Kings 9:24, it was Jehu (841–814) who killed Joram. Because Jehu and Hazael had apparently made a previous alliance (1 Kings 19:17), both men could take credit for the killing of Joram.

Jehu (841–814)

Inscriptions preserved on two monumental bulls at Calah (modern Nimrud) from the time of Shalmaneser III (ca. 858–824) announce, "At that

---

1. Andre Lemaire, "'House of David' Restored in Moabite Inscription," *BAR* 20 (1994): 30–37.
2. John D. Currid and David P. Barrett, *Crossway ESV Bible Atlas* (Wheaton, IL: Crossway, 2010), 143.

time I received the tribute of the Tyrians and the Sidonians, and of Jehu of the house of Omri."

Fig. App. 3.2. King Jehu, the Black Obelisk of Shalmaneser III

The Black Obelisk of Shalmaneser III. A scene depicting Jehu prostrating himself and presenting tribute to the Assyrian monarch accompanies this ninth-century inscription. The text reads, "The tribute of Jehu, son of Omri: I received from him silver, gold, a golden bow, a golden beaker, a golden goblet, golden cups, golden buckets, tin, a staff of the king's hand (and) javelins."

Joash/Jehoash (798–782)

The Assyrian monarch Adad-Nirari III had a major military campaign against Syria and Palestine in 805–802 B.C., and he had it recorded on a victory stele that was discovered in a Late Assyrian shrine at Tell al Rimah. The inscription mentions that "Joash the Samaritan" was forced to pay tribute to the Assyrians.

Jeroboam II (782–753)

An eighth-century seal was discovered at the Israelite city of Megiddo, and it contained an inscription that reads, "[Belonging] to Shema servant of Jeroboam."

Menahem (752–742)

In the annals of the Assyrian king Tiglath-pileser III (743–726), which are inscribed on slabs at the site of Calah, the monarch comments, "I received tribute from Kushtashpi of Commagene, Rezon of Damascus, Menahem of Samaria, Hiram of Tyre . . ."[3]

Also in the annals of Tiglath-pileser III, the Assyrian king declares, "[As for Menahem I ov]erwhelmed him [like a snowstorm] and he . . . fled like a bird, alone, [and bowed to my feet(?)]. I returned him to his place [and imposed tribute upon him, to wit:] gold, silver, linen garments with multi-colored trimmings, . . . great . . . I received from him."[4] Second Kings 15:19–20 describes the scene of the tribute that Menahem exacted from his own people in order to pay off the Assyrians.

Pekah (740–732) and Hoshea (732–722)

These last two kings of the northern kingdom of Israel are mentioned by name in Tiglath-pileser III's annals: "Israel (*lit.* Omri-Land) . . . all its inhabitants (and) their possessions I led to Assyria. They overthrew their king Pekah (*Pa-qa-ha*) and I placed Hoshea (*A-u-si-'*) as king over them. I received from them 10 talents of gold, 1,000 (?) talents of silver as their [tri] bute and brought them to Assyria." For further study, see 2 Kings 15:27–31.

A late eighth-century Hebrew seal contains an inscription that mentions the name of Israel's last king: "Belonging to Abdi servant of Hoshea."[5]

JUDAH (SOUTHERN KINGDOM)

Ahaziah (841)

The Tel Dan Inscription. On this stele, Hazael not only claims to have killed Joram of the northern kingdom, but also says he slew Ahaziah of Judah: "and [I] killed [Ahazi]yahu, son of [Joram, kin]g of the house of David." Second Kings 9:27 records the assassination of Ahaziah.

Uzziah (767–740)

Also known by the name Azariah (2 Kings 15:1), this Judean king's name appears on two seals from the eighth century that belonged to his royal officials. One is a red limestone scarab that depicts a man holding a scepter on one side with an inscription that reads, "Belonging to Shebanyahu." The reverse side pictures two winged solar discs with an inscription reading, "Belonging to Shebanyahu, servant of Uzziah." The second seal bears a similar inscription that says, "Belonging to Abiyau, servant of Uzziyau."

A stone plaque found on the Mount of Olives that dates to the second

---

3. *ANET*, 283.
4. *ANET*, 283–84.
5. Andre Lemaire, "Name of Israel's Last King Surfaces in a Private Collection," *BAR* 21 (1995): 49–52.

temple period states in Aramaic, "Here were brought the bones of Uzziah, king of Judah. Not to be opened!" According to 2 Chronicles 26:16–23, Uzziah was a leper when he died and therefore was not buried in the royal tombs (v. 23). This plaque perhaps served as a slab covering for an ossuary to which Uzziah's bones had been moved.

Jotham (740–732)

An eighth-century seal found at Tell el-Kheleifeh (ancient Ezion-geber) depicts a horned ram, and above it is the inscription "Belonging to Jotham."[6]

Ahaz/Jehoahaz (732–716)

King Ahaz (a shortened form of Jehoahaz) of Judah refused to join an alliance against the Assyrians, so he asked for military aid from Tiglath-pileser III. The Assyrians helped Judah, but it came at a price: Judah became a vassal of Assyria and paid tribute to that nation. In the annals of Tiglath-pileser III, the Assyrian king boasts, "[I received] the tribute of . . . Mitinti of Ashkelon, Jehoahaz of Judah . . . (consisting of) gold, silver, tin, iron, antimony, linen garments with multicolored trimmings . . . all kinds of costly objects . . ."

Several bullae (a clay bulla was used to seal a papyrus document) have been found containing the name of Ahaz. One impression reads, "Belonging to Ahaz, (son of Yehotam), king of Judah."[7] Yehotam refers to Jotham, who was the father of Ahaz (2 Kings 16:1).

Hezekiah (716–687)

The Prism of Sennacherib. This is a cuneiform inscription containing the records of Sennacherib, king of Assyria (705–681). A six-sided, baked-clay prism dating to 689, it narrates six important military campaigns of the king. One of them recounts the attack on Judah and the siege of Jerusalem during the reign of Hezekiah: "As to Hezekiah, the Jew, he did not submit to my yoke, I laid siege to 46 of his strong cities, walled forts and to the countless small villages in their vicinity, and conquered (them) by means of well-stamped (earth-)ramps, and battering rams brought (thus) near (to the walls) (combined with) the attack by foot soldiers, (using) mines, breaches as well as sapper work. I drove out (of them) 200,150 people, young and old, male and female, horses, mules, donkeys, camels, big and small cattle

Fig. App. 3.3.
Prism of Sennacherib

---

6. See the discussion in Nahman Avigad, "The Jotham Seal from Elath," *BASOR* 163 (1961): 18–22.
7. Robert Deutsch, "First Impression: What We Learn from King Ahaz's Seal," *BAR* 24 (1998): 54–56, 62.

beyond counting, and considered (them) booty. Himself I made a prisoner in Jerusalem, his royal residence, like a bird in a cage. I surrounded him with earthwork in order to molest those who were leaving the city's gate. His towns which I had plundered, I took away from his country and gave them (over) to Mitinti, king of Ashdod, Padi, king of Ekron, and Sillibel, king of Gaza. Thus I reduced his country, but I still increased his tribute . . ."[8]

Several bullae have been found that contain the name of King Hezekiah.[9] Perhaps the most important one was discovered in the recent excavations in the Ophel in Jerusalem. The bulla is a royal seal of the king that depicts a two-winged sun-disc flanked by ankh symbols. The inscription on it reads, "Belonging to Hezekiah, (son of) Ahaz, king of Judah."

Fig. App. 3.4. Royal Seal of Hezekiah

Manasseh (687–643)

Manasseh is listed in the campaign records of the Assyrian monarch Esarhaddon (681–669). The Assyrian king forced numerous vassals to transport building materials from their territories to Nineveh for the construction of Esarhaddon's palace. Among these are "Ba'lu, king of Tyre, Manasseh, king of Judah, Qaushgabri, king of Edom . . ."[10]

Manasseh is also mentioned in the campaign accounts of Esarhaddon's successor, Ashurbanipal (688–633). Many vassals, including Judah, were required to bring "heavy gifts" to the Assyrian king and to muster their troops to help him in battle against Egypt and Nubia.[11]

Jehoiachin (597)

The exiled Judean king Jehoiachin is named in two administrative documents from Babylon in the early sixth century B.C. One of the writings lists rations given to Jehoiachin and his family: "10 (sila) to Ia-ku-u-ki-nu, the son of the king of Judah, 2 ½ sila for the 5 sons of the king of Judah."

8. *ANET*, 288.
9. See Frank Moore Cross, "King Hezekiah's Seal Bears Phoenician Imagery," *BAR* 25 (1999): 42–45, 60; Robert Deutsch, "Lasting Impressions: New Bullae Reveal Egyptian-style Emblems on Judah's Royal Seals," *BAR* 28 (2002): 42–51, 60.
10. *ANET*, 291.
11. *ANET*, 294.

Glossary

abecedary. An ancient inscription consisting of the letters of an alphabet.

anthropoid clay coffin. A coffin with facial features, in which the dead were buried by the Sea Peoples .

archaeology. The systematic study of the material remains of human behavior in the past.

ashlar masonry. An Israelite building method employing heavily dressed stone, often arranged in a header-stretcher fashion.

balk. An unexcavated section left standing between the squares of an excavation to record the relationship of soil layers.

bamah. A religious high place or altar.

broad spectrum economy. The economy of foraging societies during the Neolithic period characterized by increased dietary breadth.

burnishing. Polishing pottery to seal pores and create a lustrous finish.

ceramic typology. Detailed pottery analysis for dating purposes.

cistern. A reservoir dug in the ground to collect and store rainwater.

city-state. A large city, ruled by a local prince or "king," with controlled territory around the urban center.

collared-rim storage jar. A vessel that has a rim that looks like a priest's collar, commonly found during the Iron 1 period in Israelite contexts.

coprolite. Fossilized feces.

core. A large stone or other natural material from which flakes have been removed in order to produce a tool.

diagnostic sherd. A pottery fragment that indicates the original vessel's style and date—normally a rim, handle, or base.

dolmen. A type of grave from the MB 1 period that looked like a table with vertical basalt rocks roofed by large rock slabs.

favissa (pl. favissae). An ancient pit near or in a temple that contained sacred objects no longer in use.

fill. A level of debris brought into a site by ancient builders in order to level an area for new construction.

flake. A small piece or chip removed from a large piece of rock (core) or other natural material in order to produce a tool.

fosse. A moat or ditch dug around an ancient tell, employed as a defensive mechanism.

four-room house. A rectangular residence with three parallel rooms divided by pillars and a broad room at the rear.

glacis. A long fortification slope running from the bottom of the mound to the defensive wall on top.

grog. Ground-up pots used as temper.

header-stretcher. A building technique in which courses of stones whose shorter ends are exposed (headers) alternate with courses whose longer ends are exposed (stretchers).

Hezekiah's Tunnel. A 1,750-foot tunnel from the Gihon Spring to the Pool of Siloam in Jerusalem dug by Hezekiah (2 Kings 20:20).

Kurkar Ridge. A sandstone ridge found along the southern coastal plain next to the Mediterranean Sea in Canaan.

locus. A specific area of work in an excavation.

midden deposit. A garbage or trash heap left by ancient humans.

mud-brick. A common building material consisting of mud and temper (straw or other substance to hold the brick together).

nawami. An aboveground tomb found in desert areas during the Chalcolithic period.

new archaeology. A recent movement that calls for an interdisciplinary approach to archaeological research.

offsets/insets wall. An outer wall built with projecting and receding sections for purposes of defense.

ostracon (pl. ostraca). A pottery sherd containing an inscription.

Pentapolis. The five capital cities of the Philistines: Ashdod, Ashkelon, Ekron, Gath, and Gaza.

realia. From Latin, the "real things," that is, the material or physical remains left by an ancient society.

robbing. The activity of new settlers removing stones from earlier structures for use in their own building projects.

rubble masonry. A technique of wall construction in which the interior between two faces of large fieldstones are filled with small stones and earth.

salvage excavation. The digging of a site being destroyed either by vandalism or for the sake of modern construction.

Sea Peoples. Groups of migrants from the Aegean area who infiltrated the eastern Mediterranean in the thirteenth century B.C., including the Philistines who settled on the coastal plain of Canaan.

seed-drill. A seed-box that is attached to a plow so that seed may be easily dropped into land being furrowed.

serekh. A rectangular frame that contained the royal emblem of the pharaoh in ancient Egypt.

shaft-tomb. A burial cave entered through a sloping shaft, prominent during the Early Bronze Age.

Shephelah. A geographical area of foothills that lie between the southern coastal plain and the central highlands of the land of Canaan.

Sitz im Leben. A German term referring to the life setting or life situation of a culture.

slash/burn agriculture. An agricultural process in which the quality of soil is improved by destroying weeds through burning and letting the ashes sink into the soil.

slip. A thin surface coat of untempered clay applied to a pottery vessel.

small find. Any man-made object that is discovered in an excavation that is not architecture, a fortification, or pottery.

stele (pl. stelae). An upright stone pillar containing a relief and/or an inscription.

stratigraphy. The study of the deposition and relationships of the occupational layers of an archaeological site.

stratum (pl. strata). A layer of earth containing the remains of a single period of occupation during which there was no major gap in culture.

tell. A mound consisting of debris from ancient cities built one on top of another on the same site.

temper. A material added to clay to provide strength and to improve the process of firing.

terracing. An agricultural method that transforms sloping land into a series of level surfaces that allows the growing of grains and fruits.

tripartite-pillared building. A public structure that has three long rooms divided by two rows of pillars.

wadi. A seasonal stream.

ware. The combination of clay and nonplastics used to make pottery.

Warren's Shaft. Part of a water system in Jerusalem that perhaps dates to the Jebusite occupation of the city and may have been the entrance that the Israelite soldiers used to capture the city during the time of David.

wash. A thin, watery coat of paint applied to pottery vessels.

Wheeler-Kenyon Method. An archaeological approach that stresses the identification of the strata in the soil of the ancient site.

Select Bibliography

Albright, William F. *The Archaeology of Palestine.* Harmondsworth, UK: Penguin Books, 1949.

———. *Yahweh and the Gods of Canaan.* London: Athlone Press, 1968.

Aharoni, Yohanan. *The Archaeology of the Land of Israel.* Philadelphia: Westminster Press, 1982.

Amiran, Ruth. *Ancient Pottery of the Holy Land: From the Beginnings in the Neolithic Period to the End of the Iron Age.* New Brunswick, NJ: Rutgers University Press, 1970.

Avi-Yonah, Michael, ed. *Encyclopedia of Archaeological Excavations in the Holy Land.* 4 vols. Englewood Cliffs, NJ: Prentice-Hall, 1975–1978.

Beitzel, Barry J. *The Moody Atlas of Bible Lands.* Chicago: Moody Press, 1985.

Ben-Tor, Amnon. *Archaeology of Ancient Israel.* New Haven: Yale University Press, 1992.

Currid, John D. *Doing Archaeology in the Land of the Bible.* Grand Rapids: Baker, 1999.

Currid, John D., and David P. Barrett. *ESV Bible Atlas.* Wheaton, IL: Crossway, 2010.

Dothan, Trude. *The Philistines and Their Material Culture.* New Haven: Yale University Press, 1982.

Finkelstein, Israel. *Archaeology of the Israelite Settlement.* Jerusalem: Israel Exploration Society, 1988.

Gonen, Rivka. *Burial Patterns and Cultural Diversity in Late Bronze Age Canaan.* Winona Lake, IN: Eisenbrauns, 1992.

Hoerth, Alfred. *Archaeology and the Old Testament.* Grand Rapids: Baker, 1998.

Hopkins, David C. *The Highlands of Canaan: Agricultural Life in the Early Iron Age.* Sheffield: Sheffield Academic Press, 1985.

Kenyon, Kathleen M. *Archaeology in the Holy Land.* New York: Praeger, 1960.

———. *The Bible and Recent Archaeology.* Atlanta: John Knox Press, 1978.

Lance, H. Darrell. *The Old Testament and the Archaeologist.* Philadelphia: Fortress, 1981.

Mazar, Amihai. *Archaeology of the Land of the Bible: 10,000–586 B.C.E.* New York: Doubleday, 1990.

Moorey, Peter R. S. *A Century of Biblical Archaeology.* Louisville: Westminster / John Knox Press, 1992.

Pritchard, James B., ed. *Ancient Near Eastern Texts Relating to the Old Testament.* Princeton: Princeton University Press, 1955.

Redford, Donald B. *Egypt, Canaan, and Israel in Ancient Times.* Princeton: Princeton University Press, 1992.

Smith, George A. *The Historical Geography of the Holy Land.* 7th ed. London: Hodder and Stoughton, 1910.

Weippert, Manfred. *The Settlement of the Israelite Tribes in Palestine.* London: SCM Press, 1971.

Wright, George E. *Biblical Archaeology.* Philadelphia: Westminster Press, 1962.

Yadin, Yigael. *The Art of Warfare in Biblical Lands.* New York: McGraw-Hill, 1963.

Index of Scripture

Index of Subjects and Names

John D. Currid (PhD, University of Chicago) is Chancellor's Professor of Old Testament at Reformed Theological Seminary. He has held several expedition staff positions, including ones at Bethsaida, Carthage, and Tell el-Hesi. He also served as the director of the Tell Halif (Lahav) Grain Storage Project. Currid has authored numerous books, such as *The ESV Bible Atlas* (with cartographer David Barrett, 2010) and *Against the Gods* (2013), both published by Crossway. He also served as senior editor for the *ESV Archaeology Study Bible* (2018) and contributed the notes to the Pentateuch in that volume.

Did you enjoy this book? Consider writing a review online.
The author appreciates your feedback!

Or write to P&R at editorial@prpbooks.com with your comments.
We'd love to hear from you.